WITHDRAWN
UTSA LIBRARIES

D1737237

EMPRESS ZENOBIA

Empress Zenobia
Palmyra's Rebel Queen

Pat Southern

continuum

Continuum UK, The Tower Building, 11 York Road, London SE1 7NX
Continuum US, 80 Maiden Lane, Suite 704, New York, NY 10038

www.continuumbooks.com

Copyright © Pat Southern 2008

All rights reserved. No part of this publication may be reproduced or transmitted
in any form or by any means, electronic or mechanical, including photocopying,
recording or any information storage or retrieval system, without prior permission
from the publishers.

First published 2008

British Library Cataloguing-in-Publication Data
A catalogue record for this book is available from the British Library.

ISBN 978 1 84725 034 6

Typeset by Pindar NZ, Auckland, New Zealand
Printed and bound by MPG Books Ltd, Cornwall, Great Britain

Library
University of Texas
at San Antonio

Contents

Illustrations

Preface and Acknowledgements

For the Roman Empire, the second half of the third century was a time of trial and fragmentation, when the centralized rule of the Emperors was challenged by the rise of breakaway states in the east and the west. The Gallic Empire was established under a succession of Roman generals, who were each declared Emperor by their troops and extended their control over the western provinces of Spain, Gaul, Britain, Germany and Raetia, from the Mediterranean to the Rhine. In the east after the capture by the Persians of the Emperor Valerian, his son and co-Emperor Gallienus was unable to mount an expedition to rescue his father or to carry the war into Persia. In these circumstances, Zenobia's husband Odenathus, ruler of Palmyra, took command of most of the east, and established peace. At a cursory glance, the successive Gallic Emperors and the Palmyrenes under Odenathus and Zenobia appear very similar, with similar methods and motives and similar unbridled ambition for permanent independence. Zenobia is variously portrayed as a rebel and usurper intent on ruling the whole Roman Empire, a national heroine, a tragic Queen brought to war by circumstances outside her control. The point is debatable, however, and is the excuse for this book.

Any author dealing with Zenobia must also cover the history of Palmyra itself, its life-supporting trade, and its government under Odenathus. The topic has been covered before, by Richard Stoneman in 1992, and more recently in 2001 the question of the Palmyrene Empire was thoroughly investigated by Udo Hartmann in *Das Palmyrenische Teilreich*, and this major work is acknowledged many times in the footnotes to this book. Hartmann's brief was the Palmyrene Empire from start to finish, in which the life of Zenobia is merely one important facet. This author was commissioned by Hambledon Continuum to write about Zenobia for an informed but not specialist audience, and does not aim at research of such terrifying intensity.

Thanks are due to several people, since a book is never the product of one person. Michael Greenwood, commissioning editor, always answered questions by return email, David Reid allowed me to borrow his photos of Palmyra, Phyllis Stoddart of Manchester Museum produced photos from mostly garbled instructions, Trish Boyle and Graeme Stobbs produced drawings and maps from similar instructions, and my long-standing friend Jacqui Taylor drew the coins which illustrate Zenobia's progress from the successor of Odenathus to Septimia Zenobia Augusta in the east. This book is dedicated in gratitude to them, and to Cleo and Tiddy whose ready feline assistance with the keyboard has to be gently discouraged.

Patricia Southern
Dunham Massey
2008

1

Zenobia in History and Legend

Zenobia, Queen of Palmyra, and self-proclaimed Empress, is one of the heroines of the ancient world who has inspired successive generations of scholars, writers, librettists and musicians, playwrights and actors. In the modern western world she is slightly less well known than Cleopatra; in the east she is still supreme, as demonstrated by the massive response throughout the Arab world to the television series called *Anarchy* (*Al-Abadid*) broadcast in Syria in 1997. The role of the Empress Zenobia was played by a very famous and beautiful Arab actress, Raghda, and her struggle against the Romans was depicted in twenty-two episodes watched by millions of people.[1] For political reasons, but by controversial calculations, Zenobia claimed descent from Cleopatra, who was neither Arab nor Egyptian, but a Macedonian Greek.[2] The writers of the television series emphasized Zenobia's iconic Arab origins, but in fact, as a Palmyrene, Zenobia combined elements of Aramaic and Arabic ancestry. The population of Palmyra was descended from an amalgamation of various tribes of different ethnic backgrounds, and their language was a dialect of Aramaic.

As the heroic and ultimately tragic Queen of Palmyra, Zenobia ranks with two other heroines of ancient history: the British Queen Boudicca and Cleopatra, who stood firm for their principles and their people, defied their oppressors, and were ultimately defeated. In each case the tragedy is all the more poignant because all three queens were the last of their lines, and after their deaths, each of their kingdoms disappeared, absorbed by Rome. These heroic women passed into legend as a result of their individual struggles and tragic fates, and the simple fact that they *were* women, who ruled as capably, and fought just as fiercely, as kings. Their enduring fame far outstrips the quantity and quality of the information about them. History is written by the victors, who combine righteous self-justification with a celebration of prowess, obliterating in the process the motives, aims and ambitions of their enemies. The Romans particularly disliked clever, martial women. A few paragraphs written by Tacitus are all that is known of

Boudicca, and even Cleopatra is only fleetingly glimpsed in laconic statements by her contemporaries Julius Caesar and Cicero. There are certain sculptures that have been identified as Cleopatra, but hardly any of them can be described as truly authentic. Her history must be reconstructed from her appearances in Plutarch's life of Mark Antony, and from her coins and administrative records.

For Zenobia's life story, there are similar fleeting glimpses. There is no reliable account of her life. The passages relating to her in the *Historia Augusta* were written retrospectively, without serious research, and with a Roman bias. There are anecdotes in Jewish and Arab sources, but no biography of her, nor is there a straightforward account of her reign from the Palmyrene, Arab or Jewish point of view. The lack of trustworthy information gives free rein to the legend of Zenobia, embellished and recast through the ages, larger than life and infinitely less mundane than the truth. The heroine can be reinterpreted over and over again as the novelists, historians, playwrights and musicians of each era reconstruct the story according to their own fashions and precepts, converting a living, breathing human being into a symbol of freedom, a champion of the oppressed, or a national icon.

As a result of the abiding interest in her story, there are several versions of Zenobia, starting with the historical queen and thereafter progressing through different interpretations of her life and character in literature, art and music through the succeeding centuries. The Zenobia of legend gradually escaped from the narrower confines of reality in both the eastern and the western worlds, diverging from her origins in the historical Zenobia of the third century AD, who was a product of her own time and place, and must be studied purely within that context, in so far as it is possible to shed the contemporary values and preconceptions of the present era.

THE HISTORICAL ZENOBIA

Zenobia is the name by which she is known to modern audiences, but there are variations of her name in the ancient sources. According to Arab sources, Zenobia was the daughter of a chief of the 'Amlaqi or 'Amalaqi tribe, and her name was Na'ilah. In Manichaean documents she is Queen Tadi. Sometimes she is called Nafsha, but this is also the name of Zenobia's sister, whose existence is doubtful. In the city of Palmyra Zenobia is attested on inscriptions in Palmyrene script, which transliterates as *sptymy'btzby*, or Septimia Bat-Zabbai.[3] The name by which she is known on her coinage is Septimia Zenobia Sebaste.

The coinage bears her stylized and Romanized portrait, but the coins do not show her true appearance. There are no firmly attested contemporary sculptural representations of Zenobia from Palmyra or anywhere else. The niches where her statues once stood are empty, with only the accompanying inscriptions to attest that there was once a portrait there. From other Palmyrene sculptures, mostly funerary portraits, some idea can be gleaned of how Zenobia may have been represented. Palmyrene women are depicted with strong, firmly outlined features, and large almond-shaped eyes gazing dispassionately into the middle distance. These portraits are idealized and impersonal, displaying those characteristics that presumably constituted beauty and nobility in the Palmyrene world. A bust or a statue of Zenobia executed in the Palmyrene style, unlike a Greek or Roman sculpture, would not be a true portrait of her, but it would convey an idea of how she dressed and presented herself. She probably wore the elaborate jewelled headdresses, rather like turbans with an elaborately embroidered headband around the forehead, depicted on most sculptures of women. The headdress covered most of the hair except for the curls flanking the face, or swept upwards at each side, covering the headband. Women are usually shown with a veil over the rear section of the turban, and they usually wear elaborate pendant earrings. Some women are festooned with several necklaces, some with large pendants, and most wear bracelets on both wrists. Their clothes are depicted in great detail, showing each pleat and fold of their long tunic dresses loosely tied just above the waist, with outer garments draped over them, one end wrapped around an arm. All display of finery seems to be concentrated in their jewellery and headdresses, while their clothes are relatively plain in design. Richly embroidered tunics and trousers, sculptured in minute and fascinating detail, are the preserve of the men.

The bare bones of the historical tale concerning who Zenobia was and what she did can be quickly told, for several reasons: because the period in which she flourished was very short, the contemporary record of her achievements is sparse, and the surviving accounts of her life derive from a much later time and are irritatingly contradictory.

Zenobia was born in AD 240, or perhaps 241; there is nothing to prove the date.[4] While she was growing up in Palmyra, one of the eastern provinces of the Roman Empire, the Romans were hard pressed and fighting on more than one front, and simultaneously the rising power of the Persian Empire posed a threat to Palmyra and the whole of the east. At 17 or 18, Zenobia married the most important noble of the Palmyrene aristocracy, Septimius Odenathus, as his second wife. Their son Vaballathus was born at some time between 258 and 260. Her husband was already recognized by the Romans as the leading statesman of the city and its environs, and he came to greater prominence when he rallied the eastern provinces after the defeat and capture of the Emperor Valerian by the Persian king Shapur I. Odenathus drove the Persians out of Syria, remaining loyal to the Romans, and was rewarded for his successes, but was assassinated by an unknown hand, probably at the end of 267 or early in 268. Not yet 30 years old, Zenobia was now a widow, determined to keep a firm grasp on her dead husband's power and his authority over the Palmyrenes, ruling in the name of her son Vaballathus. She consolidated her own territory, then extended her authority to other provinces of the east, finally taking over Egypt, then she began to style herself Augusta. Her actions were construed at Rome as rebellion, and finally she was defeated by the Emperor Aurelian. This is Zenobia's story in a nutshell, and the details have to be filled in, especially those concerning her character and ambitions, her aims and motives, and her reasons for her actions.

THE FAMILY OF ZENOBIA

Nothing at all is known of Zenobia's mother, and not much more is known about her father. A beguiling theory, based on the similarity of the name, is that her father was Julius Aurelius Zenobius Zabdilah, who was *strategos* of Palmyra during the Persian expedition of the Roman Emperor Severus Alexander in 231–2.[5] The forenames Julius Aurelius were very common in Palmyra after the reign of Caracalla (208–17), who bestowed Roman citizenship on freeborn inhabitants of the whole Empire,[6] but despite the fact that Zenobia's son Vaballathus also bore the names Julius Aurelius, there is no evidence to show that she herself was ever known as Julia Aurelia. On coins and inscriptions she always appeared as Septimia, though some scholars have suggested that she acquired this name from her husband, who bestowed it on members of his entourage after he was granted consular rank in 258.[7]

Epigraphic sources show that her father was Antiochus. On three milestones

Zenobia is described in Palmyrene as *bt 'ntywkws*, the daughter of Antiochus, and the parallel text in Greek confirms his name. Unfortunately his ancestry remains unknown. He is not attested on other Palmyrene inscriptions, so neither his political career nor his social standing can be traced. Although the name Antiochus is common enough in other ancient eastern kingdoms, it is very uncommon in Palmyra, and this factor, coupled with the evidence that Zenobia was also styled *sptymy'btzby*, or Septimia Bat-Zabbai, the daughter of Zabbai, has led to speculation by some scholars that Antiochus must be a more distant ancestor, perhaps Antiochus IV Epiphanes of Syria, descendant of Seleucus, who was one of the original companions of Alexander the Great and founder of the Seleucid Empire after the death of Alexander. Antiochus IV reigned from *c*.175 to 164 BC, continually trying to reconstitute the now diminished empire of his ancestors. He married Cleopatra Thea, the daughter of the ruler of Egypt, Ptolemy VI Philometor and his wife Cleopatra II. This association with the rulers of Egypt accords well with Zenobia's declaration that she was descended from the more famous Cleopatra VII, the consort of Julius Caesar and Mark Antony, but it seems a tenuous connection at best, dating back three centuries from her own time, to the middle of the first century BC, without any mention of the Royal titles of Antiochus or a hint of the intervening lineage.[8] A direct connection with the Seleucid and Ptolemaic Royal houses is not likely. It is more probable that the Antiochus mentioned on inscriptions was a more immediate ancestor of Zenobia, a close relative, in fact.

After the final defeat of Zenobia in 272 a rebellion broke out in Palmyra in the following year, led by an individual called Antiochus. This man may have been a Palmyrene who supported Zenobia, but who was no relation of hers and had nothing to do with her family.[9] Alternatively, he may have been her father, determined to carry on where she left off.[10] Another theory is that the rebel Antiochus was Zenobia's son, a younger brother of the better-known Vaballathus. This derives from an inscription mentioning Septimius Antiochus, son of Zenobia.[11] This causes much debate among modern scholars. Antiochus could have been truly the son of Zenobia, named for his maternal grandfather,[12] or he could have been adopted and presented as her son merely as a political expedient.[13] There is no other evidence of his existence which could corroborate any of the theories as to his origins. If he really was a younger brother of Vaballathus, he would have been still very young in 273, eminently suitable for use as a figurehead by the rebels, and quickly obliterated when the revolt was quelled by Aurelian.[14]

THE STATUS AND FAMILY OF ODENATHUS

At the time of Zenobia's marriage to him, Odenathus was already a man of authority, a leading Palmyrene citizen, honoured by Rome and pre-eminent among his peers. He was descended from an aristocratic Palmyrene family whose status was acknowledged at the end of the second century when the Emperor Septimius Severus bestowed Roman citizenship on one of Odenathus's ancestors, most likely on Wahballat, or Vaballathus, his grandfather. It was Roman policy to foster the elite among tribes or in cities, and as far as possible to rule through them. Roman citizenship was a prized reward, with legal and financial privileges and increased opportunities for further advancement in the Roman Empire, but without any obligation to renounce religion, nationality or hearth and home. Traditionally, newly enfranchised citizens adopted the family name of their benefactors, and passed this name on to their descendants, hence the name Septimius Odenathus.

The social and political prestige of Palmyrene aristocrats undoubtedly derived from their wealth as landowners, but also from their pre-eminence in the commercial life of the city. In other ancient cities, notably Rome itself, land-owning formed the basis of wealth and of nobility, but close association with trade automatically debarred families from the aristocracy and certainly prevented them from engaging in politics. Roman senators were forbidden to perform any tasks that could be construed as sordid, and work of all descriptions fell into that category. This did not prevent senators from operating large businesses or trading establishments, but they did it at one remove by employing the *equites*, the middle classes, to run their businesses for them, so that the senatorial classes could cream off the profits without actually getting their hands dirty. In Palmyra, by contrast, engaging directly in trade was not frowned on, and the wealth that accrued from commerce formed the basis of aristocratic society. No Roman senator would have organized caravans, gathered merchants together, travelled with them and protected them at their own expense as the Palmyrenes did.

Flexibility in dealing with the elite of other societies was one of the more admirable attributes of the Romans, provided of course they had something to gain. Contrary to normal Roman attitudes to people who engaged in work or trade, the undoubted commercial background of the family of Odenathus did not prevent him from reaching high rank in Palmyra, with Roman backing. By an edict of Caracalla passed in 212, all freeborn inhabitants of the Roman world were granted Roman citizenship, but the family of Odenathus had already acquired this status well over a decade earlier, testifying to their high social status in Palmyra. Odenathus was further distinguished when he was awarded senatorial rank, bestowed on him at an uncertain date by one of the Roman Emperors, perhaps Gordian III when he campaigned in the east, or Philip the Arab, who required peace and a safe frontier against the Persians and therefore promoted the man most likely to guarantee the cooperation of the Palmyrenes.

There was some confusion in the ancient sources about the genealogy of Odenathus's family. The Anonymous Continuator of Dio Cassius's Roman history wrote of the elder and younger Odenathus, which led scholars to assume that there were two, the elder one being either the father, or possibly the grandfather, of Septimius Odenathus. This turned out to be erroneous, but for a long time the assumption that there were two generations, both called Odenathus, led in turn to yet more confusion about the relationship of Septimius Odenathus to a man called Septimius Hairan, or Haeranes in Greek, known from inscriptions found in Palmyra as 'the son of Odenathus'. When it was thought that there was an elder and a younger Odenathus, it was not clear whether Hairan/Haeranes was the son of the mythical first-generation Odenathus, and perhaps the father of Septimius Odenathus, or whether Hairan/Haeranes and Odenathus himself were brothers, both of them being the sons of the alleged first Odenathus.[15]

The true lineage of Septimius Odenathus was revealed by the discovery of an inscription on a column in the Great Colonnade in Palmyra, published by Gawlikowski in 1985. The inscription is specifically dated to 252, when Julius Aurelius Ate'aqab set up a statue to Odenathus, with the text of the dedication, including the personal names, in Palmyrene and Greek. Septimius Odenathus is named as the son of Hairan/Haeranes, and the grandson of Wahballat (Vaballathus). There is no mention of another, older, Odenathus. The same lineage appears on two other inscriptions, neither of which bears any date. In the past these inscriptions could have been attributed either to the mythical elder Odenathus or to the younger one, but are now assigned to the one and only Septimius Odenathus of the 250s and 260s. One is a dedication to Odenathus by Ogeilu son of Maqqai, and the other a sepulchral text on a family vault set up by Odenathus himself in readiness for his own death and burial, and that of his descendants.[16] In the light of the more recent publication by Gawlikowski, scholars have readjusted the family tree of Odenathus, concluding that the Septimius Hairan/Haeranes named on inscriptions as the son of Odenathus was exactly what the text indicates, probably his eldest son by his first marriage, named for Odenathus's own father.[17]

There is no information about the first wife of Odenathus. Not even her name has been preserved, nor is there any source that states how long the marriage lasted. She may have died, or Odenathus may have divorced her, but there is no evidence as to her ultimate fate. More pertinently, it is not known how many children she bore to Odenathus, nor when they may have been born. One of the inscriptions concerning Septimius Hairan/Haeranes indicates that he shared his father's powers as exarch in 251, which implies that he was already an adult by then, but he may have had older or younger siblings.

According to the *Historia Augusta* Odenathus had a son called Herodes, specifically described as the offspring of his former wife, and not of Zenobia.[18] Allegedly Zenobia would not tolerate this stepson as a prince with higher rank than her own two sons, who were called Herennianus and Timolaus. There is little solid evidence for this story, and the very existence of Herennianus and Timolaus is doubtful.[19] In other passages, the author of the *Historia Augusta* states that Herodes was taken on campaign into Persia with Odenathus and Zenobia[20] and that he was assassinated with his father.[21] There is a further complication, in that epigraphic evidence attests a son of Odenathus called Septimius Herodianus. At some time after the victory of Odenathus over the Persians in 262–3, Vorodes, *strategos* of Palmyra, set up an honorary inscription to the son of Odenathus, Septimius Herodianus, who shared his father's titles of the 260s. The most likely explanation is that the name Herodes is a corruption of Herodianus, so the passages in the *Historia Augusta*, and the inscription, concern the same man.

This does not explain what happened to Septimius Haeranes, the exarch of 251. There are various possibilities. Odenathus may have had two sons by his first wife, one called Hairan or Haeranes, and another called Herodes or Herodianus. Possibly Hairan/Haeranes was killed or died at some time after the mid 250s but before the campaign against the Persians in the early 260s, and thereafter Herodianus took his place.[22] Another possible explanation is that

Hairan/Haeranes and Herodes/Herodianus may be one and the same person. No inscription has been found definitely linking Haeranes with Herodianus, but after detailed discussion Hartmann[23] draws the conclusion that there was only one son of Odenathus, called Septimius Haeranes Herodianus, with variant spellings depending on the language.

THE CHILDREN OF ZENOBIA AND ODENATHUS

Zenobia could not have made a better or more prestigious marriage, allying herself with the most wealthy and influential family in Palmyra, though she may have possessed considerable prestige on her own account. It has been suggested that as a descendant of the chiefs of one of the desert tribes, her union with Odenathus strengthened his position and unified the people of the desert and the city.[24] This may be part of her mythical ancestry invented for her in Arab tradition, but it is possible that Odenathus chose her as his bride on account of her family connections, just as the Romans made dynastic marriages to ally with other influential family groups.

There is a great deal of speculation about the number and the genders of the children of this marriage. At the end of the biographical sketch of Zenobia in the *Historia Augusta*,[25] the author declares that after her defeat and capture she lived on an Italian estate with her children, but he neglects to inform readers how many there were and what were their names. Zonaras says that Zenobia had two daughters,[26] and then makes the highly suspect statement that one of them married the Emperor Aurelian and the other married a Roman senator. With only slightly more likelihood, two sons called Herennianus and Timolaus are mentioned on more than one occasion in the *Historia Augusta*.[27] It is claimed that Zenobia was so resentful of her stepson Herodes, who was marked out for dynastic succession to Odenathus, that she entered into a conspiracy, presumably in order to remove him in favour of Herennianus and Timolaus, though this is not unequivocally stated.[28] After the death of her husband, it is alleged that Zenobia ruled in their names,[29] but in the biography of Aurelian there is a contradiction. In one passage[30] the author says that Zenobia wielded Imperial power on behalf of her sons, without giving their names, but in a later section he corrects himself by stating that she ruled in the name of Vaballathus, and not in that of Herennianus or Timolaus.[31] This statement does not deny the existence of the two boys as the younger brothers of Vaballathus, but they are not attested in any other source. Their names have not yet been discovered on any inscriptions, and neither of them is mentioned on Zenobia's coinage.[32] It has been suggested that Timolaus is the Latin version of the Palmyrene Taimallat, and Herennianus is the Latin version of Hairan/Haeranes.[33] A son of Zenobia called Hairan is attested on a seal impression from Palmyra, together with Vaballathus. Attempts have been made to reconcile this conflicting evidence. One suggestion is that Odenathus had two sons called Hairan/Haeranes, one being the offspring of his first marriage, and who died fairly young, so the same name was bestowed on Zenobia's second son, the younger brother of Vaballathus.[34] Although this suggestion neatly solves the problem of Herennianus, there is no information whatsoever to prove or disprove the existence of the son called Timolaus, or of his Palmyrene equivalent, Taimallat.

Unless further evidence is discovered, the number and identity of Zenobia's children must remain speculative. Potentially, taking into account the various sources, she and Odenathus had at least seven children in ten years of marriage, two daughters whose names are unknown, and five sons called Vaballathus, Hairan, Herennianus, Timolaus and Septimius Antiochus (see above p. 5–6).[35] It is by no means physically impossible to raise seven children in ten years, and adoptions cannot be ruled out,[36] but such a large number of offspring is doubtful because of the garbled nature of the source material, and the lack of supporting information with which to elucidate the facts. The only son who enters recorded history, who is firmly attested on numerous coins, on inscriptions, and in the ancient literature, is Vaballathus, named after the grandfather of Odenathus, Wahballat.

THE LEGEND OF ZENOBIA

Even in the ancient sources, the historical queen of Palmyra shades off into legend. The author of the *Historia Augusta* significantly devotes more words to Zenobia than to her husband Odenathus, but the quantity of verbiage hardly represents quality of information. The author admits that he documents the lives of two women, Zenobia[37] and the little-known Victoria,[38] the mother of the Gallic usurper Victorinus, simply to discredit Gallienus, who is portrayed as the worst Emperor of all time. The fact that women were allowed to rule parts of the Empire, and were not firmly suppressed, provided unequivocal proof that Gallienus was weak and ineffective. Zenobia is portrayed as a female ruler who performed her task rather better than the Roman Emperor himself.[39]

The life of Zenobia in the *Historia Augusta* is idealized rhetoric, lauding her to the skies for her sterling qualities. She was allegedly praised by Aurelian himself for her wisdom and determination, her firmness in dealing with the armies, her generosity, and her support and encouragement for Odenathus when he marched against the Persians. She emerges as a true paragon, beautiful, with striking countenance and dark eyes, but chaste, only permitting sexual relations for the purpose of begetting children. She endured hardship without complaint, rode and marched with her soldiers, disciplined them when necessary, and drank wine with her generals without succumbing to intoxication. She ruled well, in contrast to Gallienus, and when questioned by Aurelian as to why she had defied the Romans, the reply invented for her is that she never regarded Gallienus or Aureolus (the assassin of Gallienus) as true Emperors. The message is clear: that even a woman could rule better than Gallienus.

There is no hint in the *Historia Augusta* of contempt on Zenobia's part for the Emperor Claudius, because this Emperor succeeded where Gallienus failed, and ended the war with the Goths, at least temporarily.[40] In describing the life and reign of Gallienus the author of the *Historia Augusta* declared that Zenobia came to power only because that Emperor was too weak to prevent her from taking over, but in his account of the reign of the virtuous Claudius the author was obliged to avoid the uncomfortable fact that the Queen of Palmyra still ruled a large part of the east. He circumvented the problem by describing how Claudius concentrated on waging war against the Goths, wisely allowing Zenobia to protect the eastern frontier.[41] This excuse was apparently not considered valid for Gallienus, even though he spent most of his adult life fighting similar battles against the Goths and other tribes, with the important difference that he did not win a lasting victory.

In writing his account of the life of Aurelian, the author of the *Historia Augusta* no longer needed to elaborate upon Zenobia's talents in order to sharpen the contrast with the inadequacy and ineptitude of Gallienus, but he did need to present Aurelian as a successful and heroic leader and his wars as justifiable, therefore he depicted Zenobia in an entirely different light. In the life of Aurelian she is portrayed as cowardly and guilt-ridden, but proud and insolent, and treacherous enough to threaten to ally with the Persians against Rome. She is not even credited with political wisdom on her own account, but it is suggested that she was easily swayed by her advisers, who were executed by Aurelian. On the other hand, the author could not suggest even remotely that Aurelian had won an easy victory over a mere woman, so he described the Palmyrenes as numerous and emphasized their qualities as good fighters. When the war was brought to an end and Zenobia was finally subdued, she could be safely labelled most powerful, to emphasize Aurelian's victory.[42]

In the non-Roman sources, Zenobia is either crafty and scheming or fantastically talented, beautiful and powerful. In the Talmud, it is reported that an appeal was made to Zenobia to free a Jewish prisoner, but she replied dismissively that she understood that the Jewish God usually worked miracles for his faithful followers. In reality Zenobia was not indifferent to the Jewish population of Palmyra, and she fostered good relations with the Jews of Antioch and Alexandria.[43] The Arab sources lean strongly towards romance and fabulous stories. The earliest tradition dates from the sixth century AD, in the work of 'Adi ibn Zayd[44] which provided the source material for a history written by al-Tabari (AD 839–923).[45] The Arabs probably conflated Zenobia with other heroic queens. She appears in several Arab stories as al-Zabba,[46] the legendary queen of surpassing beauty and supreme courage, still evoked in the proverb describing influential, successful people as 'more powerful than al-Zabba'.

The struggle with Rome hardly signifies in the Arab traditions, which are understandably more concerned with Zenobia's relations with the tribes, chiefly the federation of the Tanukh, who perhaps represented the largest threat to Palmyrene security. Zenobia would need to keep them friendly, or to control them, and in this context Arab stories about al-Zabba dwell on her dealings with their leader Jadhima. She allegedly tricked him into meeting her, and then killed him.[47]

Thus it is largely through highly romanticized sources that Zenobia enters legend, which persists because there is sufficient sensational content in her short reign to furnish any amount of dramatization. The narrative of the *Historia Augusta* was known to medieval scholars; Chaucer was familiar with the legendary queen of Palmyra, and in his description of her he laid great emphasis on her chastity. Interest in Zenobia began to flourish in the early seventeenth century, when travellers from the western world began to visit the ruins of Palmyra, and to describe and depict what they saw.

TRAVELLERS TO PALMYRA

Among the first to visit Palmyra was Pietro della Valle, born in Rome in 1586. He set out from Venice in 1614 on a pilgrimage to the east that lasted over a decade. He travelled through Egypt from Alexandria, visited Jerusalem and Damascus, and saw the ruins of Palmyra. His ultimate destination was India, where he spent a year, returning to Rome in 1626. He wrote three books describing his travels. The first on Turkey was published in 1652, the year of his death. His accounts of Persia and India were published posthumously in 1658 and 1663. A short time after della Valle returned to Rome, an inveterate traveller called Jean-Baptiste Tavernier embarked on his second journey to the east, in September 1638, going by way of Aleppo to Persia, calling in at Palmyra on the way. In 1676 he published an account of his six voyages. The book proved very popular and was reissued in several further printings in France in 1679, 1682 and 1718, and an English edition appeared in 1678, published in London by Robert Littlebury and Moses Pitt.

This translation of Tavernier's work was published in the same year that some English merchants of the Aleppo Company visited Palmyra.[48] They made some drawings of the remains, which were reproduced as engravings in Abednego Seller's book, *The Antiquities of Palmyra*. The book was first published in 1696 by S. Smith and B. Walford, but it is the 1705 edition which is most widely known.

Much more celebrated nowadays is *The Ruins of Palmyra*, published in 1753, with over sixty large engravings showing the ruins and details of the architectural ornament that influenced architects and designers for some time thereafter. The book was an account of the expedition to Palmyra in 1751 by Robert Wood and James Dawkins. Born in Ireland *c.*1717, Robert Wood travelled to many sites in the Middle East between 1738 and 1755. He published another work on the ruins of Baalbek in Syria, in 1757. James Dawkins likewise was an experienced traveller in the east, producing several diaries and sketchbooks in which he recorded his travels.

Another artist who studied Palmyrene ruins in depth was L. F. Cassas, who toured the east in 1785. It is not known whether he had any knowledge of the work of Dawkins and Wood before he planned his expedition. He spent a month in Palmyra, producing detailed measured drawings, of which, sadly, only a few survive. He produced a plan of the city in 1801.[49]

ZENOBIA IN LITERATURE AND ART

The main impact of these travellers' books was on architects rather than historians and historical biographers, but anyone who studied Palmyra encountered the story of Zenobia, which combined all the necessary ingredients for tragedy, celebrated in verse, drama, opera and painting. In 1647, d'Aubignac wrote the tragedy *Zenobie*. The 23-year-old Tomaso Albinoni was sufficiently fascinated by the history of Zenobia to write his first opera, *Zenobia, Regina di Palmireni*, first performed in Venice in 1694. The libretto was by Antonio Marchi. Zenobia was so popular in the seventeenth century that Alain Lanavère's contribution to the 2001 Paris exhibition on Zenobia was concerned solely with this aspect of the Queen as a seventeenth-century heroine.[50] Writers such as Montaigne emphasized the heroic qualities of the Queen of Palmyra. Scholars discerned from the ancient sources that she was extremely beautiful but chaste, virtuous, full of wisdom, knowledge and learning. Like Cleopatra, she spoke several languages, including Aramaic, Greek and Egyptian, and she understood Latin though she did not speak it well. In her court circle she included among her advisers military men, scholars and philosophers, especially Cassius Longinus, a philosopher and teacher of rhetoric from Athens. He wrote an oration to Odenathus, though there is some argument about whether it was composed during the lifetime of Odenathus, or was a panegyric written after his death, most probably at the instigation of Zenobia. Unfortunately the work is now lost, although according to a letter of Libanius it was still extant in the late fourth century.[51] The seventeenth-century scholars, influenced by the account of Zosimus, attributed the formation of Zenobia's political and military policies to the strong influence of Longinus.[52]

Writers, dramatists and composers continued to celebrate the story of Zenobia in the eighteenth century, when the fashion or passion for Zenobia extended to, and was sometimes confused with, another Zenobia, queen of Armenia, faithful wife of Rhadamistus, the subject of the libretto by Apostolo Zeno and the drama by Pietro Metastasio, which was performed as a play and was also set to music by several different composers.[53] In England, Arthur Murphy, a French-educated Irish lawyer, produced a tragedy called simply *Zenobia*, about the Armenian Queen, first performed at the Drury Lane Theatre in 1768.

Zenobia of Palmyra found her niche in western art in the early years of the eighteenth century, when Giambattista Tiepolo painted a series of tableaux on the walls of the palace of the Zenobio family in Venice. Tiepolo also depicted other classical themes, with portraits of Cleopatra, Semiramis and Lucretia. There is no genealogical proof that the Venetian family had any connection with the Palmyrene queen, but it is obvious why this particular subject was chosen for the decoration of the palace. The precise date when they were painted is not known. When Alvise Zenobio died in 1817, the paintings were detached and sold. Three of them survive in museums. *Queen Zenobia Haranguing her Soldiers* is in the National Museum in Washington DC. The Prado houses *The Interview of Zenobia with Aurelian*, and *The Triumph of Aurelian* is in the Galleria Sabauda in Turin.[54]

A semi-fictional romanticized account of Zenobia appeared in France in 1758 written by Joseph Jouve, entitled *Histoire de Zenobie, Impératrice-reine de Palmyre*. Just over a quarter of a century later, in 1785, Aldemario Tegisto produced a tragedy called *Zenobia Regina di Palmira*. Inspired by the play, the Abbé Gaetano Sertor wrote the libretto of *Zenobia in Palmira*, which was set to music by Pasquale Anfossi and produced for the first time at the theatre of San Benedetto in Venice in 1789. For the next decade the opera was frequently performed, in Florence in 1790, in Warsaw in 1791, Bologna and Leipzig in 1792, Madrid and Siena in 1793, Florence for the second time and in Leghorn in 1796, and at the carnival in Venice in 1799. While this version was still being performed in the theatres of Europe, Giovanni Paisiello wrote new music for Sertor's libretto, and his opera was first performed in Naples in 1790. Sertor's *Zenobia in Palmira* inspired the young Rossini, who set to music the libretto by Felice Giuseppe Romani, *Aureliano in Palmyra*, first performed in 1813 at La Scala, Milan.[55]

Scholarly study of Zenobia can perhaps be said to begin in the mid eighteenth century, some years after the journeys of della Valle and Tavernier and the production of the various operatic works in Europe. Ernst Friedrich Wernsdorf wrote his dissertation at Leipzig in 1742, entitled *De Septimia Zenobia Palmyrenorum*. Another doctoral thesis on Zenobia was presented at Utrecht by Arend Gerard von Capelle in 1817. In Göttingen in 1852, Georg Hoyns produced a history of the so-called Thirty Tyrants, the usurpers of the *Historia Augusta*, with particular emphasis on the accounts of Odenathus and Zenobia.

In the early nineteenth century, books began to appear for the popular market, such as Mrs Anne Jameson's *Memoirs of Celebrated Female Sovereigns*, containing biographies of three queens of the ancient world, Semiramis, Cleopatra and Zenobia, as well as monarchs such as Mary Queen of Scots and Elizabeth I. Towards the end of the nineteenth century, William Wright visited Palmyra with the purpose of finding any relics of Zenobia as well as looking at the ruins, but he had to admit that he could not prove that the sculptures that he discovered were authentic portraits of her.[56] His book was published in 1895, called *An Account of Palmyra and Zenobia*. The subject of Zenobia was the perennial fascination, if not the obsession, of the Unitarian minister William Ware, whose romanticized versions of the story have had a long shelf-life. *Zenobia, Queen of Palmyra: a tale of the Roman Empire in the days of the Emperor Aurelian* was published in 1892 by Estes and Lauriat. The University of Michigan Press recently reprinted *Zenobia: or the fall of Palmyra, in letters of Manlius Piso to his friend Marcus Curtius in Rome*, originally published in 1837.

There has been a succession of modern novels and plays, among them Bernard Simiot's *Moi, Zénobie, Reine de Palmyre*, published in 1978, bearing the same title as the exhibition in Paris in 2001. Novels in English include *The Chronicle of Zenobia: the rebel queen* by Judith Weingarten (2006), *Zenobia, Warrior Queen* by Haley Elizabeth Garwood (2005), and *Zenobia, Empress of the East* by Glenn Barnett (1994). Nick Dear wrote his play *Zenobia* in 1995, portraying the Empress, after her defeat by Aurelian, as the wife of a Roman senator, living in a villa in Tivoli, just as the author of the *Historia Augusta* says. This same theme was pursued in a cooperative French–Italian–German film made in 1959, starring Anita Ekberg as Zenobia, who falls in love with the Roman general Marcus Valerius, sent to subdue the Palmyrenes by Aurelian, who scarcely appears in the film, but remains in Rome while his generals wage war on his behalf.[57] At the end of the film Zenobia walks in the garden of her Italian villa, where Valerius joins her, and the two lovers presumably live happily ever after.

All these interpretations of Zenobia are valid, in their own way. The real Zenobia is elusive, perhaps ultimately unattainable, and novelists, playwrights and historians alike can absorb the available evidence, but still need to indulge in varied degrees of speculation.

2

Palmyra and Rome

The sophisticated, cultured city of Palmyra that Zenobia knew in the mid third century AD was a late development, a product of the previous three or four hundred years before her birth. Palmyra was first and foremost a trading city, with a population not only geared to commercial activity, but also dependent on it for its livelihood. The history of Palmyra was shaped by its association with Rome from the first century BC, and in turn by the relationship between Rome and the Persians, a vigorous people who took control of the Parthian Empire in the early third century AD. The Palmyrenes dwelt on the frontier between the two Empires, but were governed by Rome and therefore adhered to Roman foreign policy with regard to the Persians.

Zenobia came to power in the second half of the third century, when she was thrust into the limelight because her husband Odenathus was the leader of the Palmyrenes, and because he held this elevated position at a time when the Romans were hard-pressed and unable to give their full attention to the problems of the east. If the Roman Emperors had enjoyed some respite from the attacks on the Rhine and Danube frontiers and had been able to mount a victorious expedition to the eastern provinces strong enough to avert, temporarily, the Persian threat, the world may never have heard of Zenobia except as a footnote to mainstream history, as the wife of the Palmyrene leader. Instead she became that leader herself when Odenathus was assassinated and she spent the next few years defending her newly acquired realm and striving to restore its security and prosperity.

The story of Zenobia cannot be told in isolation, beginning c.240 with her birth. A review of the historical background of Palmyra and the development of its life-supporting trade helps to explain the attitudes and values of the Palmyrenes and what Zenobia stood to lose if she could not find a means of reconstituting those values and revitalizing trade. Similarly an account of the events of the third century, when Rome faced the threat of disintegration, illustrates the world in which Zenobia lived and explains how she became, for a short time, the ruler of the east.

Palmyra was a settlement of considerable antiquity when Romulus founded a little village on a group of seven low hills on the banks of the Tiber, in the eighth century BC. Rome itself had prehistoric beginnings, but Palmyra still probably pre-dates it. No settlement of any description would have been possible at Palmyra, in the middle of the Syrian desert, several miles from the Euphrates and even further from the Mediterranean, without the springs that fed the oasis. Palmyra's fortune derived from its constant and reliable water supply, provided by its springs, sustaining men, beasts and crops. The main source of water was the Afqa or Efqa spring, which unfortunately dried up in 1994. The site is approached via a cave entrance opposite the modern building of the Cham Palace hotel, situated on the road to Damascus beyond the ruins of the ancient city. Passages and chambers lead off from the cave, some of them several metres long, and archaeological evidence shows that in the first and second centuries AD people bathed there in the therapeutic mineral waters. To the north-west of the city the fertile, well-watered lands afforded a comfortable self-sufficiency for the settlers and their livestock. Archaeological research has revealed the existence of large estates in this area, which supported and enriched an aristocratic land-owning class who attained important status and influence.

Stone tools found in the vicinity of the Efqa spring attest to very early activity, if not permanent settlement, from the Neolithic period, around 7000 BC. Ancient Near Eastern texts of c.2000 BC mention the inhabitants of Tadmor, the old name for the city until the Greeks renamed it Palmyra. Both names derive from words meaning 'date palm'. Bronze Age artefacts dating to the thirteenth century BC have been unearthed in the vicinity of the later temple of Bel, and somewhere between the end of the twelfth and the beginning of the eleventh centuries BC the Assyrians defeated the Arameans near Tadmor. Writing in the first century AD, Flavius Josephus recounts an old tradition that King Solomon rebuilt Tadmor, but it is unclear why the king should have been interested in a remote city in the middle of the desert, and the story has been dismissed either as unfounded legend or confusion with some other place.[1]

Apart from these sparse records, so widely separated in time, very little is known about the establishment and development of Tadmor, or the nature, extent or permanence of its population. Settlement may not have been continuous, and urbanization was slow to evolve. In the second century BC, an amalgam of Aramaic and Arabian tribesmen settled in the area, each with their own traditions and tribal gods. The four main tribes were the Komare, Battabol, Maazin and 'Amlaqi, the tribe to which both Odenathus and Zenobia are said to have belonged. The four main deities of Palmyra, Baal-Shamin, Aglibol-Malekbel, Arsu and Atargatis, are presumably to be allocated to these four tribes.[2] The unifying force that bound them together was the worship of the chief god Bel. An inscription of 44 BC attests the presence of a college of priests of Bel serving the great cult centre of undoubtedly ancient but uncertain origin. The surviving ruins of the vast temple of Bel and its spacious precincts, perhaps the most famous high point on the tourist route, date from the third century AD, but the sacred site is much older.[3]

The organization and extent of Tadmor–Palmyra before it attracted the attention of the Romans is not known in great detail, but it seems that it was not until the early years of the first century AD that the Palmyrenes began to think of themselves as a cohesive community with a clear identity and a communal political organization, influenced by Hellenistic ideals. The acquisitive urges of the Romans of the late Republic did not extend to Palmyra. When Pompey the Great ended his eastern campaigns in 64–63 BC and then reorganized the eastern territories as provinces or allies of the growing Roman Empire, he did nothing to disturb Palmyra, which remained a free city outside the jurisdiction of Rome. At this period it is assumed that the Palmyrenes were still tribal and semi-nomadic, a theory supported by the reaction of the population to an attack by Mark Antony in 41 BC.[4] The inhabitants did not stay to defend their settlement, but simply packed their belongings and trekked through the desert to cross to the opposite bank of the Euphrates, where they used their efficient archers to discourage pursuit. Most of Antony's actions and achievements in the east have been distorted by hostile sources strongly influenced by Augustan propaganda, and his real motive was said to be a desire for plunder to enrich his soldiers. Instead he found a deserted settlement and went away empty-handed.

Whatever the degree of sophistication and urbanization that Palmyra had attained by the first century BC, tribal associations remained in evidence throughout Palmyrene history. Several different Aramaic and Arabian tribes settled in Palmyra, but they are not all permanently represented in the archaeological and epigraphic record. They probably coalesced into the four main tribal groups, each with its own particular deity and temple. Throughout the history of Palmyra it was customary when erecting statues in honour of worthy individuals to install one in each of the four temples.[5] Greek influence is revealed in the corporate political organization of the city, governed by a council whose two chief magistrates were archons, and by AD 51 the community was styling itself a *polis*. Though the language used on official and private inscriptions is predominantly the Palmyrene dialect of Aramaic, many of the inscriptions are bilingual, translating Palmyrene into Greek. Later on, and less frequently, Latin versions appear alongside the Palmyrene script.

ANNEXATION BY ROME

The influence of Rome was certainly known in Palmyra at least from the reign of Augustus, but the date of formal annexation is not certain. The province of Syria had been under Roman rule since Republican times, but Palmyra remained independent for some time. Since the date of annexation is not firmly attested in any literary or epigraphic source, there has been considerable debate as to which Emperor was responsible for the decision to absorb Palmyra. The suggested dates range from the first to the third centuries, starting with Tiberius, or his adopted son Germanicus. With less likelihood, it has been suggested that Nero annexed Palmyra when his general Domitius Corbulo campaigned in the east and succeeded in making a long-lasting peace with Parthia. Vespasian, Nero's successor after the civil war of AD 69, is another candidate. During his reign the Romans were actively building roads in the territory to the east of Palmyra. A milestone dating to *c.*AD 75 proves that the road from Palmyra to Sura on the Euphrates was built by the father of the Emperor Trajan.[6] The road building alone does not necessarily signify that the area traversed by these routes was already part of the Roman Empire and administered as such,[7] but it was probably part of an overall plan to rationalize the boundary between the Roman sphere of influence and the Parthian Empire. This boundary ran for much of its length, by mutual agreement, along the Euphrates. Vespasian certainly strengthened Roman control of the lands north of Syria. The province of Cappadocia had been annexed by Germanicus before AD 17, and had been governed by a procurator; Vespasian now upgraded the province to a consular command and installed two legions. He also annexed Commagene, which had been made a province by

Germanicus, then restored to its kings, but because of the current ruler's alleged
Parthian sympathies, Vespasian brought the territory back under Roman control
and established two legionary bases at Samosata and Zeugma on the upper
Euphrates. These measures suggest that he was concerned with securing the
borders with Parthia, but do not prove that he also incorporated Palmyra into
the province of Syria at the same time.

The Emperor Trajan has been credited with the annexation of Palmyra, at
some point before or during his Parthian campaign from AD 114 to 117. Like
Vespasian he attended to the areas on the eastern edge of the Roman Empire
and the borders with Parthia. He converted Armenia and part of Mesopotamia
into provinces, so it could be argued that this is when Palmyra was taken over, as
part of the rationalization of the frontier zone. Trajan's candidacy is supported
by a statement of the Elder Pliny, that Palmyra 'had its own fate' (*privata sorte*)
between the Roman and the Parthian Empires,[8] which implies that neither
Empire controlled Palmyra and that the city remained autonomous at least until
Trajan's reign. Some authors have argued for annexation by Hadrian when he
visited Palmyra in AD 129–30, bestowing the additional name Hadriana on the
city. This has been interpreted as an indication that Palmyra was made a free
city by Hadrian, but there is no proof and it seems highly improbable. It has
been suggested that annexation was not carried out until the late second or early
third century when Severus granted Roman citizenship to a few of the leading
Palmyrenes, or when he or possibly his son and successor Caracalla elevated
the city to colonial status. Hartmann points out that such a long period of
semi-independence runs counter to the epigraphic evidence.[9] In the absence of
unequivocal proof of the date of annexation, any of these Emperors could have
been responsible for bringing Palmyra within the Roman Empire.[10]

The current consensus of opinion inclines towards an early date for the
annexation, probably under the Emperor Tiberius. There is some persuasive
evidence which supports this theory. At some time between AD 11 and 17 the
governor of Syria, Quintus Caecilius Metellus Creticus Silanus, demarcated
the western boundary of Palmyrene territory.[11] In AD 19, Minucius Rufus, the
legionary legate of *legio X Fretensis*, set up statues of Tiberius, Germanicus and
Drusus in the temple of Bel in Palmyra.[12] Germanicus was sent to the east in
AD 17, on a special mission, probably with *imperium maius*, which gave him
superior powers to the governors of the eastern provinces. He installed a pro-

Roman king on the throne of Armenia,[13] and annexed the client kingdoms of
Commagene and Cappadocia as provinces of the Roman Empire, governed by
procurators.[14] The main purpose behind these measures was to strengthen the
Roman provinces against Parthia, without going to war or actively provoking an
attack. Germanicus's work was deemed successful by the Roman senators, who
voted him an *ovatio*, and by Tiberius himself, who rejoiced that peace had been
achieved by diplomatic means.[15] Germanicus died at Antioch in October 19,
convinced that the governor Calpurnius Piso had poisoned him.[16] This accusation
was probably without foundation, but Piso was condemned, a sacrificial victim to
assuage Tiberius's sense of propriety. While he was in Syria Germanicus made an
indelible impression on the Roman army and probably on the Palmyrenes as well.
Two centuries later, the soldiers of *cohors XX Palmyrenorum* stationed at Dura
Europos still honoured Germanicus along with several deified emperors in their
annual ceremonies, listed in the document known as the *Feriale Duranum*.[17]

All these pieces of evidence – the presence of Germanicus in the east, the
work of Silanus the governor in fixing the boundaries of Palmyra, the dedication
of statues by Minucius Rufus in the temple of Bel, together with evidence that
Roman tax gatherers were operating in the city in the mid first century AD[18]
– support the theory that from this period onwards, Palmyra was part of the
Roman Empire.

There were probably several reasons for the annexation of Palmyra, the
fundamental motive being political and military concern for the security of the
province of Syria, effected by extending Roman control up to the Euphrates,
bordering on the Parthian Empire, which entailed taking in the city of Palmyra
and the territory to the east of it. During the reigns of Augustus and Tiberius,
Rome was in the ascendancy, especially after Augustus had reached a diplomatic
agreement with the Parthians in 20 BC. As part of this diplomatic coup, the
Parthians agreed to return the military standards lost by Marcus Licinius
Crassus at the battle of Carrhae more than two decades earlier. Augustus gained
enormously in prestige and had the event commemorated on the cuirass of his
famous full-length statue found at Prima Porta. It is just possible that the first
gradual and patient movements towards securing the eastern borders of the
Roman Empire began with Augustus, and the annexation of Palmyra was part
of the scheme that Tiberius and Germanicus inherited.[19]

Another motive for annexation may have been Roman interest in promoting and exploiting the undoubted wealth of Palmyra, derived from extensive long-distance trading activities, which were already established in the Seleucid period.[20] It is possible that, without the trade for which it became famous, Palmyra would still have developed very gradually in the late Hellenistic period and through the Roman era, perhaps as a small urbanized centre, self-sufficient but not nearly so wealthy as it became as a result of trade and commerce, which was its lifeblood.[21] Whether the Roman annexation was driven by military needs, territorial ambitions, trading considerations or a combination of all three, will probably never be satisfactorily resolved. Wherever Rome took control of new territories, peacefully or otherwise, it can be argued that trade routes were opened up or existing ones were purloined by the Romans. Conversely, it can be argued that conquest or annexation was executed in order to foster and develop trade. It does seem that Palmyrene commercial activities and prosperity increased from the mid first century AD onwards, arriving at a peak in the mid second century, but most of the cities of Syria and of the eastern provinces also flourished at the same time, so these facts alone do not prove that the Romans themselves encouraged or promoted Palmyrene trade, or that this was the prime motive behind annexation. It may simply be the case that the perennial concern of the Roman Emperors for the safety of their eastern provinces created the conditions necessary for trade to flourish, and the Palmyrenes took advantage of the situation.

The status of Palmyra when it became a part of the Roman Empire appears to have been somewhat anomalous. Although it was probably annexed in the first century, there is no evidence that Palmyra was immediately garrisoned by Roman troops at that time, or that troops were moved from elsewhere in Syria to control the territory between the city and the Euphrates. The first certain evidence of Roman auxiliary units in the city or its environs derives from inscriptions dated to the second half of the second century, specifically to the reign of Marcus Aurelius, naming various *alae*. Most of the Roman army units attested in Palmyrene territory were cavalry or part mounted troops, or camel units. One of the inscriptions, dated to AD 167, significantly just after the Parthian campaigns of Lucius Verus from AD 161 to 166, names Julius Julianus, prefect of *ala I Thracum Herculiana*. A unit of mounted archers, *ala I Ulpia singularium*, is attested at about the same time. There seems to have been an increase in the number of units brought into Palmyra in the late second or early third century. In some cases, inscriptions can be ambiguous. Those which name individuals may have been set up by soldiers or officers who were present on some business, and cannot be taken as proof that the units to which they belonged were actually stationed in the area; for instance Marcus Ulpius Iarais Iarhai set up an inscription in the middle of the second century to his friend Tiberius Claudius, prefect of *ala I Ulpia dromedariorum Palmyrenorum*, but there is no other confirmation that this unit was stationed in Palmyrene territory.[22]

The Roman government probably felt that there was no necessity to place troops in Palmyra in the first century. The province of Syria was well armed, with four legions accompanied by a number of auxiliary units. There were legionary fortresses in the north at Samosata and Zeugma on the Euphrates, and in the south at Raphanaea, and later at Danaba, though the dates of occupation of the last two fortresses are not certain. The post of governor of Syria was one of the top-ranking Imperial appointments, usually filled by eminent men of experience who had reached the consulship. Their responsibility extended to the control of Judaea, garrisoned by auxiliaries under a procuratorial governor. In AD 70, after Vespasian and then his son Titus had quelled the Jewish revolt, one of the Syrian legions was moved to Judaea and stationed in Jerusalem. When Trajan annexed the kingdom of Nabataea in AD 106, he renamed the conquered territory as the province of Arabia and stationed a legion at Bostra, an insignificant settlement until the foundation of the legionary base. During the first century, Palmyra was thus gradually surrounded on the north, west and south by Roman legions and auxiliaries under the command of the provincial governors of Cappadocia, Commagene, Syria itself, and of Judaea and Arabia.

THE PALMYRENE MILITIA

Throughout the Roman period, the Palmyrenes possessed an important privilege that was denied to many other cities of the Empire, in that they were allowed to recruit and organize their own army. It was not completely unknown in the east for communities to raise their own militia with Roman approval,[23] but these other military forces were perhaps not as extensive nor as long-lived as the Palmyrene army. The Palmyrenes were famed for their skill as archers, using horses and camels to enable them to traverse the desert rapidly, but they also employed infantry soldiers armed with swords and lances, and protected by small round shields, as depicted on relief sculptures.[24]

Recognizing and exploiting the skill and expertise of the Palmyrenes in policing and patrolling large and sparsely populated areas, the Romans recruited them for the auxiliary forces of the Roman army. Vespasian reputedly commanded eight thousand Palmyrene archers in his army in Judaea, though it is not known how they were organized.[25] Palmyrene units were recruited by Trajan, who raised at least one Palmyrene camel unit, *ala I Ulpia dromedariorum Palmyrenorum*, referred to above. Palmyrene units in the Roman army are attested at least from Hadrian's reign in north Africa where the desert conditions would be familiar to them, and in the province of Dacia, where they patrolled large areas which were not under organized military threat but where mobile tribesmen could harass the population and impede transport. In the second half of the second century Palmyrene archers were stationed in Parthian territory, on the right bank of the Euphrates at Dura Europos, after it was taken by the Romans in 164 under Lucius Verus. These troops were formed into a regular Roman unit, *cohors XX Palmyrenorum*, by the third century.[26] In all these cases, in Africa, Dacia, and Palmyra itself, the Palmyrene units seem to have recruited many of their replacements from their homelands, rather than from the native population as was the normal practice for many other auxiliary units. Men from other ethnic backgrounds were not totally excluded from Palmyrene units, but recruitment from the homelands continued, attested by the fact that over an extended period the soldiers of Palmyrene units put up inscriptions in their own language and script, accompanied sometimes by translations into Latin.

The organization of the Palmyrene army is imperfectly understood, but it is known that commanders used the Greek title *strategos*, attested on inscriptions from Dura Europos where two different commanders are named *strategos* of the archers.[27] Permanent garrison posts were established, such as those at 'Ana (or Anatha) and at Bijan[28] on two of the islands in the Euphrates. The epigraphic evidence shows that Palmyrene cavalry units were present at 'Ana, at Hirta, and Gamla.[29] These places are attested by their ancient names on inscriptions, but the modern locations are not always known. Certain other sites, such as Birtha, or Birth-Asporakan, later renamed Zenobia (modern Halebiye), and the caravan station at Hit on the Euphrates, may have held troops, and some of the sites discovered by archaeological research, such as the rectangular buildings at

Umm as-Salabikh, 120km south-east of Palmyra, and Quasr as-Swab, a further 80km away, may have been military posts[30] situated at intervals along the routes used by the caravans.

These Palmyrene military posts may have been established purely in the interests of trade, since they were positioned on the caravan routes,[31] but it is unlikely the Palmyrene troops were limited to what amounted to convoy duty. Although Roman troops were permanently stationed to the west of Palmyra and also in the region of the city and the oasis, in the desert to the east there was a marked absence of Roman military installations[32] implying that the territory between Palmyra and the Euphrates was controlled by the Palmyrene troops, who checked the raids of the nomads, and helped to protect the frontier between the Roman and Parthian Empires. Full-scale warfare against the Parthians, and their third-century successors the Persians, was a Roman preserve, but for the protection and policing of the frontier, and for keeping the nomads under control, it would have been wasteful to use Roman troops when there were competent soldiers available who could do the job at least as well as the Romans, or perhaps even rather better. There is no evidence as to the recruitment or organization of the Palmyrene units, but it is possible that the city selected, equipped and paid their own troops and the *strategoi* trained and disciplined them. The degree of autonomy enjoyed by the Palmyrene commanders is not known. They may have operated within broad terms of reference outlined by the Roman governor, while making their own decisions on local matters.

In addition to the regular Palmyrene military units patrolling the desert and protecting the trade routes, it is suggested that privately organized guards were hired or appointed to accompany the caravans of the merchants and traders.[33] When danger threatened the caravans it seems that it was not always the regular Palmyrene troops who came to the rescue. Many of the honorary inscriptions and statues at Palmyra were set up to render thanks to individuals who had protected the caravans and brought them out of danger, presumably from attacks by the nomads or robbers. An example is So'adu, who was honoured on several different occasions for his assistance to the caravans. At least twice he may have engaged in military actions to avert danger: once in AD 132, when he was honoured for saving the merchants in circumstances which are not specified, and on another occasion in AD 144 he was thanked for rescuing a caravan when it was attacked by robbers. On both these occasions So'adu was awarded four statues in each of the four temples at Palmyra. The inscription from AD 132 also honours him for helping his fellow citizens at the Parthian trading centre of Vologesias, so it is assumed that So'adu was a resident of the Palmyrene colony that grew up there. Since there is no evidence that he was a commander of a unit of the Palmyrene army, his actions in saving at least two caravans may have been performed as part of his duties in an official post concerned with trade, perhaps with access to a body of caravan guards appointed for the purpose, though this is to go beyond the evidence.[34]

ORGANIZATION OF PALMYRENE TRADE

The fact that Palmyra, with its fertile lands and an abundance of water, lay on the route from Mesopotamia to the Mediterranean enabled the city to function as a trading centre. The older model of Palmyrene trade, now revised, was based on the reasonable assumption that traders gravitated automatically to the route through Palmyra, so that all the Palmyrenes had to do was to await the arrival of the caravans, levy a tax on them as they passed through, extract a fee for use of the water from the springs, and also make fortuitous profit from the goods and services offered to the people who rested there. There seemed to be some support for this hypothesis when the list of taxes known as the Palmyrene Tariff (*Portoria Palmyrenorum*) was discovered in 1881. Although the inscription is dated to AD 137, the Tariff combines information from the first century[35] and itemizes the tax due on goods passing through the market. At first sight the Tariff could be taken as proof that caravans passed through the city and the goods carried were taxed, but the list does not include the sort of luxury items which were associated with Palmyrene long-distance trade, such as spices and perfumes. The tax is levied on dried fish, lard, olive oil and wool, among other things. There is also a section dealing with dues payable on the import of slaves and prostitutes, which casts a rather more lurid light on Palmyrene trade. The common denominator for all the items listed in the Tariff is the fact that although they were brought in from outside Palmyrene territory, they were all destined for home consumption in the local market in Palmyra itself, and were not goods in transit from east to west, or vice versa.[36] Although there were agricultural lands around the city, the home-grown produce was not sufficient to support the population. Like any other city of the Roman Empire, Palmyra required the infrastructure of imports of food and the ancient equivalent of consumer goods, and also like any other city the Romans collected the taxes levied on such transactions, with the exception of the produce from Palmyrene territory, which was exempt.

In recent years scholars have challenged the theory that it was solely the fortuitous geographical position that gave rise to the trade of Palmyra, that trade would have sprung into existence simply because of the water supply and fertility of the surrounding area. Instead it is suggested that the Palmyrenes actively established and promoted the route through their city and provided all kinds of assistance for the caravans. This should not imply that they invited merchants and traders from other lands to participate in the trade. None of the epigraphic evidence suggests that any traders other than the Palmyrenes themselves carried goods along their routes. Palmyrene commerce seems to have been an exclusive operation from start to finish, undertaken by Palmyrenes for the benefit of Palmyra and its inhabitants.[37]

There were other very well-established routes used by traders to import goods from the east to the Mediterranean world, and in turn to export Greek and Roman artefacts. Merchants used these routes before Palmyrene trade began to flourish in the second century AD, and they continued in use while the Palmyrenes prospered. There is no evidence that certain routes came to prominence only after Palmyra fell in the later third century, so it cannot be said that the Palmyrenes competed with or stifled the trade of other communities.[38]

THE CARAVANS AND THEIR LEADERS

The development of trade involved complex administration. In order to facilitate the transport of goods, the Palmyrenes provided finance and leadership, animals for transport and for riding, and ships for the sea journeys from the Persian Gulf to India. Relief sculptures from Palmyra depict camels and ships.[39] Palmyrene colonies were established in the important trading centres, in Parthia, Mesopotamia, and eventually in Egypt, and there were perhaps agents or reliable connections in other places. In Mesene, Palmyrenes were appointed to official posts, one as satrap of Tylos (modern Bahrain) and one as archon of Phorath.[40]

It has been proposed that several different people were involved in the organization of each caravan that set out from Palmyra, such as bankers to finance expeditions and lend money to merchants who did not have access to ready cash, and patrons who attended to the other fine details of organizing an expedition, including the appointment of a leader who perhaps acted as guide and protector in addition to the Palmyrene troops stationed along the routes.[41] More recently this theory has been revised by the suggestion that in fact all the above roles were combined in one person, the *synodiarch* mentioned in the Greek versions of Palmyrene inscriptions. Another Greek term, *archemporos*, appears to be synonymous with, or a later version of, *synodiarch*.[42] In this proposed model, the *synodiarch* would be a rich landowner, already wealthy, who could provide the transport animals, raise the finances necessary for backing for a group of merchants to form a caravan, and then organize, lead and protect the caravan on its journey to and from its destination.[43] In return, the *synodiarch* gained in social and political prestige, and could also make a financial profit by levying fees for his services from individual merchants, and by engaging in trade himself.

Several honorific inscriptions were set up in Palmyra by grateful merchants, dedicated to various people who had helped them on their journeys. Some of these inscriptions name certain individuals who had led the caravans, such as 'Ogeilu ben Maqqai, who was honoured for leading caravans on several occasions[44] and Julius Aurelius Salamallat, *archemporos*, who was honoured in AD 257–8 for bringing back a caravan at his own expense.[45] In the mid second century a series of inscriptions were set up in honour of Marcus Ulpius Iarhai, who appears to have taken on several different roles in assisting caravans, at least once helping traders on a ship coming from India, and on other occasions as leader of a caravan. The caravan trade was a family concern. Iarhai's son Abgar led one of the caravans which he helped 'in every way' according to an inscription.[46]

Some of the men who were thanked and honoured on inscriptions were not the leaders of the caravans but individuals who had rendered some kind of assistance, which is unfortunately not always specified. In some cases, individuals mentioned on the honorary inscriptions at Palmyra were themselves natives of the city acting in some capacity, official or otherwise, perhaps as agents based in foreign cities. Other inscriptions concern widely different personnel from diverse places, among them a councillor at Antioch, an official at the port of Phorath (who may have been of Palmyrene origin), and a Roman centurion, all of whom presumably helped the traders in some way within their brief or competence, perhaps legally or financially, cutting through red tape or generally facilitating the passage of the caravan through ports and along the route.[47] These people were not *synodiarchs* from Palmyra and had no direct concern with the organization of the caravans which they assisted.

LUXURY GOODS

The principal types of commodities conveyed through Palmyra were luxury goods from the east for the Roman market, and in the other direction traders carried prestigious Roman exports. Spices, perfumes and silk found a ready market in the Roman Empire, brought from far distant places by land and sea. Appian says that the Palmyrenes traded in Arabian and Indian goods that came through Persia.[48] The import of silk formed a large part of Palmyrene commerce, both for home use and most probably for export to Rome. The collection point was on the coast of India, and transport would then be by sea to Charax and through Mesene, or overland into Parthia. The production of silk originated in China, where its manufacture was a closely guarded secret. Chinese annals of the later Han dynasty (*Hou Han-Shou*) imply that the Parthians tried to maintain a monopoly on the silk trade, dissuading the ambassador Kan Ying from attempting to reach Rome by the sea route by convincing him that it was much too far. The Parthians allegedly prevented the Romans from reaching China, because they did not want the two Empires to come into contact with each other, and then establish direct trade routes which bypassed Parthian territory, thus depriving the Parthians of lucrative profits and tolls. This theory of Parthian control is entirely dismissed by modern authors, not least because in the Roman period a Syrian merchant called Maes Titianus was able to travel unmolested through Parthian lands, reaching a place called the Stone Tower, deep inside Asia, perhaps on the borders of China itself. The products and luxury goods of the Far East were perfectly accessible to the Palmyrenes, and through their agency these items reached the Roman world.[49]

Competition with other traders does not seem to have adversely affected the Palmyrenes. Egyptian traders also visited India, using the ports at Barygaza and Barbarikon[50] together with the traders on the Palmyrene routes, but it is thought that the Egyptians and the Palmyrenes operated separately and independently and did not compete with each other.[51] Similarly the Palmyrenes did not absorb the trade of the Nabataeans, which ran through Petra, but declined after 106 when Trajan's governor Cornelius Palma annexed the kingdom. The theory that the Palmyrenes harnessed the trade that used to benefit their so-called rivals remains unproven and has been challenged, on the basis that the Nabataeans traded in incense via Arabia, whereas the Palmyrenes did not deal in the same commodities, and it cannot be conclusively shown that the goods carried on the Petra route were definitely taken over by the Palmyrenes.[52]

TRADE ROUTES

The precise routes used by the Palmyrenes are not firmly attested in any literary account. There are two major sources for eastern trade routes in general, but neither of them is specifically concerned with Palmyra. The *Periplus Maris Erythraei* by an unknown author of the first century BC, probably a Greek-speaking merchant based in Egypt, describes the Red Sea trade with Africa, Arabia and India.[53] Another work dealing with routes and depots is the *Parthian Stations*, written by Isidore of Charax in the late first century BC. The work may have been produced for Augustus. It is of slightly more relevance to Palmyrene trade, dealing with routes from India along the Euphrates and through Syria. It is interpreted almost as a manual of trading posts, but it has been pointed out that this is never stated unequivocally, and it is not certain whether the places listed are posts of military or administrative origin. The work does provide evidence of established routes, but it cannot be stated that these are definitely trade routes.[54]

Using passages from other literary works, and the information from papyrus records and inscriptions, archaeologists and historians have been able to piece together evidence from different sources to identify Palmyrene trade routes with a large degree of probability. In the early first century, the Palmyrenes conducted their trade via the ancient cities of Babylon, on the Euphrates, and Seleucia, on the Tigris opposite the later Parthian capital of Ctesiphon. The activities of the Palmyrenes were tolerated by the Parthians.[55]Although there was probably no opposition to Palmyrene trade at these cities, in the second half of the first century or in the early second century the Palmyrenes found other centres. Seleucia on the Tigris was burnt by Trajan in AD 116. It was rebuilt, but then it was completely destroyed by Avidius Cassius in AD 166 and never properly recovered. From about AD 140 the Palmyrenes had already diverted to the trading centre of Vologesias, founded by Vologeses, King of Parthia from c.AD 51 to AD 80.[56] The major problem concerning this centre is that it is not certain where it lay. It may have been sited very close to Seleucia on the Tigris, built there with the express purpose of creating competition with the older trading centre, which was a Hellenistic city that had retained its own forms of government when the Parthians took it over. Scholars have recently argued that this is not the case. In her study of the cities founded by Vologeses, Marie-Louise Chaumont suggested that a different city called Vologesocerta was founded near Seleucia on the Tigris, and that Emporium Vologesias, used by the Palmyrenes and other traders, was built south-west of Babylon, on the western bank of the Euphrates.[57]

Many of the inscriptions still extant at Palmyra refer to commercial activities, and a large proportion of them mention the port of Spasinou Charax, the capital of Mesene.[58] Charax was founded by Alexander the Great, and took its additional name in 126 BC when it declared independence under Hyspaosines, the first king.[59] Inscriptions attest the presence of resident Palmyrene officials at Charax, some of whom set up dedications to the Roman Emperors. This poses a problem for historians, since Mesene was supposedly a Parthian vassal state, but some scholars have suggested that the Romans had somehow converted it to a client state of their own, a suggestion which certainly simplifies matters and explains why certain Palmyrenes were able to demonstrate loyalty to Rome in a city that was allegedly under Parthian control.[60] The theory cannot be dismissed, but there are certain elements of doubt, in that the citizens of the Palmyrene colony in the trading centre at Vologesias also set up a temple to the Augusti, demonstrating their loyalty to Rome.[61] It may be that the Palmyrenes of the trading centres were allowed certain privileges and liberties, and were not strictly subject to the law of the land. In AD 150–1, the Parthian King of Kings, Arsaces Vologeses, campaigned in Mesene and took it by conquest. If Mesene was a Roman client state, it might be expected that Roman reaction should have been instant, but there seems to have been no military response. Moreover the Parthian attacks did not seriously disrupt Palmyrene trade, since there are a number of caravan inscriptions from the years AD 156 to 159. However, as Young points out,[62] the quantity of inscriptions perhaps does not signify a healthy growth in the total number of caravans passing through Charax, but instead may indicate that the merchants required and received help much more frequently than usual because they met with more problems as the Parthians assumed a more aggressive stance.

When the trade routes from Palmyra were fully established, the northward route would probably head for Sura,[63] while eastwards and southwards the favoured routes for outgoing caravans would probably run through one of the stations on the Euphrates, at Dura Europos, or at Hit. The road to Hit was good, properly made, and there were caravanserais spaced along it where the traders could rest and where they could find protection. The next part of the route was most likely by water transport, down the River Euphrates as far as Volgesias or to Charax on the Persian Gulf. From this port Palmyrene ships made the journey to India and brought back some of the goods destined for the western or Syrian market. The journey back was probably to the same destinations, although navigation on the Euphrates would depend on the seasons and the level of the water, and may have necessitated a variation in the points where the outgoing and incoming caravans joined or left the river.[64] The routes westwards from Palmyra are harder to trace,[65] since any of the Mediterranean ports could have been used to convey the goods to Rome and beyond. Some items may have been traded in Syria itself.[66] There is only tenuous evidence of Palmyrene commerce on the western route, such as the inscription from Antioch[67] honouring Marcus Aemilius Marcianus Asclepiades, a councillor of the city and also collector of the *tetarte*, the 25 per cent tax levied by the Romans on imported goods. This evidence proves that one Palmyrene caravan arrived at Antioch, but since it was one of the most frequented trading centres on the route to the west the Palmyrenes probably used it more frequently than this inscription suggests.

PALMYRA, ROME AND PARTHIA

The smooth operation of Palmyrene trade depended on good relations with Parthia, or Persia as it became known in the third century. Palmyrene merchants regularly passed through Parthian territory on their way to and from the trading centres, and do not seem to have been harassed by Parthian troops. On the contrary there is some evidence that in their own lands the Parthians provided guards for the caravans.[68] More important, Palmyrene trade depended on Roman relations with Parthia, and here political and military factors overrode the needs of trade. Despite Pliny's statement[69] that in times of conflict Palmyra was the first concern of both Empires, neither the Roman Emperors nor the Parthian kings showed any consideration for merchants and their caravans once wars broke out.

A perennial bone of contention between Parthia and Rome was the kingdom of Armenia. Neither Empire seemed to be willing or strong enough to take it over in its entirety and administer it directly, because to do so would stretch resources of manpower and money, and would involve the creation of a well-defended frontier which would invite constant attacks from the other power. The alternative was to leave the kingdom nominally free, but with a puppet ruler who would be amenable to suggestion. Consequently the Romans and Parthians imposed or deposed kings of Armenia, depending on which power was in the ascendancy at the time, and on occasion went to war in order to remove the candidate installed by the opposition and replace him with one of their own.

War between Rome and Parthia was a fairly regular occurrence with varying degrees of severity. The Romans, anxious at all times to preserve the safety of their frontiers, were often the aggressors, reacting to perceived threats. Nero conducted campaigns in the east through Domitius Corbulo, from AD 58 to 63. One advantage gained from these campaigns was that for the next half-century the kings of Armenia were loyal to Rome. In AD 110 the Parthian king Osroes imposed his own candidate on the Armenian throne. The Roman response was delayed, until Emperor Trajan invaded and annexed Armenia three years later. This brought the Romans to the frontier with Mesopotamia, so Trajan's next task was to wrest control of this territory from the Parthians. He may have intended to annex the whole land between the Tigris and the Euphrates, but he succeeded only in keeping a firm grip on the northern part. He was preparing to continue the war when he died in AD 117, and his successor Hadrian immediately abandoned the new conquests. He was reviled by his contemporaries for giving up territory, but in the east it was a wise move, since later attempts to annex Mesopotamia brought further conflict with the Parthians and then the Persians.

After Trajan's death there was peace for half a century, until the Parthian king Vologeses III invaded Armenia, defeated the Romans in Syria and started to plunder the country. There is no evidence to suggest that Palmyra suffered in these attacks, but trade was interrupted for several years. In AD 162 Lucius Verus, the Imperial colleague of Marcus Aurelius, made war on the Parthians via his generals, principally Avidius Cassius, who was of Syrian origin. This general captured Seleucia and the Parthian capital Ctesiphon, but was prevented from following up his victory by the outbreak of a serious plague in his army. By 166 the Romans had regained control of northern Mesopotamia, and set up a Roman candidate on the throne of Armenia.

Despite the Roman successes, it was another three decades before trade resumed in Palmyra. There is a complete dearth of caravan inscriptions from AD 162 to 192, significantly all through the reign of Vologeses III, who was presumably not well disposed to Palmyrene merchants in his kingdom.[70] By the time that the caravan inscriptions started to reappear, an endemic insecurity had set in, caused largely by escalating aggression between Rome and Parthia, and to a lesser extent by civil war among the Romans.

THE RISE OF SEPTIMIUS SEVERUS

After the assassination of Commodus in AD 193 the scramble to fill the vacuum developed into war. Roman armies in various parts of the Empire declared for their generals and prepared to fight it out. The general who moved most quickly was Lucius Septimius Severus, who marched to Rome and became Emperor, but there were two serious rivals: Clodius Albinus in the west, proclaimed by the legions in Britain, and in the east Pescennius Niger, governor of Syria and proclaimed by his troops. Severus dealt with Niger first and brought war to Syria. The effects on the province were far-reaching. After his defeat at the battle of Issus, Niger tried to find refuge in Parthia but was captured and killed. He had been enabled to stand against Severus because he commanded three legions and a number of auxiliary troops and had access to the resources of the whole of Syria. Severus himself had come to power in exactly the same way, at the head of an army, but he was determined that no one else should be able to emulate him. He divided Syria into two smaller provinces: Syria Coele in the north, with a consular governor and two legions, and Syria Phoenice in the south, with only one legion, whose legate was also the governor of the province, with the ancient city of Tyre as his capital. A section of Phoenice was sliced off and added to Arabia. Henceforth, no Syrian governor would command more than two legions, and would have only restricted access to the wealth of the provincial cities. Potential usurpers need large quantities of money and men, so Severus limited the opportunities for provincial governors to rebel. The policy of division and downsizing was applied to other provinces, notably Pannonia on the Danube and Britain, where Clodius Albinus commanded three legions.

Not content with ensuring that no other governor could aspire to become Emperor quite so easily, Severus embarked on a vendetta to punish the eastern cities which had supported Niger. Antioch was deprived of its status as capital and downgraded, while Laodicea was upgraded and took its place as capital of Syria Coele. Fortunately for Palmyra, which was assigned to Syria Phoenice, there had been no question of disloyalty to Severus. The city and its inhabitants were rewarded. Severus fostered the leading families. He bestowed Roman citizenship on an ancestor, probably the grandfather, of Odenathus.[71] Other Palmyrene families demonstrate the connection with the house of Severus, distinguished by their names Julius Aurelius. The first attested use of the name Aurelius is dated to 213, after Caracalla granted Roman citizenship to all freeborn inhabitants of the Empire and the new citizens took his name. The additional name Julius was adopted in honour of Severus's wife Julia Domna, who came from the Syrian city of Emesa (modern Homs).[72]

In the course of restoring order after the elimination of Niger, Severus overran the client kingdom of Osroene, where rebellion had broken out. He quelled the revolt and annexed the territory. The new province of Osroene incorporated the city of Nisibis as its capital, and may have extended as far as the Tigris.[73] Next Severus continued his campaign into northern Mesopotamia, without achieving very much except to make a demonstration of Roman power. Perhaps if he had remained in the east for some considerable time, he may have been able to consolidate his gains and avert war, or alternatively he could have gone to war and, if victorious, arranged a long-term settlement with Parthia. He lacked the time for such a tremendous undertaking, because he could not allow Clodius Albinus, still a rival Emperor, to gain more time and power, so from AD 196 to 197 he returned to the west to fight the final battle for supremacy in Gaul. The Parthian king Vologeses V took advantage of his absence and mobilized. He surged through Mesopotamia, invaded Armenia, and put Nisibis under siege. Severus's generals relieved Nisibis, and on the approach of the Emperor himself the Parthians retreated, pursued by the Romans all the way to Ctesiphon, which was sacked. According to Dio, Severus failed at Hatra, which he besieged twice but could not take the city.[74]

Attention to the frontiers was called for. The province of Osroene was reduced in size and administered from the new capital at Carrhae, which was made a *colonia*. Since the legionary fortresses of Samosata and Zeugma on the upper Euphrates were no longer on the frontier with Parthia, detachments were sent to Dura Europos. The province of Mesopotamia was created, although as in Trajan's day the Romans controlled only the northern half of the territory. The city of Nisibis became the capital of the new province, and two newly raised legions, I and III Parthica, were based at Singara near the Tigris and Resaina in the west.[75] Severus was proud of his achievements, and advertised the annexation as a bulwark for Syria, but the historian Dio, as epitomized by Xiphilinus,[76] pointed out that having extended their Empire to take in the peoples bordering on the Parthian Empire, the Romans now fought their wars for them, using up valuable resources for very little return. There may have been a hint of sour grapes in Dio's statement, but he was right: the annexation of Mesopotamia sowed the seeds of future discord with Parthia.[77]

CHANGES IN THE PALMYRENE MILITIA

The reorganization of the frontiers affected Palmyra indirectly. It may be significant that as Severus attended to the military dispositions of the two Syrian provinces, new developments occurred at about the same time in the organization of the Palmyrene troops. Two new commanders were appointed, first attested in AD 198–9, the *Strategos* Against the Nomads, and the *Strategos* of the Peace. Protection of the caravans was presumably the main task of the *Strategos* Against the Nomads. The first known postholder was Ogelus 'Ogeilu, son of Maqqai, who was honoured on more than one occasion. According to one of the honorary inscriptions set up by grateful merchants, this man combined his duties as *strategos* with his responsibilities as *synodiarch*. The text of the inscription specifically mentions his activities in his *strategia*, and also that he ensured the safety of the caravan from his own means as *synodiarch*.[78]

There is some controversy about the nature and extent of the duties of the *Strategos* of the Peace. Some scholars suggest that he may have been responsible for patrolling the desert around Palmyra, protecting the whole area from attacks by the nomads while his colleague protected the caravans. Others consider that his activities were confined to the city and its immediate territory, to police internal conflicts. This is more likely, since the text of the earliest known inscription outlines his responsibilities as the 'Strategos who makes peace within the boundaries of the city'.[79] It is quite possible that disorder had started to escalate within the city. Trading activities had been at a standstill for the last three decades. The Roman civil war and the Parthian campaigns of Severus would scarcely have facilitated commerce, and although there seems to have been opportunity for improvement after AD 192, the lesser merchants had probably gone bankrupt, and even the wealthy landowners would have felt the strain. This financial stress combined with the ever present Parthian threat was not guaranteed to produce a contented populace.

THE LATE SEVERAN DYNASTY AND THE RISE OF THE PERSIANS

The perceived threat from the Persians, if not endemic warfare, was constantly present after the death of Severus in 208. He was succeeded by his son Caracalla, whose eastern campaign was ended when he was assassinated in 217. Two of his actions concerned Palmyra, indirectly when he authorized the *Constitutio Antoniniana* in 212, declaring all freeborn inhabitants of the Empire Roman citizens, and directly when he raised the status of the city to a colony, along with Emesa, the birthplace of his mother Julia Domna.[80] Severus elevated several cities to the status of colonies, including the two new provincial capitals in Syria Coele and Phoenice, Laodicea and Tyre, and also Nisibis, Carrhae, Resaina and Singara, but there is no proof that he also honoured Palmyra in the same way. The new colony was granted *ius Italicum*, exempting the Palmyrenes from paying the tribute to Rome that other provincials paid. This would reduce their expenditure at a time when their commercial enterprises were severely curtailed. The third century was a period of tremendous insecurity for Palmyra, and trade declined. For the years between 212 and 274, only four caravan inscriptions are known.[81] There may have been increased nomadic raids, at a time when neither the Romans nor the Parthians were strong enough to restore order.

The Emperor Macrinus, the man who had ordered the murder of Caracalla and then took his place, probably did not anticipate that the Syrian family of Julia Domna would prove so resolute in regaining power. In the year following the death of Caracalla, Macrinus was removed and the grandson of Julia Domna's sister Julia Maesa, a teenager called Varius Avitus Bassianus, was declared

Emperor, better known as Elagabalus. An infamous but fortunately brief episode of Roman history ended when the cousin of Elagabalus succeeded him as the Emperor Severus Alexander in 222.

An uneasy peace between Parthia and Rome had been maintained, largely because the Parthian Royal House was engaged in fierce internal squabbling. Vologeses V quarrelled with his brother Artabanus V, and the kingdom was virtually split between them, but unfortunately for the Romans this schism provided an ideal opportunity for a strong, ruthless, ambitious leader to make the first move towards usurpation. While Artabanus V was preoccupied in western Parthia securing the frontier with Rome, in the eastern territories an Iranian nobleman called Pabag, of the house of Sasan, quietly took over the kingdom of Istakhr near Persepolis. His son Ardashir gradually absorbed several other vassal states of the Parthian king. This was an overt challenge to Artabanus, but the king could not turn his attention to the empire building going on in the east, being fully occupied in war with Caracalla, and his brother Vologeses was no help to him. The interval afforded enough time for Ardashir to consolidate his gains and to form alliances with the vassal states he had not yet conquered. He experienced some failures – for instance he could not reduce Hatra – and the kings of Media and Armenia successfully resisted him. Undeterred, he marched into Mesopotamia, probably in 220, and took Ctesiphon. Within the next three years Vologeses was dead, and Artabanus was killed in battle in 224, at an unidentified place called Hormizdagan. Ardashir was now supreme and unchallenged. By 226 he was crowned *Shahanshah*, King of Kings.

Ardashir set out to reconstitute the ancient Persian Empire. He fostered a strong unifying religion, Zoroastrianism, based on the worship of Mazda, or Ahuramazda, the supreme Iranian god. A potential weak point in his regime was the organization of the Persian army, which followed the same lines as its Parthian predecessor. When he came to power, Ardashir had a body of experienced troops, but there was no tradition of a standing army with a core of professional officers. The army was called together when a campaign was to start, like the Roman army of the Republic, which meant that although there may have been an army in the field for most of the time, the soldiers could serve for the specified time and then go home to their farms and estates. Nonetheless, the perceived threat from the vigorous new regime was taken very seriously in the Roman east, and by the Syrian descendants of the house of Severus.

When Ardashir invaded the Roman province of Mesopotamia in 230 or 231, the Romans tried to negotiate, but ended by mounting an expedition under Severus Alexander in 232. The Romans advanced in three columns, but were not successful on any front and had to retreat. Fortunately Ardashir had lost far too many troops to pursue. The result was stalemate, and there was no conclusive treaty and no clearly marked boundaries were drawn, leaving the situation ripe for further wars. Severus Alexander made some efforts to reinforce the Syrian provinces, moving a legion to Danaba to guard the road from Palmyra to Damascus, and bringing another from Palaestina to Syria Phoenice.

THE ROMAN RESPONSE

Almost continuous conflict ensued, which is difficult to date securely. The chronology of the Roman Empire and most of the ancient world is a little murky up to the death of Severus Alexander in 235, but it becomes downright impenetrable in subsequent years, so that it is impossible to be certain in which order events occurred. In broad general outline, the Persians recovered by 237, invaded Syria and took several cities, including Nisibis, Carrhae and Hatra. On the death of Ardashir in 242, his son Shapur succeeded him, even more determined than his father to take back from Rome the territories which had formed the ancient Persian Empire. Delighting in the number of cities he captured from the Romans, he included a list of them in the record of his achievements carved into the rock face at Naqs-i Rustam, a few kilometres north of Persepolis.[82] The text, known as the *Res Gestae Divi Saporis*, is written in three languages, and the siting of the inscription was not fortuitous, since it is located near the rock-cut tombs of Darius I, Xerxes, Artaxerxes and Darius II, the great kings of the former Persian Empire.

The youthful Roman Emperor Gordian III and his Praetorian Prefect were ready to face Shapur by 243, and succeeded in driving the Persians out of Syria, but once again there was no follow-up, because Timesitheus died, and Gordian was murdered, probably by Philip the Arab, who succeeded him. Philip quickly arranged peace with Shapur, which he celebrated on his coinage with the legend *Pax Fundata cum Persis*,[83] and went to Rome, leaving his brother Priscus in command in the east, with the title *rector orientis*.[84] The title implies civil, legal and military powers.[85] Priscus had been prefect of Mesopotamia under Gordian III and continued in this post under Philip, who also made him simultaneously governor of Syria Coele.[86] A petition delivered to Priscus at Antioch on 28 August 245 provides evidence of his titles at that time,[87] making it clear that he held power over a large area combining more than one province, but Zosimus says that he was much too harsh in exercising it.[88]

The post of *rector* which Priscus held was not a permanent one, so whatever he was able to achieve to support the peace treaty arranged by Philip was not sustained by the appointment of a new *rector*. Shapur had not given up his quest to reconstitute the Persian Empire and the potential threat still remained as strong as ever. The Romans and the provincials were aware of this, and the danger was exacerbated by the fact that for the decade from 244 to 254, when Valerian embarked on his Persian expedition, no Roman Emperor, and no campaign army, was present in the east. Serious incursions of the Goths across the Danube occupied the Romans somewhat nearer home, and there were no troops and no time to spare for the problems of the eastern provinces. From 246 until the end of 247, Philip successfully fought off attacks on the Danube provinces by the Quadi and Carpi, adopting the victory titles *Germanicus* and *Carpicus*. Perhaps misled by these successes, he made a serious mistake. The Romans ruled by a combination of armed force, diplomacy, trading sanctions and embargoes, and for a long time had controlled some of the tribes beyond their frontiers by prestige gifts and the payment of subsidies in cash or in food supplies. Philip put an end to the subsidies paid to the Goths in 248, directly precipitating the Gothic invasion of Moesia and Thrace. The Roman general Pacatianus who was sent against them, with a widely extended command over Pannonia and Moesia, used his power and control of the armies to have himself declared Emperor. At about the same time, the armies of the eastern provinces declared for Jotapianus in 248 or 249. The provinces of Syria Coele, Syria Phoenice and Cappadocia supported him, but it is not known whether the attempted usurpation involved the Palmyrenes.

Civil war resulted among the Romans, until Decius emerged as Emperor in 249. A persecution of the Christians began, interrupted by another invasion of the Goths across the Danube in 250. Decius was killed when he brought them to battle at Abrittus (modern Razgrad in Bulgaria). The governor of Moesia, Gaius Vibius Afinius Trebonianus Gallus was declared Emperor, and quickly made peace with the Goths, presumably reinstating the subsidies paid to them.

This might have ensured peace on the Danube had it not been for the revolt of
Aemilianus, raised by the acclamation of the legions, but when Gallus despatched
Valerian to subdue Aemilianus, the legions declared for Valerian instead. A
short civil war ensued, in which Gallus and Aemilianus were killed, leaving only
Valerian, who became Emperor with his son Gallienus in autumn 253. Towards
the end of the following year, Valerian left Rome for the eastern provinces, while
Gallienus attended to the problems of the west. For the first time in many years
it seemed that there was hope for peace throughout the Empire, with two adult
Emperors sharing power and responsibility.

THE DECLINE OF PALMYRENE TRADE

The cumulative effect of the prolonged troubles was disastrous for Palmyra. The
decline of trade meant economic disaster, but the Palmyrene caravan leaders
could not continue to function in such uncertain times. Caravans from Spasinou
Charax probably ceased at the end of the second century. The last inscription
specifically relating to this port is dated to 193. This does not necessarily mean
that there was an abrupt end to visits by Palmyrene caravans at this precise date,
but it is significant that caravan inscriptions on this route never resumed in
the third century. Goods from the port at Charax may have been conveyed by
other traders to the larger centres where the Palmyrenes could collect them.[89]
Palmyrene caravans continued to visit Vologesias until 247.[90] Thereafter there
is no proof that the Palmyrenes used this route, though a caravan returned
safely from an unnamed starting point in 257/8, led by Salamallathus at his own
expense.[91]

At the beginning of the third century there is some evidence that the
Palmyrenes were using alternative routes other than Charax, bringing their
traders through South Arabia and across the Red Sea into Egypt. Palmyrene
sailors are attested working on the Red Sea route, and an inscription dated to
212 from Tentyra near Coptos in Egypt names a Palmyrene, Aurelius Maccaeus.
Another records a dedication to a Palmyrene god by Aurelius Belacabus in 216.[92]
The evidence is not substantial enough to suggest that this route was used for
any length of time.

ODENATHUS, CHIEF OF THE PALMYRENES

Against this background of rising Persian aggression and declining trade, Odenathus came to greater prominence in Palmyra. He had lived all or most of his adult life in a period of turmoil, at a time when Palmyra had passed its peak. The monuments and buildings of the city revealed how successful the Palmyrenes had been in the past, but attempts to resuscitate commerce on the same scale as before were fraught with hazard. The constant threat of hostilities by the new Persian regime, and the concomitant threat of war between the Romans and the Persians, stultified trading activities.

Odenathus attained Roman recognition and senatorial rank, first attested in the early 250s, so it is postulated that he had performed some signal service to the Romans, perhaps in the 240s during the Persian war of Gordian III or when his successor Philip made peace. This is based on informed speculation. There is no evidence to prove that he assisted the Romans in any way before 260, or to clarify beyond doubt why he was granted senatorial status.[93] This status is not attested in its Latin form, but it is denoted in the bilingual Palmyrene and Greek inscriptions by the Greek word *lamprotatos*, the equivalent of Latin *clarissimus*, most illustrious, which by the third century always signified senatorial rank, just as *egregius* signified a member of the *equites*. Senatorial status was a rare honour. There was only one other man of senatorial rank in Palmyra, Septimius Haddudan, who opposed Zenobia and the rebels who tried to defy Aurelian after the fall of Palmyra. He appears to have been elevated to this status only after the rebellion was defeated.[94]

Adlection to the Roman Senate did not necessarily bestow on Odenathus any special powers, and he does not seem to have played a significant commanding role in the ordinary day-to-day government of Palmyra. When the city was made a colony, Roman administration replaced the older Hellenistic form of government. Instead of the two annually appointed archons, the two chief magistrates were Roman-style *duumviri*, called *strategoi* in Greek. The Palmyrenes continued to elect these magistrates until *c.*264, which indicates that Odenathus did not usurp the government, substituting himself for the *strategoi*, even when he was given other titles and possibly special functions, which served to underline his supreme position.

The earliest evidence that Odenathus was elevated to a position as leader of

the Palmyrenes derives from an inscription dated to 252, where he is designated
in Palmyrene as Ras Tadmor (*rs' tdmwr*), or Chief of the Palmyrenes. The Greek
title, not complete, is restored as exarch (*exarchos Palmyrenon*). The precise date
when Odenathus was granted this title is not known, but on another inscription
of 251 his son Haeranes carries the same titles, so it is clear that Odenathus shared
power with his son, and that the acceptance of the position and titles pre-dates
252 by at least one year.[95]

Opinion is divided as to whether Odenathus was already a senator when he became Ras Tadmor. In an inscription which is unfortunately undated, Odenathus
is designated as senator but not as exarch or Ras Tadmor, so it could be argued
that senatorial status pre-dates his position as leader of the Palmyrenes.[96]
Hartmann disagrees, dating Odenathus's position as Ras Tadmor to the 240s after
the death of Gordian III, and the senatorial status to the 250s.[97] Since there is as
yet no firm evidence as to the dates when Odenathus became a Roman senator
and leader of the Palmyrenes, it is not beyond the bounds of possibility that both
events occurred at the same time. It is possible that after the death of Gordian
III the Palmyrenes took what action they deemed necessary for their immediate
protection and made Odenathus their leader, on their own terms and without any
suggestion of assuming any Roman office. Then when Philip the Arab concluded
peace with the Persians and left his brother Priscus in charge of the east, he may
have sanctioned and ratified Odenathus's position by adlecting him to the Senate,
so that he could rely on a strong but not wholly independent ruler to protect the
Palmyrene sector of the desert and the frontier with Persia.

Neither the Greek title exarch nor the Palmyrene Ras Tadmor carried with
it any known official position or normal magistracy in the government of
Palmyra. Ras usually denoted the chief of a tribe, but in Palmyra there are no
known forerunners with this title, which is associated exclusively with Odenathus
and his family.[98] The epigraphic evidence provides no hint as to whether or
not there were any civil or military functions attached to the title Ras Tadmor.
It could simply be an honorary description, in recognition of Odenathus's
influence and patronage.[99] No one can say with any certainty what his powers
were, but two inscriptions confirm his supremacy among the Palmyrenes. An
undated inscription, in Palmyrene only without a Greek translation, refers to
Odenathus as Ras Tadmor and mentions the gift of a throne made by 'Ogeilu son
of Maqqai Haddudan Hadda, the father of Haddudan who was made a senator

in the 270s. The throne has inescapable connotations of kingship or at least the powers of a supreme chief, without the actual title of king. In April 258 the guild of goldsmiths and silversmiths set up an inscription in honour of Odenathus, with the text in Palmyrene and Greek. He is referred to as consular and lord; the Palmyrene term is *mrn*, meaning lord, for which the Greek equivalent is *despotes*, which implies something more than mere influence and patronage.[100]

The extraordinary title Ras Tadmor, with no historical antecedents, appears during extraordinary times, when there was a need for extra vigilance and greater defence, especially while the Roman Emperors were preoccupied with wars in other parts of the Empire. In these circumstances the Palmyrenes may have created a new post with an unprecedented title to denote unprecedented supreme power, including military command.[101] Hartmann points out that in the eastern kingdoms the title exarch carries connotations of military power, and the designation Ras, usually denoting the chief of a tribe or city, can also involve military command.[102] There is no absolute proof, but it is probable that Odenathus was both civil and military leader. His command may have extended over the whole of the Palmyrene army, and covered all the territory between the city and the Euphrates, in which case the military *strategoi* would have been subordinate to him.[103] Sceptics point out that there is no evidence that Odenathus or the Palmyrenes took part in any military action against the Persians before 260, but lack of evidence is not absolute proof of inaction.[104] The Palmyrenes may have appointed a commander to prepare for potential operations which never came about. It is possible that Odenathus overhauled the Palmyrene army, recruiting desert nomads, and perhaps increasing the number of heavy armed cavalry, nicknamed the *clibanarii*, which means ovens, because fighting in heavy armour in desert conditions was tantamount to being baked in an oven.[105] These troops were probably recruited from the 240s onwards. Their use is attested at Dura Europos, which fell in 256, which means that *clibanarii* were in use before that date.[106] An important consideration is that if Odenathus had experience of command before 260, in a post sanctioned by Rome, it helps to explain how he was able to take control of his own army and the Roman troops so quickly and so effectively after the capture and imprisonment of the Emperor Valerian.[107]

The title Ras Tadmor is not related to any official Roman post such as *legatus* or *praefectus*, so at this time it probably concerned only the Palmyrenes and not the other cities or Roman military posts in Syria Phoenice. The choice of

Odenathus as the leader of the Palmyrenes and the title granted to him was presumably sanctioned by the Roman Emperor, otherwise it could have been construed as an attempt at usurpation. Further promotion of Odenathus after the 250s indicates that he was favoured by Rome.[108]

SHAPUR I, KING OF KINGS

About two years after the first appearance of Odenathus as Ras Tadmor, the Persian king Shapur took advantage of the preoccupation of the Roman Emperors, who were either fighting civil wars or repelling invasions on other frontiers. While they were occupied elsewhere, Shapur attacked the eastern Roman provinces, and the kingdom of Armenia, probably in 252, or in 253.[109] His excuse was that the Roman Emperor lied and did wrong over Armenia. With no definitely established chronology it is impossible to be certain which Emperor is meant. Some authors opt for Philip the Arab,[110] and others suggest Trebonianus Gallus,[111] who was preparing to launch a punitive campaign when he was killed in the civil war that brought Valerian to power. The problems of the east were bequeathed to Valerian and his son Gallienus.

In his memoirs, Shapur boasted of defeating a Roman army at Barbalissos and killing 60,000 Romans,[112] but no hint of such a disaster appears in Roman sources. Shapur also claimed that he had devastated Syria and captured thirty-seven cities with their surrounding territories.[113] He may have captured Nisibis,[114] and destroyed Antioch. This is a debatable issue, but Zosimus says that Antioch had to be rebuilt when Valerian arrived in Syria in 254.[115] The coinage was interrupted there in 253, implying that normal life and commercial activity had ceased.[116] The enormity of the destruction and the threat of further depredations, with no help forthcoming from Rome, made a profound impression on the Syrian and other eastern cities. In this context, the so-called usurper Uranius Antoninus, priest king of Emesa, took control of his own troops and probably some civilian volunteers, and fought back, driving Shapur out of Syria.[117] Uranius is scarcely acknowledged in the ancient literature, and is known mainly from his coins, issued in the Seleucid year 565, which equates to 253–4.[118] He connected himself with the Imperial dynasties by taking the names Lucius Julius Aurelius Sulpicius Severus Uranius Antoninus, and he assumed the titulature of the Roman Emperors, probably because the title *Imperator* and the Imperial insignia facilitated his command of an army and the coordination of the defence of his city and territory. The Syrians accepted him, but he was not a usurper in the strict sense of the term. He was concerned solely with the protection of his homelands and not with ousting the legitimate Roman Emperor and taking his place.[119] His ultimate fate is unknown, and it is not wholly out of the question that after averting the danger, he retired into private life in Emesa when the Emperor Valerian arrived in Syria.[120]

There is no evidence that Odenathus or the Palmyrenes took part in any fighting as the Persians invaded or as they withdrew after Uranius Antoninus drove them out,[121] even though the cities or fortresses captured by Shapur included places that concerned them directly, such as 'Ana or Anatha, the caravan base on the island in the Euphrates, Sura on the west bank of the Euphrates north of Palmyra, and Birtha-Asporakan, which sometime later was renamed Zenobia, and is now known as Halebiye.[122] The city of Palmyra itself was probably not threatened, and it is possible that the caravan stations on the Euphrates had already been given up, so there would have been no need to precipitate attacks by going onto the offensive. Perhaps a defensive stance was all that was necessary to pre-empt hostilities on the desert frontier.

THE EMPEROR VALERIAN AND ODENATHUS

In the Syrian provinces, the civilians and the army commanders alike no doubt felt great relief when Valerian arrived in 255, preparing for a campaign against the Persians, but before it could begin, Valerian had to repulse yet another invasion of the Goths that threatened Byzantium and the surrounding provinces. By 257/8 he was ready to take the war into Persia. The chronology of events for the years prior to 260 is very uncertain, allowing for widely divergent opinions as to the date of Valerian's Persian expedition, but at about the same time that he was preparing for war, at the end of 257 or early in 258, Odenathus was elevated to consular rank, and the titles exarch and Ras Tadmor went out of use.[123] Odenathus is not attested as consul in Latin, but the evidence derives from inscriptions where the Greek *lamprotatos hypatikos* equates with Latin *clarissimus consularis*, denoting a senator who had reached the consulship.[124]

There were parallels where other eastern rulers were given consular rank, such as Abgar, king of Edessa, who was described as *hypatikos* on inscriptions.[125]

Whether Odenathus was made suffect consul *in absentia* or was simply given the rank and insignia of a consul (*ornamenta consularia*) remains unclear,[126] but whichever is correct, consular rank shows that Valerian found Odenathus and the Palmyrenes loyal and trustworthy. Whether there were any instructions that accompanied the promotion from the Emperor is not known, but it is unlikely that this was simply an empty honour with no substance behind it. Odenathus was perhaps entrusted with the defence of Palmyra and the desert zone bordering on Parthian territory. It has been suggested that Odenathus's new title may have bestowed on him wider authority than the protection of Palmyra and the frontier. An inscription from Tyre, the most important city in Syria Phoenice, shows that Odenathus was recognized and honoured there, distinguished as *clarissimus* but with no other indication of rank, and no specific date, so this inscription is not necessarily related to the period 257/8 when Odenathus was granted consular rank.[127] If the honorary inscription was set up prior to 257, it reveals that the influence of Odenathus had spread as far as the capital city if not the whole of Syria Phoenice, but if it dates to the period after 257, it may signify that Odenathus had been appointed as governor of the whole province. Christol argues against this[128] but Hartmann brings other factors to bear, in that five of the consular inscriptions are all dated to the Seleucid year 569, a period when no other governor of Phoenice is attested, so this may represent Odenathus's year of office as consular governor.[129]

None of this speculation can be proved beyond doubt. As consul, Odenathus would outrank the legionary commanders and any other official in Syria Phoenice, and he would be empowered to command armies. If he was raised to the consulship in 257/8, without any intention of putting him in charge of the province and its troops, then the bestowal of such high rank was extremely fortuitous, not least because it gave him power to govern civilians and command troops. Odenathus and the Palmyrenes would be fully aware of this when, in summer 260, news arrived that there had been a battle between the Romans and the Persians between Edessa and Carrhae, and Shapur had captured and imprisoned the Roman Emperor and many of his officers.[130] All the hopes of the Romans and the provincials that peace might be restored were suddenly shattered. A leader with power and credibility was required to pick up the pieces. Septimius Odenathus held the rank, the powers and the long-standing influence to become that leader.

1. There are no truly authenticated depictions of Zenobia from Palmyra or anywhere else, except for her stylized coin portraits, usually showing her with a determined expression befitting the ruler of the east, and older than she really was. This portrait is adapted from coin issues, representing the Queen as a Roman lady emulating the Roman Empresses in her clothing and hairstyle. In Palmyra she would probably have been portrayed in the elaborate headdress and veil of high-ranking Palmyrene ladies, with elaborate drapery and jewellery. Drawn by Jacqui Taylor.

2. Caius Publius Licinius Valerianus was over 60 years old when he became Emperor in 253, sharing power with his adult son Gallienus. The invasion of the eastern provinces by the Persians under Shapur I, probably in the same year, required a firm response from the Romans. Gallienus took charge of the western Empire while Valerian marched to the east to mount a campaign which ended in disaster when Shapur captured the Emperor and some high-ranking Roman officers. The Roman army rallied under Macrianus and his two sons, who were declared Emperors. This is the context of the rise to power of Odenathus, lord of Palmyra. Photo courtesy of the Ny Carlsberg Glyptotek, Copenhagen.

3. This portrait of Gallienus dates from the later period of his reign, showing him in stylized form with worry lines between his eyes, a characteristic of most late third-century Emperors. Photo courtesy of the Ny Carlsberg Glyptotek, Copenhagen.

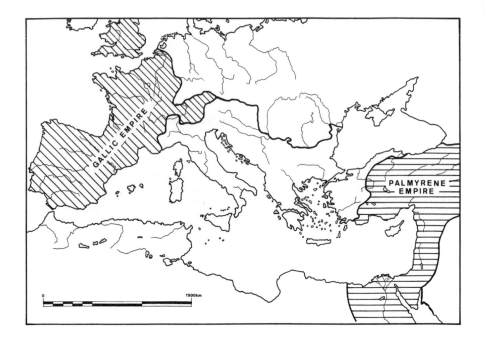

4. Map of the Roman Empire *c.*260. After the defeat and capture of Valerian the Empire almost broke up into three parts, with the Gallic Emperors controlling the west, Gallienus confined to the central portion covering Italy and the Danube provinces, and the Palmyrenes under Odenathus controlling the eastern provinces. Under Zenobia, the Palmyrenes briefly extended their control to Egypt and Asia Minor. Drawn by Graeme Stobbs.

BLACK SEA

CAPPADOCIA

Caesarea

MESOPOTAMIA

Tigris

Antioch

SYRIA

Palmyra

Euphrates

Emesa

Damascus

MEDITERRANEAN
SEA

Jerusalem

Alexandria

EGYPT

R. Nile

RED SEA

▪–▪–▪ Border of Roman Empire

▓▓▓ Kingdom of Palmyra AD 260–72

5. Map showing Zenobia's Empire in more detail. Beyond the territory controlled by Rome, the Palmyrenes were traditionally responsible for patrolling the desert up to the Euphrates and keeping the peace, a task which became even more necessary after the capture of Valerian and the rise to power of Odenathus. The extent of Odenathus's rule is debatable. He may have held a position of influence over Egypt and Asia Minor, without actually controlling these areas, but Zenobia consolidated Palmyrene control by means of conquest. When Aurelian arrived in the east, she had not succeeded in taking the whole of Asia Minor. Drawn by Jacqui Taylor.

6. Drawing of the rock carving from Naqs-i Rustam showing the Persian king Shapur I and two defeated Roman Emperors. Philip the Arab, cloak flying, kneels before the king, while Valerian stands by the king's horse, both hands firmly grasped by Shapur as a sign of his defeat and submission. Valerian is depicted in similar fashion, with his hand or sleeve in Shapur's grasp, in other forms of Persian art, for instance on similar rock sculpture at Bishapur, and on an intaglio. Philip survived and paid an indemnity to the Persians, but no one knows the true fate of Valerian. Drawn by Trish Boyle.

7. Gold aureus issued late in Gallienus's reign, perhaps in 266 or 267. The obverse bears a fine portrait of the Emperor, and the reverse shows the goddess Victory riding in her chariot, surrounded by the legend *Ubique Pax*, 'everywhere peace'. Though the Empire was not yet united, there was no active state of war with the west or the east, and the message on this coin suggests that even if Gallienus had not formally recognized Odenathus as ruler of the east, he was at least content with the way in which the Palmyrenes kept the peace in the eastern provinces. Drawn by Jacqui Taylor.

8. The Tetrapylon marked the point where the main street of Palmyra, lined with columns and known to modern historians as the Great Colonnade, met a smaller street leading north-eastwards to the temple of Baal-Shamin. The columns of the Tetrapylon are much restored, but originally were made of pink granite from Egypt. Photo courtesy of David Reid.

9. These two photos were taken looking towards the north-west, from inside the vast courtyard of the temple of Bel, the largest and most important temple complex in Palmyra. The temple courtyard was enclosed within a wall and a colonnade that ran all around the interior. Many of the columns have collapsed, but the section shown in this photo reveals what the colonnade looked like, with pediments for statues or busts facing into the courtyard, which contained, besides the great temple itself, a sacrificial altar, a ritual pool and a banqueting house. Photos courtesy of David Reid.

3

Septimius Odenathus: Restorer of the East

The period after the defeat and capture of Valerian can be justifiably termed a crisis, not just for Palmyra, but for Syria and the eastern provinces, and indeed for the whole Empire. The central authority for the east was unexpectedly removed at one stroke, and there was no hope of assistance from the west. Valerian's son Gallienus, with whom he had shared power, was now sole Emperor, beset by problems on all sides. He was fully occupied with the protection of the Rhine and Danube frontiers from external threat as tribesmen of the northern regions made hit and run raids, sometimes penetrating far into Roman territory, looting and destroying their way south and back again. There were other more peaceful tribes who merely wanted to settle permanently on the Roman side of the frontiers, but were prepared to fight for the privilege. The incursions were widespread and could not be immediately contained, and as a result the armies and the population of the threatened areas took steps to protect themselves. In some cases, self-protection escalated into a bid for home rule. Gallienus had just defeated the attempted revolts of Ingenuus, governor of Pannonia, and another usurper called Regalianus, but while he campaigned in the Danube area, the tribesmen of the Iuthungi and Alamanni invaded Italy. The governor of Raetia drove some of them out, and Gallienus himself defeated a band of Alamanni near Milan in summer 260. At the same time, increased pressure from the Franks and Alamanni on the Rhine frontier helped to bring about the secession of the western provinces of Gaul and Germany, which combined to form the *Imperium Galliarum* under their own Emperor, Marcus Cassianus Latinius Postumus. Faced with all these problems, there was very little likelihood that Gallienus could gather an expeditionary force and leave Italy himself, or delegate precious troops and capable officers, to exact retribution from the Persians. The rescue of Valerian by means of a military action was out of the question.

Even if another army could be raised for a campaign to drive the Persians out of the eastern provinces, it would take months to organize it and transport it, and during those crucial months more damage would be inflicted by the Persians. Instant action was required on the spot, whether or not Gallienus intended to bring an army to the east at sometime in the future. There was widespread destruction in Syria, and the cities of Carrhae and Nisibis, the capitals of the newly established Roman provinces, had fallen. Several other cities had been destroyed and the Persians were still at large, probably operating in several groups, plundering and destroying their way through Cappadocia and onwards to the coast of Cilicia.

MACRIANUS AND HIS SONS SEIZE POWER

The Roman soldiers fleeing from Shapur had lost most of their officers, and would need a mustering point and a central authority to rally them. They found both at the campaign headquarters in Emesa, where Macrianus was stationed, though some sources state that he was at Samosata, where Valerian had launched the Persian campaign. Macrianus was probably *praepositus annonae expeditionalis*, the officer in charge of supplies of food and equipment for the campaign, and he had presumably not been at the front when the disaster occurred.[1] He gathered the army together and took command, which meant that he had to assume the authority of the Emperor.[2] It was the old dilemma, such as Uranius Antoninus had faced a few years before, in that the title and trappings of Roman Imperial power were necessary if the assumed authority was to be meaningful and effective, but unlike Uranius, whose interests were localized and wholly centred on the protection of his own region and people, in the case of Macrianus the restoration of order and arrangements for the protection of the east eventually turned into a bid for supreme power over the whole Empire.

On taking command, Macrianus appointed an officer called Ballista (perhaps a nickname, as he is called Callistus in some sources) as his praetorian prefect, and started to strike back at the enemy. The Romans checked the Persians on the coast of Cilicia. Ballista captured Shapur's harem and cartloads of booty which the Persians were carrying home. This was only a partial success, since there were more marauding bands still in the east, so there were probably several brief encounters between Romans and Persians, as a sort of guerrilla warfare was conducted to mop up the remaining groups.

Odenathus and Zenobia may have been watching from the wings as the

Romans began to recover. There is no evidence as to their whereabouts or activities. The main priorities for Odenathus would be the protection of Palmyra and the frontier zone, and perhaps making the necessary preparations in case there should be a Persian attack. It has been suggested that Odenathus may have been the governor of Syria Phoenice in 257–8, a theory not without dispute,[3] but if this is true his tour of duty as governor would have provided him with greater experience than nearly all the other officials in the province, with the possible exception of the current governor of Syria Phoenice, about whom there is no information. Since he had access to his own army, Odenathus may have reprised his role as governor and commander in the emergency after the defeat of the Romans. His responsibilities probably embraced more than his leadership of the Palmyrenes, perhaps extending to other cities and communities in Syria Coele and even other provinces. Communities far and wide would look to him to organize their protection.

Odenathus may have operated independently at first, eventually communicating with Macrianus, but there is no evidence that he collaborated with the Roman commander, or took orders from him. No one can be certain what happened since the whole episode from the summer of 260 until the spring of 261 is only sparsely documented. Odenathus was clearly in command of troops, perhaps his own army with a number of Roman units, when he inflicted a defeat on Shapur's army as it was returning to Persia. This skirmish occurred somewhere between Zeugma and Samosata, which means that Odenathus was operating some distance to the north of Palmyra. His victory was welcome, but not complete. Shapur and most of the Persians escaped to fight another day, but Odenathus is credited as the leader who drove the Persians out of Syria.[4]

Towards the end of 260 or at the beginning of 261, Macrianus made his bid for Imperial power. He did not appoint himself Emperor, but elevated his two sons, Macrianus the younger and Quietus, to the rank of *Augusti*. He left Quietus with the praetorian prefect Ballista at Emesa, and marched with the younger Macrianus towards Italy. He removed numbers of soldiers to accompany him, which must have considerably depleted the complement of troops in the provinces.[5] Fortunately the situation in the east was peaceful for the time being, and Shapur did not launch another attack.

Odenathus seems to have played no part in the attempted usurpation. It is feasible that he had kept his army together after ousting Shapur. The Palmyrene army would be answerable to him, but it is impossible to say whether he based it in the north, distributed it in garrisons on the frontier, or returned with it to Palmyra. There is no evidence about any other troops that he commanded so it remains a matter of opinion whether there were Roman units under his command, but since he was fighting so far away from Palmyra in the vicinity of legionary bases, it is probable that he had some legionaries with him, who may have been torn between loyalty to Gallienus and a wish to join Macrianus.

In spring 261 Macrianus and his son arrived in the Balkans, where they were defeated by Gallienus's cavalry commander Aureolus. At about the same time Odenathus moved against Quietus at Emesa. According to the *Historia Augusta* he began the campaign after he had heard of the defeat of the usurpers by Aureolus.[6] This is probably correct, since Odenathus may have waited upon events to ensure his own safety and that of his native city. If he had declared openly for Gallienus, only to find that Macrianus and Quietus had succeeded in their bid for Imperial power, the results might have been disastrous for Palmyra. On the other hand, if he made no move at all against Macrianus, then Gallienus would have been suspicious of his inactivity. He did move eventually but it seems certain that the news of the failure of the two Macriani had already reached the east by the time Odenathus and his army approached Emesa, since the followers of Quietus had begun to melt away. Odenathus did not have to engage in much fighting. The citizens of Emesa despatched Quietus and then joined Odenathus.[7] There is an unsubstantiated tradition that Ballista was at first released by Odenathus, but then went on to stage a revolt of his own, and was defeated by the Palmyrenes.[8] These were hardly resounding victories but they were important because they left only Odenathus as the most successful and most powerful authority in the east, who was fortunately loyal to the Emperor Gallienus.

There is an account in a later source that at some unspecified time Odenathus tried to arrange a treaty with the Persians. It came to nothing in the end. It is recorded that Odenathus sent valuable gifts which the Persian king threw into the river, unequivocally rejecting whatever proposals Odenathus had made. There is no secure dating evidence, so some modern authors have suggested that this story belongs to Shapur's earlier invasion of 253,[9] but at that time there were two Roman Emperors looking after the affairs of the Empire and consequently there was more than just a hope that one of them would begin a campaign in the east to settle the score, repair the damage, and prepare for future defence.

In the 260s there was no such hope, and Odenathus's attempt to come to some arrangement with Shapur at this time would be understandable as an exercise in damage limitation. Though scholars are divided on this issue, the context of the alleged embassy to the Persians may have been in 260, immediately after the capture of Valerian and before Odenathus knew of the intentions of Macrianus, in which case it could be construed as an act of self-preservation, concerned only with Palmyra and the resuscitation and peaceful pursuit of its commerce for the foreseeable future.[10] If not at this moment, then perhaps the embassy was sent after the repulse of Shapur from the eastern provinces, and the elimination of Quietus, when Odenathus was the only leader with sufficient power and influence to command troops and organize some sort of truce on his own initiative.

Whenever it was made, the attempt to negotiate does not necessarily imply that Odenathus had changed his allegiance to Gallienus, but without a strong Roman presence to protect him and his people, he perhaps deemed it necessary, as a result of his previous incontestable connections with Rome, to declare to the Persians his own intentions to remain neutral, keep the peace and not provoke an attack. Had the embassy been successful, he may then have been able to arbitrate between Rome and Persia, still with an ulterior motive for the full restoration of Palmyrene trade. Viewed from Rome, if Odenathus had acted on his own initiative in sending an embassy to the enemy for the purposes of making a treaty, it would look suspiciously like secession. An unproven theory is that Odenathus sent an embassy to the Persians when he already held a position of authority, sanctioned by the Emperor Gallienus, giving him authorization to act for the whole of the east.

ODENATHUS, RESTORER OF THE EAST

In modern works concerning Odenathus and his rise to power, he is generally described as *dux Romanorum*, which taken literally means that he was leader of the Romans, and *corrector totius orientis*, indicating that he was given responsibility for the whole of the east. Unfortunately none of the evidence that has been used to reconstruct these titles applies directly to Odenathus himself during his lifetime. All the indications derive from a posthumous inscription set up three or four years after his assassination, and from the titles held by his son Vaballathus.

It is certain that Odenathus possessed sufficient power and influence to exercise military command and that he used this power to gather an army, probably embracing Palmyrene and Roman troops, to chase the Persians out of Syria. It has been suggested that from now onwards Odenathus did not reside at Palmyra, but set up his headquarters at Emesa. This city resisted the Persians in 253, and it was the headquarters of Quietus and Ballista. If this is correct, the army or part of it was probably based there.[11] Odenathus retained his power and influence after the eviction of the foreign enemy and the elimination of the usurpers Quietus and Ballista. It is most probable that these powers were endorsed and sanctioned by the Roman Emperor Gallienus. What is less certain is whether this Imperial sanction was expressed by the titles that are traditionally associated with Odenathus. The evidence derives from literary, epigraphic and numismatic sources which are not mutually reconcilable. The inscriptions do not give any of Odenathus's supposed titles in Latin, so historians must rely upon the Greek terms and their Palmyrene equivalents to reconstruct the probable official Roman designations.

LITERARY SOURCES

Although the *Historia Augusta* is not perfectly reliable as a source of historical information, there is a hint of consistency in the work about the powers that Odenathus attained, and there seems to be an indication that he accumulated these powers in successive stages.[12] The vocabulary of the literary sources does not correspond exactly to the words of the titles that are generally attributed to him. The author of the *Historia Augusta* states that Odenathus assumed Imperial power over the east after the capture of Valerian,[13] implying that this was an unofficial arrangement at first, with no evidence that he was formally granted *imperium* by the Emperor Gallienus after the capture of Valerian and Shapur's defeat of the Romans. Full honours are said to have come after the suppression of the usurpers, and the author consistently says that Odenathus was made *Imperator*. Having defeated Quietus, so the story runs, Odenathus was made Emperor of the whole of the east (*totius … orientis factus est Odenathus Imperator*).[14] This is unlikely to have any basis in fact, and may simply be attributable to a rather casual use of terminology, although some modern authors have taken it seriously and suggested that the troops hailed Odenathus *Imperator* after he had driven the

Persians out of Syria.[15] If this is correct, Gallienus may have confirmed the title as that of a military commander, or he may have chosen to ignore it, confident that Odenathus was not about to declare himself Emperor. No other ancient source, either literary or epigraphic, confirms that the title *Imperator* was ever bestowed on Odenathus. Although *Imperator* does appear among the titles of Vaballathus, it did not apply to him until after the conquest of Egypt in 270.[16] It is fairly certain that Vaballathus did not inherit this title *Imperator* from Odenathus, since it is reasonable to assume that if her husband had held it, Zenobia would surely have exploited it from the first moment after Odenathus's death.

In another passage in the *Historia Augusta* Odenathus is called *Imperator* once again, with the comment that by his actions Odenathus had shown that he was worthy of this high office, but the author's main concern here is not historical accuracy or even justly deserved praise of Odenathus, but to create a device to mark the contrast between the worthy provincial leader, who truly merited the title *Imperator*, and the Emperor Gallienus, who is consistently portrayed as ineffective and indolent, and totally unworthy of his title.[17] Warming to the Palmyrene leader, the author claims that during the consulship of Gallienus's brother, the younger Valerian, and another relative called Lucillus, which dates the event to 265, Gallienus performed a praiseworthy act in allowing Odenathus to share the Imperial power, which is not accurate. The author of the *Historia Augusta* considers this alleged shared power an appropriate reward after Odenathus had recaptured Nisibis and Carrhae, restored Mesopotamia to the Roman Empire and besieged, and possibly even captured, the Persian capital of Ctesiphon. In essence, Odenathus did share power with Gallienus, but as a subordinate in charge of the eastern provinces, and not as co-ruler of the Empire. The author of the *Historia Augusta*, writing some time after the events, takes it for granted that Odenathus was given the title Augustus, which is untrue, and insists that Odenathus's son Herodian was also made *Imperator*.[18] This perhaps implies that the Roman audience of the later Empire would believe that Odenathus and his son were *Imperatores* and *Augusti* in spirit if not in fact.

DUX ROMANORUM

Zonaras says that Odenathus was made *dux Orientis*, but this is the only literary source to assert that Odenathus held the title *dux*.[19] There is no epigraphic source that states that Odenathus held this title, but his son Vaballathus adopted it a few years after the death of his father, as attested on his coins by the initials DR, or on the Greek coins by the title *strategos* of the Romans. Scholars have argued that this is unlikely to be a newly invented title for Vaballathus, who was still a child when his father was killed.[20] In support of this argument it is pointed out that Vaballathus would hardly be credible as a military leader unless the title was inherited from his father.[21] The assumption is reasonable, especially since Zenobia, as the widow of Odenathus and regent for her young son, would have every reason to preserve her husband's titles and powers in order to maintain command of the armies, but she would not be likely to risk incurring ridicule by bestowing on a 10-year-old boy a high military rank which had no precedents within her family or indeed in Palmyra. More important, it was a Roman title, and at first she avoided using anything other than acceptable Palmyrene or Greek titles that would not cause resentment at Rome.

From the third century onwards the Roman *dux* was usually a military commander with wide-ranging powers over sections of the frontiers that typically embraced more than one province. The emergence of the military *duces* was a response to the mounting threats on the frontiers, requiring an overall commander who stood outside the government of the individual provinces so that his authority was not restricted to one small area of the frontier. He was empowered to give orders to the provincial governors. The authority of the *duces* was usually limited to the military sphere, though there were exceptions where the *dux* was also the governor of a province and took charge of civil matters, but in normal circumstances civil government generally remained in the hands of individual provincial governors.

The territorial responsibilities of the *duces* were usually outlined in their titles, such as Marcus Cornelius Octavianus, equestrian governor (*praeses*) of Mauretania Caesariensis, who was made *dux per Africam Numidiam Mauretaniamque* by Gallienus. In this role Octavianus controlled the long frontiers of three provinces in north Africa. Gallienus appointed two other men as *duces*: the equestrian Marcianus, and Aurelius Augustianus, commander of troops from two legions in Macedonia. Hartmann relates this appointment to the invasions of the Heruli in 267 or 268, where an overall commander would be needed to organize defence of a large area against a very mobile enemy.[22]

Assuming that Odenathus's postulated title *dux Romanorum* was bestowed on him by the Emperor, it may have been part of Gallienus's measures to upgrade certain officers to attend to the sort of task that the *duces* traditionally fulfilled. He needed to delegate command in certain areas because he could not bring his own campaign army to deal with invasions and unrest in all parts of the Empire at the same time. The wording of the title *dux Romanorum* implies that Odenathus was empowered to command Roman troops as well as the Palmyrene army, but it is not known whether he was restricted to Syria Phoenice, or the two Syrian provinces, or whether he was immediately placed in charge of the military forces of whole of the eastern frontier from Bithynia Pontus through Cappadocia to Arabia. Except in the work of Zonaras, who states that Odenathus was made *dux Orientis*, the Palmyrene leader was not designated by a title that specified his control of the frontier zones of the eastern provinces. If he had possessed a clearly defined territorial brief in his title, modern scholars would be spared the discussion about the exact boundaries of his authority.

There are several questions that remain unanswered. Was his command definitely expressed by the title *dux Romanorum*? Was this power of command officially granted to him by Gallienus? If so, at what date was it granted, or did Odenathus simply adopt it as a means of taking command, and was it eventually sanctioned by the Emperor? The solution to these problems would help to clarify, among other things, how far and for how long Odenathus acted on his own initiative as consular leader of the Palmyrenes. For some time after the capture of Valerian the eastern commanders, including Odenathus, would be left to their own devices, without instructions from Rome. Defence required immediate action whether authorized by the Emperor or not. Communications between the Roman Emperor and the eastern provinces would be too lengthy to wait for messages to reach Gallienus and a reply to be received before embarking on any action. It is not beyond the bounds of possibility that Odenathus took control and styled himself *dux* after reviewing, and rejecting, the other available Roman titles that indicated overall command. He probably felt the need to designate himself by some recognized military title to convey his authority and his intention of taking control, but he would wish to avoid assuming an inflammatory title that might be indicative of attempted usurpation. He would remember the example of Uranius Antoninus, who called himself *Imperator*. Odenathus was not a provincial governor or *legatus Augusti*, nor did he hold any official command of troops with any of the usual military titles. The literal meaning of the Latin *dux* is simply leader; innocuous enough, perhaps, if *Romanorum* was not attached to it.

Whether Odenathus acted on his own initiative, or collaborated with Macrianus or indeed took orders from him, is not elucidated. It is possible, but not very likely, that he had already been appointed *dux* and had full Imperial authority to attack the Persians as they returned home via Syria. A more likely scenario is that Odenathus gathered whatever troops he could muster, consisting of his own Palmyrene army, probably augmented by groups of Arab tribesmen, together with some of the Roman units from the vicinity of Palmyra and from Syria Phoenice, hence the *Romanorum* of his alleged title. Independent activity is consistent with the passages in the *Historia Augusta*, where the author claims that Odenathus assumed power, with no hint that such power had already been granted to him by the Emperor.[23] After the defeat of the Persians, Gallienus may have rewarded Odenathus with the title of *dux Romanorum* which legalized his de facto but anomalous position as commander of the Palmyrene and Roman troops.[24] Syncellus, followed by Zonaras, both state that after the repulse of Shapur, Odenathus was made *strategos*, which equates with the Roman title *dux*.[25]

It would be interesting to know, but impossible to discern, whether the revolt of Macrianus precedes or post-dates Odenathus's command. Initially, Macrianus may not have intended to play the part of usurper, but it is implied in the *Historia Augusta* that he had this in mind from the very first moment. The story is that he held a conference with Ballista, debating what to do after the capture of Valerian, and was immediately chosen to rule by the soldiers. Then, as if there was no interval while battles and skirmishes took place, it is stated that he immediately declared his sons Emperors, and marched on Rome.[26] Everything depends on the chronology of events, which will probably never be established beyond doubt, but it is possible that while Macrianus was still organizing the defence of parts of the east, Odenathus was given control of the frontier regions and all the Roman forces in Syria Phoenice and Syria Coele, as would have been consistent with the usual responsibilities of the *dux*.[27] This would have placed Macrianus in a subordinate position. Such an Imperial snub, following his success in gathering and rallying the scattered Roman troops, organizing defence and launching attacks on the Persians, would have been a bitter pill to swallow. For Macrianus, the prospect of being demoted and taking orders from the consular leader of the Palmyrenes may have influenced his attitude and precipitated the rebellion.

When Odenathus moved against Quietus, he may already have been officially confirmed as commander of all Roman forces within a specified area. After the suppression of the rebellion, there was then a power vacuum, or at least an immediate vacancy for an overall commander in the eastern provinces to repair the damage and attend to future defence. Odenathus had shown that he had considerable military ability, the troops seemed ready to obey him, and the eastern communities seemed to respect him. Moreover he was loyal to Rome. His *curriculum vitae* showed that he was perfect for the appointment.

CORRECTOR TOTIUS ORIENTIS?

The author of the *Historia Augusta* describes how Odenathus defeated Quietus, and was then made Emperor of the whole of the east (*totius ... orientis factus est Odenathus Imperator*).[28] The terminology so closely resembles Odenathus's postulated title *corrector totius orientis* that it lends weight to the argument that he received this title after the suppression of the revolt of the two Macriani and Quietus. The use of the word *Imperator* in the literary account is mistaken, but may be just a slip of the pen by the author who wanted to emphasize Odenathus's power, using terminology that his readers would accept and understand.

From the late first century, *correctores* had been appointed in the eastern provinces for the purpose of regulating the legal and financial affairs of the free cities. These officials were not subject to the provincial governors, and they were granted *imperium*, which would enable them to command troops if necessary, even though their responsibilities were primarily in the civilian sphere, covering financial and legal matters. In the third century, *correctores* were appointed in Italy, sometimes in charge of regional affairs, or in the case of Pomponius Bassus, *corrector totius Italiae*, of the whole of the country.

Odenathus is not irrefutably attested as *corrector totius orientis* during his lifetime, but it is generally accepted by modern scholars that he held this office. The evidence derives from inscriptions, a posthumous honorary dedication accompanying a statue set up to him by Zenobia's generals Zabdas and Zabbai in August 271, and milestones with the names and titles of Vaballathus.

The inscription belonging to the statue dedicated by Zabdas and Zabbai is securely dated by the Palmyrene system to the month of Ab in the Seleucid year 582, which is equivalent to August 271. The text is in Palmyrene script only, the Greek translation having disappeared or been erased.[29] Odenathus is described as *mtqnn' dy mdnh' klh*, which is said to correspond to *corrector totius orientis*. The last three words of this Palmyrene title refer clearly enough to 'the whole of the east', but a problem arises over the use of the Palmyrene term *mtqnn'*, which is related to an Aramaic verb meaning 'to restore to order'. As it stands, the Latin *Restitutor* is a more appropriate equivalent.[30] This title was commonly used in the third century, along with *Renovator* and *Conservator*,[31] usually applied retrospectively after some achievement in driving out enemies, repairing damaged frontiers and rescuing cities, or even whole provinces. On this basis, the posthumous inscription to Odenathus may entail nothing more than retrospective praise for having restored the east after the Persian invasions.[32] The inscription does not prove beyond doubt that Odenathus held an official Roman title, conferring certain powers on him.

The wording on the milestones, however, is more definite. Vaballathus is described as *pnrtt' dy mdnh' klh*. The appellation *pnrtt'* is not a Palmyrene word, but a direct transliteration of the Greek term *epanorthotes*, usually interpreted as the equivalent of the Latin *corrector*.[33] There are, however, some problems with the epigraphic evidence and its interpretation. The use of two dissimilar words in different Palmyrene inscriptions, *mtqnn'* and *pnrtt'*, perhaps to denote the title *corrector*, demands explanation, but Hartmann points out that there are other cases where a Palmyrene transliteration from Greek and also a Palmyrene equivalent are used on inscriptions to mean the same thing. Another consideration is that Odenathus held a previously unknown position in Palmyra, with no established term to describe it, so this may account for the variation in terminology.[34] These suggestions cannot be fully refuted, but still do not amount to conclusive proof that Odenathus was ever given the Latin title *corrector* or its equivalent.

For Vaballathus, the terminology used on the milestones leaves no doubt that he held the official title *epanorthotes*, but it is not a straightforward or uncontested process to relate this to Odenathus and the Roman title *corrector*. It cannot be conclusively proved that Vaballathus inherited the title *epanorthotes* from Odenathus. The same argument can be applied as for Vaballathus's use of the title *dux*, in that after the assassination of his father, he was too young to exercise full military or administrative powers in his own right, so it is highly likely that Zenobia would use and emphasize all the titles and attendant functions that Odenathus had enjoyed, for the sake of continuity, and to underline her own credibility as regent. Once again the suggestion is perfectly credible but does not constitute absolute certainty.

Another problem concerns the relationship between the Greek *epanorthotes*, the Palmyrene transliteration *pnrtt'* and the Roman title *corrector*, which has been challenged. It cannot be assumed that the Greek title is an exact translation of *corrector* with all the connotations of powers and functions that the Romans would have derived from it.[35] Whatever his titles were, it is undeniable that Odenathus did hold considerable power in the east, condoned by the Roman Emperor, but this does not necessarily imply that he supplanted the provincial government entirely, since governors of the individual eastern provinces continued to be appointed by Gallienus.[36] Odenathus's position was probably similar to that of Priscus, brother of Philip the Arab, who was *rector totius orientis* in the 240s. The similarity of the title *rector*, which is definitely attested, with *corrector*, which is not so readily proven, furnishes a very beguiling comparison but it is somewhat tenuous, especially since the sources do not describe the instructions that were given either to Priscus or to Odenathus. The brief from Gallienus may have given the Palmyrene leader very general instructions to keep the peace and defend the frontiers, leaving all the details of how it should be done to Odenathus, or he may have been very precise in outlining where Odenathus's powers began and ended. Unfortunately no one can say whether there were temporal and territorial limits to Odenathus's powers. The sources do not mention any specific length of tenure, such as five or ten years, or until such time as Gallienus was able to attend personally to the affairs of the east. That may perhaps have been taken as read, but it can never be known how Odenathus himself, and then Zenobia, viewed his command of the east, and whether they even considered that it might not be permanent and his powers might one day have to be relinquished.

The territorial limits to Odenathus's command as ruler of the east have been considered and disputed by modern scholars. The term *totius orientis* may have been clear to contemporaries, but 'Oriens' can be interpreted very differently by historians nearly two thousand years later. It has been suggested that Odenathus controlled only Palmyra and the desert zone up to the Euphrates, with no powers in the rest of Syria,[37] but the boundaries of *Oriens* may have corresponded to those of the later Diocese set up when Diocletian reformed provincial government, just over two decades later. If this is the case, Odenathus may have controlled Arabia, Palestina, Syria, Cilicia, Mesopotamia and the island of Cyprus. There is some evidence that Odenathus held some power in the city of Antioch, and possibly this extended to the two Syrian provinces.[38] Egypt seems to have remained outside the direct control of Odenathus but there may have been a section of the population who were sympathetic to the Palmyrenes.[39]

It is disputed whether Odenathus held *imperium maius*, which would give him powers that outranked other Roman officials,[40] so that he would be able to give orders to the provincial governors, reorganize the provinces, oversee repairs of the damaged cities, and regulate finances and the food supply, which would have considerable bearing on the pay and supply of the troops.

THE CAMPAIGN AGAINST THE PERSIANS

Not content with driving the Persians out of Syria and the eastern Roman provinces, Odenathus mounted an expedition into Persian territory, or perhaps two campaigns, in 261–2, and again in 267, though the dates are disputed.[41] Of all the ancient literary sources, only Zosimus explicitly states that there were two expeditions,[42] but there are some tenuous hints in other sources.[43] The aims of the expedition or expeditions must remain speculative, but revenge for the destruction of Palmyrene trading centres may have played a part. Another reason may have been to launch a pre-emptive strike to discourage Shapur from making any further attacks in the near future. Despite the assertion in the *Historia Augusta*[44] that the sole intention of Odenathus was to rescue Valerian, this probably did not feature in the motives of the Palmyrene leader at all.

Zosimus says that Gallienus asked Odenathus to assist in the east while he campaigned in Thrace.[45] Some communication with Gallienus presumably took place, either as a declaration of intent on the part of Odenathus, which then received Imperial sanction, or possibly instructions arrived to which Odenathus responded. The statement of Zosimus implies that the Palmyrene leader was in command of a large army, but the troops that Odenathus mustered are not documented. It has been suggested that he had only his own private army but it is doubtful that he would embark on a major campaign with only these troops.[46] Odenathus, as leader of the Palmyrenes, would presumably command the whole of the Palmyrene army, and he perhaps augmented it by recruiting contingents of Arab tribesmen, good fighters who were accustomed to desert conditions and the Euphrates region. Later sources are somewhat dismissive of the soldiers of Odenathus's army, giving the impression that he had assembled a group of peasants and armed them.[47] It was not out of the question in the third century for civilians to fight alongside the armies in times of extreme danger, but these rather derogatory descriptions probably do not tell the whole story, and should not imply that Odenathus took an untrained rabble into Persian territory. Zosimus says that he joined the remaining Roman troops to his own army.[48] He may have used Arab tribesmen, who were highly mobile, as scouts and light skirmishers, while the core of his army was made up of Roman legions and auxiliaries and the Palmyrene troops.

Probably in spring 262 Odenathus set off on the first Persian campaign, eventually reaching Ctesiphon and laying siege to the city. Virtually nothing is known of the route or routes followed by his army, or the events along the way. Ctesiphon may have been captured, but the sources disagree on this point. According to the *Historia Augusta* the lands all around the city were devastated and battles were fought with the Persian satraps who came to the relief of their capital,[49] then Odenathus withdrew, carrying off prisoners and booty.[50]

It seems that there was no formal peace treaty with the Persians.[51] It is feasible that Odenathus was empowered to arrange such a treaty, though ultimately it would be sanctioned by Gallienus. The achievements of the expedition were not inconsiderable. The cities of Carrhae and Nisibis and the province of Mesopotamia were restored to Roman control.[52] By the end of 263 Gallienus added *Persicus Maximus* to his victory titles and held a triumph in which he displayed the Persian captives respectfully sent to him by Odenathus.[53]

KING OF KINGS

For Odenathus the rewards were perhaps not as great as he had hoped, since Dura Europos and the other Euphrates trading stations were not restored, so the full resumption of trade was not to be facilitated, although the caravans continued until the fall of Palmyra in 274. The Persian campaign definitely increased Odenathus's prestige, embodied in his new title King of Kings, which was also bestowed on his son Herodianus. This occurred probably at the end of 263, and according to an inscription it took place near the River Orontes, so it is assumed that there was a ceremony at or near the chief city on that river, Antioch.[54] Once again the evidence does not apply to Odenathus directly, except in the posthumous inscription set up in 271 by Zenobia's generals.[55] Herodianus is directly attested as King of Kings on the honorary inscription set up by Julius Aurelius Septimius Vorodes,[56] but in some sources Odenathus is described merely as king.[57] It is unlikely that Odenathus would have been simply king while his son was King of Kings, though not all scholars agree on this point.[58] It seems logical to assume that he held this title from the end of the Persian campaign, sharing power with his son.

This elevation to supreme Royalty was a deliberate act, possibly undertaken after consultation with Odenathus's immediate entourage, perhaps even with other leading men of the eastern cities. Unlike the eastern city states of Emesa or Edessa, where there was a long lineage of kings, there was no hereditary kingship in Palmyra and no tradition of Royalty. No Royal palace has ever been identified in the city. Even as Ras Tadmor, Odenathus was not a hereditary chief and no palatial house has been identified as his residence.[59]

The designation King of Kings carried much weight in the east, and would be thoroughly understood by the Persians, who used the title themselves. The challenge was aimed at Shapur, not at the Romans.[60] It was not an attempt by Odenathus to usurp power or to oust Gallienus. He employed eastern methods to govern the eastern populations, using titles to which they were accustomed and in which they had faith. Although all the evidence for the use of the title derives from Palmyra itself, the full meaning would be appreciated in all the eastern cities and settlements.[61] In the absence of the Roman Emperor to act as a shield between the eastern provinces and the Persians, it was probably reassuring to know that there was an authoritative individual who could organize protection for the provinces and keep order within them.

At this period of her husband's supremacy, Zenobia remains in the background, unnoticed in the historical record, but to her contemporaries she probably assumed a much more prominent role. She accompanied Odenathus on campaign, gaining political advantage that would be of service to her later, and no doubt boosting the morale of the soldiers; the Palmyrene and Roman troops were probably dazzled by the young wife of their commander. According to later sources, Zenobia's reputation for bravery and for enduring hardships was as great as her husband's, but this may not be entirely due to retrospective hyperbole.[62] Familiarity with the army would be a useful attribute, and by sharing the tribulations of the soldiers on the march she no doubt laid the foundations of their respect and obedience that enabled her to retain power after her husband's death.[63]

After the Persian expedition, when Odenathus became King of Kings, it is reasonable to assume that Zenobia would adopt the title of Queen, as she is designated in the later literary sources,[64] but these are retrospective accounts and provide no indication of the date when Zenobia was first styled Queen of Palmyra. The earliest attested use of the title dates from two or three years after Odenathus's death,[65] but while he still lived she would hardly be blind to the dignity and status that the Royal title would bring to them both, especially after the success of the Persian campaign.[66]

This was the zenith of Odenathus's career. His achievements should not be underestimated. For the next few years after the Persian campaign the activities of Odenathus are not itemized in any source, but on the basis that no news is good news, the very silence of the ancient sources speaks for the success of his government of the eastern provinces. The Persians were dormant, beset by internal problems of their own, and did not launch a punitive expedition into Syria. Externally there seems to have been no threat to the eastern territories, and no internal unrest is recorded, save for a short-lived rebellion in Palestine, and a revolt in Egypt staged by the prefect Mussius Aemilianus, which was outside Odenathus's control, and was put down by Aurelius Theodotus, one of Gallienus's generals.

Whether it was due to Odenathus's wise government, or whether it was fortuitous, no would-be usurper from the eastern Roman provinces made a bid for Imperial rule, which suggests that recovery after the Persian invasions was fairly rapid, and that the army and the personnel of the provincial government were acquiescent in the rule of Odenathus if not contented with him.

The supremacy of Odenathus in the east is undeniable and he seems to have ruled wisely and well. Being an easterner himself he would understand the subtleties of governing the various eastern peoples. The author of the *Historia Augusta* labours the point somewhat, insisting that all would have been lost if Odenathus had not assumed power after the capture of Valerian, and that he would have been able to restore the whole of the east if he had lived longer.[67] The population of the cities and villages could rely on him to organize their protection from the Persians, and to maintain internal security. His reliability extended to his relationship with the Emperor Gallienus.[68] He controlled and governed the east but made no attempt to usurp Imperial power in the region, and never assumed standard Imperial titles. He was content with the designations that he had assumed and in which he had been confirmed, or that had been directly granted to him. None of his titles implied standard Roman appointments and so he was differentiated from normal Roman provincial governors and Imperial officials. Gallienus was careful to avoid giving Odenathus titles such as *praefectus* or *praeses*, which belonged to regular Roman governors.[69]

Odenathus and Zenobia collected an entourage, as would be natural for leading citizens of any community, and formed a court circle of friends and advisers, some of whom took the name Septimius, a clear indication of their adherence to their king and patron.[70] One of the best-known members of the court and the recipient of high offices was Septimius Vorodes, or Worod, who features in a number of inscriptions.[71] He may have adopted the name Septimius after *c.*258–9, if he is the same Vorodes as attested on an inscription giving his name as Aurelius Vorodes.[72] In 262 he was *procurator ducenarius* of Caesar,[73] and at the same time military commander,[74] with the usual Greek title *strategos* until *c.*264, but he is also described from 264 to 265 as *argapetes*, derived from the Parthian *hargbed*,[75] meaning commander of a fort or perhaps governor of a city. In the case of Vorodes it probably indicated a high command, embracing both military and civil control of Palmyra. The post was unusual, and the Parthian title may have been employed in the absence of any ready-made Palmyrene or Greek term to describe it.[76] By 266 Vorodes was clearly in charge of civil affairs, as administrator of justice (*dikaiodotes*) and public notary (*agoranomos*).[77] No other Palmyrene official was honoured by so many dedications during the supremacy of Odenathus. It is suggested that Vorodes acted as deputy for Odenathus, and probably controlled the state when Odenathus was absent.[78]

Since Vorodes is allegedly an Iranian name, and he bore a Parthian title in the Palmyrene government, it has been suggested that he may have been either a refugee who escaped from the Parthian court when Ardashir came to power,[79] or that he was the leader of a pro-Persian faction in Palmyra,[80] or even, less credibly perhaps, a Persian spy or double agent. Hartmann dismisses the concept that Vorodes was of Parthian origin, insisting that he was a member of the Palmyrene aristocracy, loyal to Odenathus and suitably rewarded.[81] He may have had some dealings with the Persians, however. In the *Res Gestae Divi Saporis*, the Persian king lists the names of all the officials who had submitted to him, one of whom is Warzabad, the Persian equivalent of Vorodes, who is also labelled *agoranomos*, an office which Vorodes held in Palmyra, first attested in 266. Opinion is divided as to the identity of this Vorodes, some authors insisting that the coincidence is so great that it is almost certain that this is the Palmyrene Septimius Vorodes.[82] He may have been an ambassador from Odenathus to the Persian court, possibly the leader of the embassy referred to by Petrus Patricius,[83] which opens up insoluble debate about the chronology and purpose of this event. The supposed connection with Persia from the end of Odenathus's reign has been taken as support for the statements of Zosimus and the *Historia Augusta* that Zenobia considered asking for assistance from the Persians against Aurelian, and that she contemplated finding refuge with them after her defeat.[84] Ultimately this must remain hypothetical, since the identification of Warzabad as Vorodes involves much speculation based on insufficient evidence.[85]

THE LAST YEARS OF ODENATHUS

Palmyra under Odenathus is often depicted as a secessionist state, comparable to the Gallic Empire in the west, where Postumus and his successors declared themselves Emperors and set up an independent state in opposition to the legitimate Emperor. The comparison is not valid for the reign of Odenathus, except in so far as Gallienus lost immediate personal control of two large parts of the Empire, but Odenathus was neither a rival nor a threat to Imperial security, or at least he did not declare his independence in such a blatant manner. Gallienus continued to appoint his own governors to the eastern provinces, and though there is no complete list of them, there is sufficient information to suggest that government of the individual provinces continued as before, with the insertion of an extra tier of overall administrative and military command in the form of the Palmyrene leader.[86] In the west Gallienus did not enjoy these privileges, and had lost not only the control of the entire government, but also the revenues of the western provinces and access to the armies. He may not have trusted Odenathus, but he was still Emperor of Rome and nominally in command of the eastern provinces, with Odenathus acting as his powerful subordinate.

The chronology of the last few years of Odenathus's rule is dubious and much disputed. Probably in the spring of 267 he mobilized for his second Persian campaign. No source except Zosimus specifically says that there were two campaigns. The *Historia Augusta* hints at a second expedition[87] but other authors descibe only one; they may well have conflated two campaigns, but the available information is too scanty to be certain.[88] The motive for another assault on Persia may have concerned an attempt to secure the trade routes preparatory to rehabilitating commerce, but for this there is not the slightest evidence. It does not seem to have been a retaliatory campaign, since no recent hostilities from the Persians are recorded.

The Palmyrenes probably reached Ctesiphon once again but did not capture the city, because the whole campaign was abruptly ended and the army marched back northwards to stem an influx of tribesmen into Asia Minor. This area would form part of Odenathus's responsibilities as ruler of the east. The *Historia Augusta* describes a hit-and-run raid of the Scythians, and indicates that this was contemporary with Odenathus's Persian campaign.[89] This can hardly be the first campaign of 262–3, especially since the author had already described this expedition in an earlier passage of the same biography.[90]

The Romans used the name Scythians indiscriminately to describe a variety of tribesmen of different origins, and the term is sometimes interchangeable with Goths, though strict ethnic purity is not to be expected among the groups of peoples who pressed on the Roman frontiers in the third century. The tribesmen combined and recombined in fluid gatherings, and probably never knew themselves by the names applied to them by the Romans. The tribesmen who built ships and used them to cross the Black Sea were probably Heruli, and the date was probably 267–8. The Heruli aimed for the coast of Bithynia-Pontus and attacked Heraclea (modern Eregli in Turkey). According to Syncellus, Odenathus and his son Herodianus marched there to relieve the city, but the tribesmen had already started back for the coast and were going home, laden with booty which they loaded onto their ships.[91] Many of them perished in a sea battle, perhaps conducted by Odenathus, or were shipwrecked. Shortly after this, Odenathus and his son Herodianus were assassinated. There is no solid evidence for the exact location or the precise month of the event, nor is there any reliable information about the identity of the murderer or murderers, or the motive for the assassination.

Syncellus says that Odenathus and his son were killed while they tried to counter the tribal incursion into Pontus, but Zosimus says that Odenathus was celebrating the birthday of one of his friends at Emesa when he was murdered.[92] Other sources neglect to mention where the murder took place. No ancient historian gives a clue as to the exact date of the assassination, which has been disputed. Various scholars have placed it anywhere between 266 and 268. Considerable confusion arose because in the summer of 272, when he had driven the Palmyrenes out of Egypt, Aurelian decided to redate the beginning of his reign, pushing it back for a few months, claiming that his accession should be dated directly after the death of Claudius, not after the elimination of Quintillus. This would mean that his reign was politically correct, following on seamlessly from his predecessor without the contretemps posed by the proclamation of Quintillus, who was not only eliminated in the physical sense but was thus eventually wiped from the administrative record as well. From the end of June 272, when Aurelian was recognized as sole Emperor with undisputed control of the east, the Egyptian papyri, which always counted the rule of the Roman Emperors from late August of one year to late August of the next, dutifully recorded the revised dating for Aurelian's reign, reckoning the period from August 271 to August 272 as his third year. Extrapolating backwards from this third year, scholars calculated that his first year was extremely short, belonging to the period August 269 to August 270, directly after the death of Claudius Gothicus. The problem was exacerbated by the fact that coin issues indicated that the first year of Aurelian was equivalent to the fourth year of Vaballathus, so naturally, using the available evidence, the first year of Vaballathus was reckoned as 266 to 267, and thus it seemed clear that the murder of Odenathus must have occurred at that time.

In reality, Aurelian's revised dating was a convenient fiction, and more recent research into the complexities of the Egyptian papyrus records has shown that while the Palmyrenes ruled Egypt, the original, unaltered date for the first year of Aurelian's reign, which was equated with the fourth year of Vaballathus's rule, was actually August 270 to August 271. This means that Zenobia and Vaballathus dated the first year of their supremacy to the period between August 267 and August 268, providing unequivocal support for the theory that the assassination of Odenathus occurred at some point during this same period. It probably occurred towards the end of 267 or at least some months before the early autumn of 268 when the Emperor Gallienus was assassinated.[93] If Odenathus was killed just after the battle with the Goths as indicated by Syncellus, then the murder probably relates to the date of the incursions of the so-called Scythians, and Udo Hartmann takes some pains to equate the invasion of the Heruli across the Black Sea in 267 to 268 with the death of the two Palmyrene kings who marched towards the Pontic coast to stop the tribesmen.[94]

Probably none of the fine details of the assassination will ever be known. There is scarcely any agreement in the ancient sources as to how, where and why the assassination occurred.[95] The *Historia Augusta* consistently claims that it was a cousin of Odenathus who killed him, naming him in two biographies as Maeonius, who allegedly seized power for a very short time after committing the crime.[96] The exact relationship is not recorded and Maeonius is otherwise unknown. Zonaras accuses a nephew of Odenathus, who killed him and Herodianus after an argument concerning a hunting incident.[97] Syncellus says it was another Odenathus who killed his namesake the king. This man may or may not have been a relative.[98]

With the exception of Zonaras, none of the ancient authors attempts to outline a motive for the assassination. The conspiracy theory hinted at by one or two of them is not helpful. If it was a plot, the sources do not help to identify the guilty parties. The *Historia Augusta* suggests that Zenobia once conspired against her husband but does not accuse her of complicity in the assassination. Zosimus says that there was a conspiracy, but does not name individuals or a group, and does not suggest any motive.[99] The Anonymous Continuator of Dio tells a strange tale of a certain Rufinus who acted independently in eliminating Odenathus, claiming that it was all done on behalf of Gallienus who condoned his actions.[100] This tale absolves Gallienus of instigating a plot but makes it clear that he desired the removal of the Palmyrene ruler. John of Antioch accuses Gallienus outright of forming a conspiracy to have Odenathus killed.[101]

The alleged conspiracies are unexplained because no reasons for the murder of Odenathus and his son are given. Hints at Zenobia's involvement can be dismissed, especially the modern interpretations that she was impatient with the pro-Roman policies of her husband and wished to pursue her own anti-Roman policy with megalomaniac ambitions to rule the whole Empire.[102] Had this been the case, it is difficult to explain why there was no irrevocable reversal of Odenathus's policies for at least two years after his death.

Other suspects who may have had a motive for the murder of Odenathus include the Persian king Shapur, the Roman Emperor Gallienus, and unknown easterners, probably Palmyrenes, who perhaps bore a grudge against their leader for any number of reasons. The Persians can be acquitted, since it would not have benefited them to remove Odenathus without installing a pro-Persian candidate of their own, as they usually did when dealing with Armenia. Such an action would have been only a stopgap, eventually reversed by the Romans when they could turn their attention to the east. There is a stronger case for Gallienus as the main suspect,[103] on the grounds that Odenathus had become far too powerful and represented a danger to the already disintegrating Empire. From the limited evidence it seems that Odenathus had been uniformly loyal to Gallienus and had shown no signs of wishing to rule the whole Roman world. His title King of Kings was customary in the east and was not designed to eclipse the Roman Emperor, but there may have been more covert indications of greater ambition, now lost to modern audiences, that Gallienus interpreted as a threat.[104] Some authors have interpreted the construction of fortifications at Adraha and Bostra in the province of Arabia as a pre-emptive strike against the overweening ambition of Odenathus, a supposition which Hartmann dismisses.[105] Although logical behaviour was not always an outstanding attribute of Roman Emperors, it would have been ill-advised, while there were so many other pressures on all the frontiers, to assassinate Odenathus, and risk causing chaos when the eastern provinces suddenly found themselves without the leader who had organized their corporate defence. In addition to his distrust of Odenathus, perhaps the Emperor considered that the east was pacified and that normal provincial government could be resuscitated, but without Odenathus, who could be safely removed, and the Palmyrenes would return to the task of protecting the frontier with Persia. Then the revenues of the east could be channelled into Rome to finance the strengthening of the frontiers and the attempt to win back the Gallic Empire. It is not impossible that Gallienus instigated a conspiracy, but perhaps not very likely. Even if he was not universally popular, Odenathus could command the support of a large part of the east, so a simple assassination, without the backup of an army to ensure the substitution of a strengthened, purely Roman government, would seem to be the height of folly. Assassination of the Gallic Emperor Postumus or of his successors would hardly have solved the problem of the *Imperium Galliarum*. Gallienus was scarcely in a position to remove the Palmyrene king and then take over the eastern command in person or to install another all-powerful general.

If it was not the Persian king or the Roman Emperor who killed Odenathus, other suspects must be considered. Opposition to Odenathus from the eastern provinces is not noted in any of the sources, so it is not possible to say whether any of the aristocrats from the city states of Bithynia, Cappadocia, Syria, Arabia or the lesser provinces had any reason to assassinate the Palmyrene leader. In Palmyra itself, jealousies may have been steadily accumulating among the family of Odenathus or among the nobility that led ultimately to a plot or a sudden vengeful attack fuelled by anger.[106] An unpremeditated crime of passion cannot be altogether ruled out in the assassination of Odenathus and his son. Assassins are not uniformly cold, calculating or logical individuals with a burning ambition to replace their victims on thrones or in positions of power. The murderer of Odenathus may not have entertained a political or military motive. He may have been a misguided fanatic.

A more likely theory is that the Palmyrene leader was killed by Palmyrenes who were discontented with the political developments in their city. When Odenathus was Ras Tadmor, he did not interfere with the day-to-day government and administration of Palmyra, but towards the end of Odenathus's reign there were changes. The democratic system may have been replaced. From about 264 the annual elections of the chief magistrates seem to have been given up,[107] and though the Palmyrene Senate and People survived at least until 266, when they dedicated a statue to Vorodes,[108] their power and influence had probably been curtailed by the King of Kings and his coterie of all-powerful civil and military officials such as Vorodes himself. A significant factor is that Septimius Vorodes, who had been *strategos* of the colony of Palmyra, *procurator ducenarius*, and administrator of justice, is not attested in the historical record after 267. No one knows what happened to him, so it is possible, as scholars have argued, that he was made redundant by Zenobia when she assumed power, but she seems to have retained other close associates of her husband, such as her generals Septimius Zabdas and Septimius Zabbai, who were most likely given their names by Odenathus as a reward for their services. It is equally possible that when Odenathus and Herodianus were killed, there may also have been a purge of high-ranking members of the immediate court circle. Vorodes may not have been the only official to disappear.

Only in the case of Maeonius is it recorded that the murderer tried to usurp the power of Odenathus. The conspirators, if such there were, had probably not planned what to do once the murder was committed, much as the assassins of Gaius Julius Caesar failed to make any plans to take immediate control of the government of Rome in 44 BC, and then stood back bewildered when the Republic did not spring back to life as soon as the tyrant was dead.

Zenobia's whereabouts at the time of the assassination are unknown. It is probable that she had accompanied her husband to Bithynia Pontus, in which case she would be able to take control immediately after the murder and rally the army to her side, her first consideration, in the dire circumstances, being for her continued existence and that of her son. Survival was essential, whether or not she intended to assume the full powers of her husband and stepson. There is support for this scenario in the account of Syncellus, who implies that there was a rapid turnover of events and the whole episode was quickly over and done with, more or less on the same day. Syncellus says that the murderer of Odenathus and Herodianus was immediately killed by the soldiers, who handed over the government to Zenobia. In the Roman Empire of the third century, where the soldiers made and unmade Emperors with monotonous regularity, this was a hackneyed theme, but it may actually be the truth. It would explain how and why Zenobia was able to assume power so quickly and comparatively easily after her husband's death, and it indicates that the army, probably composed of Roman and Palmyrene troops, was ready to support her and not the assassin or conspirators.

If Zenobia was in Palmyra when the assassination occurred, there would be an unavoidable and probably dangerous delay between the removal of the Palmyrene leader and the emergence of Zenobia as regent for Vaballathus. The support of the army was vital, and if most of the troops were in Bithynia Pontus, or perhaps at Emesa, while Zenobia was many miles away, the soldiers may not have thought of handing over the government to her, sending messengers to her and awaiting a reply. In the interval they could have chosen one of their officers, or any candidate for leadership could have engineered his own proclamation. The likelihood is that Zenobia was on the spot when her husband was killed, and she acted quickly to secure her own position.

By accident or design, Zenobia remained alive, and so did her son Vaballathus, which may simply indicate that she and the boy were considered unimportant by the assassin or the alleged conspirators. If this was so, he or they grossly underestimated the Queen.

4

Zenobia Widowed

Zenobia's first concern after the murder of her husband and stepson would be to secure the safety of herself and her son Vaballathus. Although it could be argued that the assassination of Odenathus ultimately benefited her,[1] rumours that she had planned the assassination, and had therefore also planned her assumption of Odenathus's powers, can be discounted. Though she clearly had her own supporters, such as the generals Zabdas and Zabbai who are attested at a later date, there is no reason to believe they were waiting in the wings with instructions to seize power.

No contemporary source elucidates what she did in the first moments after the death of Odenathus, but it is likely that she sought and secured the support of the troops serving in her husband's army, which may have comprised Palmyrene and Roman soldiers. Without their united support nothing further could have been achieved, and without immediate action and a visible demonstration of power on her own part, Zenobia may have failed to engender that united support. If she had not acted rapidly there would probably have been a scramble for control and a disintegration into factional strife. Zenobia was probably well known to the troops, especially if she had accompanied Odenathus on campaigns, prominently displayed, sharing hardships, and demonstrating courage. This is part of her legend, but it may be founded on fact. It is possible that Zabdas and Zabbai rallied the army on her behalf and helped to keep order. The troops probably had no difficulty in declaring for her.

There were several important tasks awaiting Zenobia's attention. Control of the army was paramount, but like other rulers who achieved their positions with the support of soldiers, Zenobia no doubt realized that attaining power is only half the battle. The real challenge lies in retaining it. She needed to sound out and cultivate the governors of the Roman provinces, then the rulers of the independent eastern kingdoms, and beyond these immediate neighbours she must come to some understanding with the Roman Emperor and protect her frontiers from any future incursions by the Persian Shahanshah.

THE REPRESENTATION OF VABALLATHUS AS RULER

It is not reported that Zenobia had to fight for supremacy, and there was probably no delay in achieving it. For those who argue for a lapse of time between the death of Odenathus and the installation of Vaballathus in his father's place everything depends on the date of the assassination. Christol cites Egyptian documents which reveal that Vaballathus was acknowledged at some time between 29 August 267 and 29 August 268, so if the death of Odenathus occurred in 266 or the spring or even the early summer of 267, then there seems to have been a delay in proclaiming him as the ruler of Palmyra.[2] Sartre says that there was some delay before Vaballathus appeared as *Imperator*,[3] which is perfectly true, but this does not mean that there was any delay in his taking over from Odenathus. The delayed use of the title *Imperator* was deliberate policy on the part of Zenobia, because such a firm indication of the assumption of Roman powers would be to risk Roman retribution. At this early stage she did not wish to usurp power.

The difficulty over the supposed delay in the elevation of Vaballathus as his father's successor disappears if the assassination of Odenathus occurred only a short time before that of Gallienus, who was murdered in late summer 268. Since there is no absolute proof of the date of Odenathus's death, the matter becomes one of opinion, but it would seem sensible for Zenobia not to hesitate for an instant after the death of her husband, but to assume power immediately in the name of her son.

Vaballathus was only about 10 years old, so it would be obvious that the real power lay with Zenobia as regent, and her generals. She probably exercised some restraint in how she represented her son to the army and the people, and she seems to have chosen his titles with care. On the earliest known inscriptions attesting his rule[4] Vaballathus is styled in Palmyrene as *mlk mlk'*, King of Kings, as were his father and his stepbrother Haeranes. He is also styled as *pnrtt'*. As discussed in the previous chapter, this is not a Palmyrene word, but a direct transliteration of the Greek *epanorthotes*. This title has been interpreted as a translation of the Latin *corrector*, but the interpretation is not without debate.[5]

King of Kings was a purely eastern concept and had very little to do with

Rome. It made a statement to the Persians but it was never intended as a challenge to the Roman Emperor, and it was not taken up in any of the sources as a serious attempt to usurp power. The title *epanorthotes* is more problematic. If it was indeed the case that Gallienus named Odenathus as *corrector*, and if it is true that *epanorthotes* is its equivalent in Greek, then Vaballathus ought not to have assumed this title. It was not an inheritable office automatically handed down from father to son, and it would require the authorization of the Emperor to bestow the title once again on another individual. There is no evidence that Gallienus granted the title to Vaballathus, and since he had no right of inheritance of a Roman office and its powers, the continued use of such a title after the death of the original holder would be regarded in Rome as a provocative act, if not a declaration of intent to usurp power in the east.

However, the case for the prosecution of Vaballathus as usurper is not so clear. The questions surrounding the exact Latin equivalent of *epanorthotes* have already been mentioned, but it is worth reiterating the salient points. The title *epanorthotes* was possibly an honorary epithet, and it may not have bestowed specific powers on Vaballathus. It is not even certain that Vaballathus ever inherited the title from his father, since Odenathus is not designated by this specific Greek title *epanorthotes* on any of the extant inscriptions. Furthermore, the assumption that *epanorthotes* equates to the Latin *corrector* is probably without foundation. Neither Odenathus nor Vaballathus is ever attested unequivocally in Latin as *corrector*. Concerning Odenathus there is even more room for doubt about his alleged role as *corrector*. On the inscription dedicated to him posthumously in 271, he is described by the Palmyrene title *mtqnn'*, which has been interpreted as the equivalent of *corrector*, but the term was not in general usage, and is better translated by the honorary epithet *Restitutor*, common to Roman Emperors who had restored peace to a province or region.[6] It is fairly certain that wide-ranging powers *were* bestowed on Odenathus by Gallienus, but it is not certain that these powers were expressed by the title *corrector*.

On the available evidence it cannot be proven that Zenobia had always harboured the ambition to rule the whole Roman world from the first moment that she took power, and that she advertised her intentions by the deliberate elevation of her son Vaballathus. The titles which Zenobia chose to display were customary in the east, and were not derived from official Roman administrative appointments. Inherited rule was perfectly acceptable to the people of the eastern provinces, and Zenobia was as discreet as possible about the way in which it was expressed. This may be the reason why, until 270 and after, there is no evidence of *Dux Romanorum* or *Imperator* among Vaballathus's titles.[7] Zenobia deliberately avoided the use of such blatantly Roman military titles, nor did she attempt to express them by means of a Greek or Palmyrene equivalent.

As for herself, Zenobia assumed only legitimate titles which were hers by right. On the milestone inscriptions, in the Palmyrene version, she is called the most illustrious and pious Queen, which was a perfectly legitimate title for the widow of the King of Kings. Her name is given as Septimia Bat-Zabbai, but in the Greek version she is Septimia Zenobia and the Greek word used to describe her status is *lamprotate*, the equivalent of *clarissima* in Latin, which translates as most illustrious but also indicates senatorial rank. Though she could not be a senator herself, it was perfectly acceptable to describe herself thus, since she had been married to the senator Odenathus.

GAINING THE SUPPORT OF THE EASTERN KINGDOMS AND PROVINCES

Using eastern titles in eastern languages, Zenobia reconciled the army and the eastern kingdoms and provinces to her rule. She opened up opportunities to the eastern nobility to take offices in her government.[8] Religious tolerance was a necessity if she was to weld together so many disparate units. She came from a city where several cults existed side by side and was accustomed to dealing with a multilingual and multicultural society. She accommodated Christians and Jews alike. Her legendary association with Paul of Samosata, the heretical Bishop of Antioch, has been exaggerated, deriving mostly from much later sources.[9] Paul was excommunicated after a Synod in 267–8 for heretical teaching, which was influenced by Jewish doctrine and inclined towards a monotheistic viewpoint that acknowledged God but denied Jesus Christ. According to Athanasius, writing in the fourth century, he found protection with Zenobia, who is described as Jewish.[10] There is no evidence that Zenobia took Paul under her wing or invited him to her court, but she may simply have supported him as Bishop of Antioch in the interests of religious tolerance, in a squabble that perhaps seemed to her to be purely an internal affair of the Church.[11]

It was probably in a spirit of enquiry and learning that Zenobia received the emissaries of the Manichaeans at Palmyra. The new religion of Manichaeism had been very recently founded by Mani of Babylon, who was executed by the Persians in 276. Mani's teaching was derived from Gnosticism, and was based on the dualistic principles of the eternal conflict between good and evil. The association with Zenobia is not firmly attested, but she was said to have extended her protection to the bishops of the new cult. It did not take root in Palmyra, and the visit may have been a brief affair, given greater emphasis than it merited in the later sources.

The territorial and ethical boundaries of Zenobia's rule have never been decisively described. It has been argued that she controlled only Palmyra and Emesa and their surrounding territories[12] but if this was the case it is remarkable that in 270, over the course of only a few months she suddenly extended her control from these confined areas to the whole of Syria, and then embarked on the absorption of Arabia and Egypt. It is more likely that she continued from where Odenathus left off, and already had control of Syria, Mesopotamia and Asia Minor,[13] and that she retained this power unchallenged. During the first two years of Zenobia's rule the Antioch mint issued coins bearing only the head of Gallienus, and then of Claudius, but nothing for Quintillus, and with no acknowledgement of the Queen or Vaballathus from 268 to 269 onwards. This has been interpreted as a definite indication that she had no control over the city of Antioch or the rest of the province of Syria Coele, but it is more likely that she did not find it necessary during the reign of Claudius to issue coins in the name of Vaballathus. When he died there were two rival Emperors, and in the changed circumstances, she had to make a choice. She did not acknowledge Quintillus, perhaps ensuring that the mint did not issue coins for him, then when she reopened it she used the opportunity to declare for Aurelian, but at the same time to declare the position of Vaballathus as his subordinate in the east.[14] The theory that she did not control Antioch is in any case offset by the statement of Zosimus that she had a residence there. It had perhaps been established by Odenathus when he chose to elevate himself and his son as King of Kings at or near Antioch. Eutropius says that Zenobia inherited all Odenathus's powers, and according to the *Historia Augusta* in the reign of Gallienus she took control of the east, which implies more than just Palmyra and the desert up to the Euphrates.[15]

What exactly is meant by control is debatable. As far as is known, Roman governors continued to be appointed to the various provinces, so Zenobia was not responsible for day-to-day administration, dispensation of justice or the collection of taxes, but she was probably empowered to give orders to the provincial governors for the purposes of corporate defence. At least three Roman governors, all of equestrian rank, were compliant or even actively supported her, and she did not interfere with their activities in day-to-day government. Salvius Theodorus, *praeses* of Syria Phoenice under Claudius and therefore contemporary with Zenobia as Queen, set up an inscription to the Emperor with no mention of the Palmyrene rulers, so to all intents and purposes normal Roman administration was still functioning and Zenobia did not insist on constant acknowledgement of her status or equal rank with the Roman Emperor.[16] Julius Marcellinus was Prefect of Egypt from 270 to 271, and Statilius Ammianus, who was governor of Arabia during the supremacy of Odenathus, succeeded Marcellinus as Prefect of Egypt from 271 to 272.[17] There is some argument as to who made this appointment, whether it was Aurelian[18] or Zenobia,[19] but since Ammianus was active under Odenathus, without recorded hostility to the Palmyrenes, it may be that Zenobia had more or less inherited him and that he was a trusted ally.

No signs of unrest are recorded in the ancient sources when Zenobia took over from her husband, not even from later authors who were hostile to her, and who would certainly have made some mileage out of the fact that there was opposition to her in the east from the very beginning. Only oblique hints of opposition are found in the *Historia Augusta*. In the biography of Claudius, the author says that several appeals were made to the Emperor for deliverance from the men of Palmyra,[20] but there is no mention of the originators of these appeals and no details of what the men of Palmyra were supposed to have done. Another insinuation is found in the letter allegedly written to the Senate by Aurelian, where the Emperor is made to say that the Egyptians, the Armenians and the Arabs were in such fear of Zenobia that they never rebelled against her.[21] Included in this list are the Saracens, the late Roman name for the nomadic Arabs, whom Zenobia recruited as allies. Some of them appeared as captives in Aurelian's triumph.[22] Significantly, the author does not make Aurelian say that the eastern communities in Syria were afraid of Zenobia, though Zosimus reports that when Aurelian approached Palmyra in pursuit of the Queen, he easily won over the eastern cities. The people of Antioch welcomed Aurelian, as did the cities along the Orontes and then Emesa,[23] but even if this is true it may simply mean that the eastern cities chose to change their allegiance and to declare their support for Aurelian because he was clearly going to be the victor, and he promised leniency to those that submitted to him. The Syrians cannot seriously be accused of duplicity towards Zenobia. Their submission need not imply that they had always opposed her but had been firmly oppressed and too weak to resist her until this point, when rescue was imminent. It simply means that survival was paramount, a concept that Zenobia herself understood perfectly.[24]

The first potential dissidents who could have mobilized against Zenobia when she assumed power were the Roman provincial governors and the commanders of the Roman armies, but there does not seem to have been the slightest hint of opposition from the Roman authorities within Syria and the provinces. It is not recorded that Zenobia marched on the headquarters of any provincial governor to overpower him, nor is it recorded that a Roman governor or an army commander attempted to remove the Queen by diplomatic means, by the substitution of another ruler more acceptable to Rome, or by military action. Hartmann suggests that the governors of the provinces of Syria Phoenice, Syria Coele, Palestina and Mesopotamia, and the commanders of the Roman armies, recognized and supported Vaballathus as the successor of Odenathus.[25]

RELATIONS WITH ROME

Opposition from Gallienus is taken as read by the ancient authors, but the report that he sent an army against Zenobia under the praetorian prefect Heraclianus[26] may not be entirely accurate. The story is somewhat garbled. In the life of Gallienus, it is said that Heraclianus set out against the Persians to finish off the war that Odenathus had been forced to abandon, but on the way he was defeated by the Palmyrenes, something of a non sequitur unless the Persian campaign was a subterfuge and the real purpose was to dislodge Zenobia, in the confused period immediately after the death of her husband.[27] Modern authors assume that the Palmyrenes were not fooled by the ostensible purpose of the Persian expedition and reacted accordingly, chasing Heraclianus out of the east with the loss of most of his troops.[28]

Interpretations of this story are varied. There is general agreement that the praetorian prefect Heraclianus was in Milan in 268, and that he was one of the conspirators who arranged the assassination of Gallienus. Whatever was the exact date of the murder of Odenathus, in 267 or 268, there would be only a very short time span to organize a military expedition between the assassination of the Palmyrene leader and that of Gallienus, and even if Heraclianus had accomplished such an expedition, after such an ignominious and rapid defeat Gallienus would no doubt have deprived him of his post as praetorian prefect, so that he would hardly appear in this role in summer 268 if he had been trounced by Zenobia a few months earlier. One suggestion is that an eastern expedition was planned, with the dual purpose of replacing Odenathus and of finishing off the Persian campaign that he had started, but this plan was never carried out because the invasion of the Heruli occupied all the Emperor's time and resources, then immediately afterwards the cavalry commander Aureolus made his bid for Imperial power, quickly followed by the assassination of Gallienus and the acclamation of Claudius as Emperor.[29] Another more attractive suggestion, made by David Potter, is that the author of the *Historia Augusta* deliberately placed all the misfortunes in the reign of Gallienus to round off his biography of this disastrous Emperor, so that he could begin his biography of Claudius with a record that was squeaky clean from the start.[30] When it is remembered that the Emperor Claudius was claimed as an ancestor by that studied embodiment of perfection, Constantine, this scenario becomes more likely. It is possible that there really was an expedition to the east under the praetorian prefect Heraclianus, but it was despatched by Claudius, and its failure was glossed over and retrospectively dated to the reign of Gallienus.

The removal of the Emperor Gallienus and the installation of Claudius seemed initially to have little effect on Palmyra, though the paucity of the sources is in part to blame for this impression. Zenobia would need to reassess her position and perhaps make overtures to Claudius, though there is no evidence to suggest that she did so. It is likely that Claudius made some official pronouncement regarding Palmyra, even if only to pre-empt criticism from his advisers and from various Roman officials, who considered that Gallienus had neglected the affairs of the east and therefore would not tolerate a laissez-faire attitude from his successor. The new Emperor may have allowed Zenobia to continue as Queen and regent for her son, ruling on the same basis as her husband, so that she was recognized as having control of the eastern frontier and the responsibility for its defence, a task which Claudius was not in a position to undertake personally.[31] In a letter supposedly written by Aurelian to the Senate, the author of the *Historia Augusta* says that Claudius allowed Zenobia to retain her power and take charge of frontier defence in the east while he fought the Goths, a decision which he made wisely (*prudenter*).[32]

PROTECTION OF THE EASTERN FRONTIER

Whether or not Zenobia was officially asked by the Emperor to secure the eastern frontier with Persia, it was in her own interests to do so. She fortified some of the settlements on the Euphrates. Among others, two of these sites were rebuilt by the Emperor Justinian in the sixth century, and were mentioned by Procopius in his account of Justinian's work.[33] One is at Halebiyeh, on the right bank of the Euphrates, at a point where the river flows through a narrow canyon. Procopius says that it was built by Zenobia and named after herself, which was a normal Hellenic tradition. Hartmann postulates that it may be close to the old site of Birtha, or Birtha-Asporakan, which was destroyed in 253 by Shapur.[34] The visible ruins, dating primarily from the reign of Anastasius, comprise a trapezoidal fortification with thirty bastions, and the citadel at the eastern side. The later fortifications of the sixth century are not so well preserved. The eastern rampart was originally too close to the river, and had to be rebuilt more than once, and it was this proximity to the river that helped the nineteenth-century British archaeological expedition, led by F. Chesney, to identify the fortress as that of Zenobia,[35] because it was exactly as described by Procopius, who says that the river flowed at the base of its eastern rampart.[36]

Three kilometres south of Halebiyeh, on the opposite bank of the Euphrates, Zenobia also fortified another settlement at Zalebiyeh.[37] It is likely that the Palmyrenes used these fortified cities as bases and perhaps stationed troops in them permanently, but this remains a suggestion without firm proof. It has been pointed out that since Dura Europos was destroyed in 256 and not rebuilt, these fortresses may have taken its place.[38]

Zenobia's programme of fortification does not sit well with the allegation, made in ancient times, that she had made an agreement of some kind with the Persians. The evidence is merely circumstantial. In a letter supposedly written by Zenobia to Aurelian she makes the threat that she expected to receive Persian reinforcements for her army.[39] The Romans considered that this was not an idle threat because Aurelian was said to have displayed captive Persian soldiers in his triumph after the fall of Palmyra, though where and how he captured them is not elucidated.[40] Just before her own capture, the Romans said that Zenobia was preparing to flee to the Persians. It was also claimed that Zenobia was worshipped like the Persian leaders, and that she drank wine with their generals.[41] In the context of Palmyra, with its blend of Hellenic, eastern and Parthian or Persian customs, these allegations are not surprising. Zenobia probably kept a watching brief on her Persian neighbours, and she no doubt dealt with them politely and circumspectly, but this is not conclusive proof that she allied with the Persians against Rome. This is provocative rhetoric for the Roman audience, to illustrate how the Palmyrene Queen represented an enormous threat to stability by allying with Rome's greatest enemy.

Far from making an alliance, Zenobia may have fought against the Persians. There may have been some encounters between the Persians and the Palmyrene army on the borders of Palmyrene territory. There is no record of actual attacks by the Persians, nor of Palmyrene military activity, but probably in 269 Claudius took the victory title *Parthicus Maximus*,[42] and Vaballathus adopted *Persicus Maximus* as part of his own titles. Hartmann suggests that these titles are linked, perhaps commemorating an unrecorded skirmish with Shapur's troops, perhaps near the Euphrates or upper Tigris, where Shapur may have tried to regain control of northern Mesopotamia.[43]

QUEEN AND REGENT

Protection of the frontiers may have helped to instil confidence in the peoples of the east, sufficient to engender support for Zenobia as Queen and regent for Vaballathus. In the past the Palmyrenes had rendered good service in ensuring peace in the desert and along the Euphrates,[44] so the continuance of this service and the assurance that the Queen would continue the work of Odenathus in this respect would reassure the population of the eastern cities. Zenobia's title as Queen was legitimate as the wife of Odenathus the King, and though there was a strong tradition in the east of powerful ruling queens, Zenobia represented herself as regent for Vaballathus, and did not claim to rule independently in her own right.

Legendary role models of whom she would have been aware include Dido, Queen of Carthage; Semiramis, the widow of Shamsi-Addad of Assyria and regent for her young son in the late ninth century BC;[45] and the Queen of Sheba, familiar from the Bible and Islamic tradition.[46] Cleopatra was a more pertinent role model who dealt warily with Rome to keep her country intact while fostering her son Caesarion as her intended successor. Zenobia's association with Cleopatra was not just romantic hyperbole. In claiming descent from the last Queen of Egypt she also claimed a strong connection with Egypt, and perhaps cultivated her knowledge of the Egyptian language as part of this connection, representing herself to the populace as the rightful successor to Cleopatra and ruler of her country. Antonia Fraser points out that it demonstrates Zenobia's intelligence.[47] Politically, descent from Cleopatra would enhance her position in Egypt.

Closer to Zenobia's own era, the Syrian women of the Severan dynasty provided a more pragmatic object lesson in empire building.[48] Julia Domna, the wife of Septimius Severus, was born in Emesa, the daughter of Julius Bassianus, the priest of the sun god Heliogabalus. She was highly regarded by the army, with an official status as *Mater Castrorum* or mother of the camp, granted to her by her husband. Zenobia's relationship with the troops may have emulated this status without the title. Julia Domna committed suicide after the assassination of her son Caracalla in 217, but her female relatives succeeded in wresting supreme power from the usurper Macrinus in 218. Julia Domna's sister Julia Maesa, and Maesa's two daughters Julia Soaemias and Julia Mamaea, arranged the declaration of the 13-year-old Varius Avitus Bassianus, the son of Julia Soaemias, as Emperor. It had all ended badly, largely because of Bassianus's fierce devotion to his Syrian deity, whose name he adopted as the Emperor Elagabalus. The Romans were fairly tolerant of other religions, but in this case the rites and cult practices proved too extreme for the Senate and People of Rome, and the power of the Syrian women was resented. Four years after his accession Elagabalus was assassinated and his more sober cousin Severus Alexander succeeded him. If Zenobia drew any conclusions from this slice of political history, she probably realized that rule by women, especially foreign women, was not welcomed with open arms at Rome, and that the survival of the chosen male figurehead depended on a low profile and a non-intrusive, non-threatening representation, and above all on seamless assimilation with Roman forms and customs.

In the Arab world as well as in the Roman Empire there were precedents for woman as rulers, who were more happily accommodated in the east. There were various pre-Islamic Arab queens of the first millennium BC, of whom little is known, except that their brief appearances in history and legend reveal that rule by a woman was not anathema to the ancient Arabs.[49] Nor were the Jews averse to women rulers; as Stoneman points out there were Jewish queens such as Bathsheba and Jezebel.[50]

Zenobia has been portrayed as a warrior queen, like the British Boudicca, leading her armies into battle.[51] It is a portrait derived in part from the ancient authors who described how she accompanied the armies of Odenathus, and in part from the willing and eager romanticization of the Palmyrene Queen by modern admirers, who see her as the champion of the oppressed in her struggle against Rome. She was said to rule with the vigour of a man,[52] and to perform her tasks just as competently as her husband.[53] She was said to have accepted the diadem, a symbol of Royalty in the east, but to the Romans this held a somewhat more sinister significance as an assumption of Imperial power, corroborated by the fact that Zenobia readily adopted the Imperial cloak (*sagulum*) of her husband.[54] Thomas Bauzou interprets the cloak as the *paludamentum*, the red cloak of Roman military commanders,[55] but whether it was to be taken literally that she actually wore the cloak, or merely metaphorically, meaning that she took over the role of Odenathus, is not important, because either way it implies that she assumed military command. This does not necessarily mean that Zenobia rode into battle clad in armour and wielding weapons. As Queen and regent for her son that would have been somewhat reckless. The image of a female leader risking her life in such a way evokes a tragic heroine staking all on a last battle because she had nothing left to lose. Zenobia had everything to lose, not just power but the guardianship of her son, who would probably not have lived long if she were to be killed. She had a duty to survive.

She did not need to ride into battle in order to exercise command. Ultimate responsibility for political and military decisions rested with her. When military actions began, she probably accompanied her army in person, but she entrusted the conduct of campaigns to her generals Zabdas and Zabbai. Septimius Zabdas features in the history of Zosimus as the general in chief of the army, whereas Zabbai's role was commander of Tadmor, presumably with responsibility for the safety of the city and environs of Palmyra.[56] These two generals with different spheres of influence perhaps evolved from the earlier *Strategos* Against the Nomads and *Strategos* of the Peace. When Aurelian attacked the Palmyrenes, Zabdas was the commander at Antioch and after the Palmyrene defeat he led Zenobia and the army to Emesa.[57] The *Historia Augusta*, describing the

Palmyrene invasion of Egypt during the reign of Claudius, names one of the commanders as Saba,[58] and in the life of Aurelian he is named Zaba,[59] two slightly distorted versions of Zabdas.

QUEEN AND COURT

Both Zabdas and Zabbai were members of Zenobia's court and were among her most important advisers. Together they dedicated the statues of Odenathus and Zenobia, set up in the Great Colonnade at Palmyra, for which only the inscriptions remain.[60] The other members of her court society included philosophers and men of letters, whom she gathered around her just as Julia Domna had done half a century earlier. Perhaps the most famous of Domna's protégés was Lucius Flavius Philostratus, the sophist also known as 'the Athenian', from whom she commissioned his best-known work, the *Life of Apollonius of Tyana*.

Zenobia's most famous protégé was Cassius Longinus, a celebrated teacher of philosophy and rhetoric at Athens, where he had founded an Academy in *c.*230. Some years later the philosopher Plotinus set up another school in Rome, and the two scholars were in correspondence with one another, often through their pupils. Plotinus said that Longinus was less of a philosopher than a rhetor and literary critic, but the rivalry, if such it was, between him and Plotinus was not of an embittered academic nature. In 263 Longinus sent his star pupil Porphyry to the school in Rome to continue his studies with Plotinus, and he was anxious to obtain a complete set of Plotinus's works.

Highly educated and passionate about learning, Longinus was labelled in antiquity as a living library and a walking museum.[61] He had been teaching at Athens for over three decades when the city was attacked by the Heruli in 267. The city was successfully defended and an account of the siege was included in the history of the Gothic wars by Publius Herennius Dexippus, who is credited with organizing the defence, though this impression is conveyed largely through the way in which he built up his own role in his chronicle of the attack.

It may have been after the siege that Longinus left Athens for the east. The fear of further attacks may have influenced many Athenians and perhaps curtailed intellectual life. However philosophical a teacher and pupil may be, it is hard to teach and hard to learn when existence is threatened, and in preparing for continued defence there are usually other priorities than learning. Longinus perhaps felt the need to retire and go home. He was probably in his sixties, and he had been born in the east, most likely at Emesa.[62] He may have been the nephew of the rhetor Frontinus of Emesa, who also taught at Athens.[63] Arriving in the east, Longinus settled in Syria Phoenice, though he is not firmly attested there until 270.[64] The lack of precision about the date of his arrival allows some scholars to postulate that he was a member of the court circle of Odenathus, especially since he produced an oration for the Palmyrene leader.[65] It is not known if this was composed during the lifetime of Odenathus, or whether it was written at the behest of Zenobia after the death of her husband.[66] The work is now lost and its former existence is known to the modern world only by its reputation, as reported in a letter of Libanius.[67] If Longinus was already settled in Syria at the time of Odenathus's death, he may have been part of Zenobia's intellectual inheritance from her husband, but since the sources associate him solely with Zenobia[68] it is more likely that the invitation to the Palmyrene court originated with her. He was appointed as tutor to Vaballathus, whose reputation would gain much from his association with such an eminent teacher.

Various scholars have tried to discern the reasons why Longinus joined Zenobia's circle. He may have agreed to write the oration for Odenathus, intending to return home afterwards, but then was perhaps caught up in events and remained with Zenobia till the end.[69] He has been accused of giving in to the seduction of wealth and ease,[70] or of abandoning the intellectual life in favour of embarking on an experiment to mould and influence the new Palmyrene government on philosophical principles. Neither of these two extremes sounds wholly plausible. He was an unlikely mercenary, selling his talents to the highest bidder, and though he has been credited with an enormous influence over Zenobia he may not have exercised it as a frustrated politician hoping to be able to rule the eastern half of the Roman Empire at one remove.

For some scholars, both ancient and modern alike, Longinus was the evil genius behind Zenobia's territorial expansion and her supposed intention to rule the whole Empire. He has been described as the ideological support behind Zenobia,[71] and the man who fanned the flames of the Queen's ambition,[72] as though she was totally unable to think for herself and required a renowned philosopher to outline her next moves for her, or to martial her thoughts and form a plan of action, or even to write her letters, as implied in the *Historia Augusta*.[73] Some scholars have taken the inference even further, to interpret the events of the last years of Zenobia's reign as a nationalist Syrian uprising, or an anti-Roman movement with no other purpose than to throw off the yoke of Roman rule and take over the Empire. Zenobia's plans embraced neither of these things as an end in itself, and the blame for her actions from 270 onwards cannot be laid entirely at Longinus's door.[74]

Other members of Zenobia's intellectual circle remain shadowy or may even be fictitious, such as Nicomachus, who receives a casual mention in the *Historia Augusta* as the man who translated into Greek a letter written by Zenobia to Aurelian, dictated in the Syrian language.[75] Nicomachus is not known from any other source, and since Longinus was said to have been engaged to teach Greek to Zenobia, it is questionable whether she would have needed a different scholar to help her translate her letter. Without actual proof, historians are forced to speculate as to which scholars and literary men may have been involved with Zenobia. Nicostratus of Trapezus is a likely candidate, a historian who wrote an account of events from the time of Philip the Arab to the capture of Valerian, rounding it off with the victory of Odenathus over Shapur. He may have been engaged by Zenobia, serving a similar purpose to Longinus, in providing a history of Odenathus.[76]

On firmer but not absolutely certain ground, Callinicus of Petra was said to be associated with Zenobia, and it is alleged that his history of Alexandria was dedicated to her. This conclusion is derived from the fact that he wrote the work at about the time when Zenobia conquered Egypt, and he dedicated it to Cleopatra, claimed as one of Zenobia's more illustrious ancestors. The connection is perhaps likely but it does not constitute proof that Callinicus was attached to Zenobia's court.[77]

It is easy to sneer at Zenobia's attempts to create an intellectual centre and to gather the scholars of the day around her. Palmyrene literary and scholarly life has been described as impoverished when compared to other Syrian centres such as Edessa and Tyre, and the celebrated cities of Antioch and Alexandria.[78] Richard Stoneman provides a glowing picture of the scholarly traditions of Hellenized western Syria,[79] and compared to this rich literary tradition the Palmyrene court was decidedly the poorer. Longinus explained the lack of facilities in a letter to his pupil Porphyry, in which he urged him to join him for the sake of his health, because the excellent climate would be beneficial to him. He asked Porphyry to bring, or to send, copies of Plotinus's works, because there was a such a chronic shortage of copyists that he had been forced to take one of them away from all his other jobs to devote himself entirely to copying Plotinus, until the set was complete.[80] Clearly writing and publishing was not one of the major industries in Palmyra, but Zenobia was determined to make a start. Longinus was probably keen to help her, perhaps hoping to found a school at Palmyra, just as his contemporary Amelius Gentilianus, a pupil of Plotinus, had founded a Neoplatonic school at Apamaea. All great learning enterprises, even the great library at Alexandria, had to begin somewhere, by obtaining books by gift or purchase, or copying them, and finding librarians to organize it all and teachers to attract pupils. If Zenobia had remained in power for longer and had been able to hand down that power to succeeding generations, the intellectual life of Palmyra may have blossomed and eventually come to rival that of the other eastern cities. She had only about five years at the most to devote to the task, and so her attempts seem puny and derisory, but this is to judge a project only just begun, without considering what might have been.

Zenobia was still under 30 years old when she was widowed, and for the next two years after the murder of her husband she continued to play the same part as Odenathus, protecting the eastern frontier and ensuring the safety of the eastern provinces from attacks by the Persians. The Palmyrene army kept the desert nomads in check, securing the routes and communities bordering on the desert.

Though Vaballathus was only about 10 years old, he was presented as the successor of Odenathus. Zenobia relied on her husband's prestige and good name to ensure the acceptance of their son as the next ruler of the east, under her tutelage. She engaged Cassius Longinus, the best tutor and mentor she could find to educate the boy destined to be King of Kings in reality and not just in name. She brought him up to speak Latin, and though she herself could not speak it with ease, she did so when necessary, recognizing no doubt that without this language she and her successors would be at a disadvantage when dealing with the Romans and their politics.

With a respect for learning, Zenobia tried to establish a literary and philosophical circle that may have developed and flourished if enough time had been allowed. She also educated herself, allegedly learning Greek with Longinus as tutor, though perhaps this means that she studied Greek literature, and perhaps philosophy, with him rather than the language, since she was said to read Roman history in Greek. According to the *Historia Augusta* her knowledge of the history of the east and Alexandria was extensive, and she was fluent in Egyptian.[81]

If she harboured any tremendous ambitions to usurp the Roman Emperor, Zenobia kept such plans well hidden in the first years after the death of Odenathus. It is arguable that she did not in fact plan for anything more than the continued rule of the east in place of her husband. Everything was low-key and undemonstrative. She claimed only non-Roman titles for herself and for Vaballathus, using eastern forms and terminology, expressing the titles that she did use in Palmyrene and Greek, not in Latin. She did not claim supremacy over the whole of the east by elbowing aside any reference to the legitimate Emperor. If the governor of Syria Phoenice could set up an inscription bearing only the names and titles of the Emperor Claudius with no mention of Zenobia, it is likely that the privilege applied to the other governors. The mint at Antioch issued coins in the name of Gallienus and then Claudius without hindrance from Zenobia. It is likely that she exercised forbearance in accord with the low profile she had adopted in the use of titles and forms of address. There were no detectable signs of rebellion in Zenobia's attitude, nor in her actions, in her first years as a widow. Then, in 270, something changed, perhaps prompted by a deteriorating relationship with the Emperor, or the growth of insecurity in the east, or the need to revive commerce. Whether or not Zenobia's activities of the next two years constituted a revolt is a matter for some debate.

5

Septimia Zenobia Augusta

For the best part of three years after the death of Odenathus, Zenobia concentrated on her own sphere of influence, remaining within the confines of her own territory, the extent of which is arguable, but probably included the Syrian provinces and Mesopotamia.[1] She attended to the defence of the eastern frontier against Persian incursions, building fortifications, which are attested by their archaeological remains and in literature of the late Empire. As part of the defence of the frontier she may have strengthened the Palmyrene army by recruiting soldiers from among the Arab tribes and the population of the eastern provinces, which is unfortunately impossible to prove. Shapur and the Persians remained quiet, perhaps as a result of Zenobia's measures to deter attacks, and the restrictions imposed by their own internal problems. Shapur was no longer a young man, perhaps not likely to engage in strenuous campaigns while he concentrated on the succession, as much a problem for the Persians as it was for the Roman Emperors. He needed to ensure that his son Hormizd succeeded him without a struggle. A new and younger king would perhaps turn his attention to the Euphrates border, but in the meantime, Zenobia could rely on her frontier fortifications and her troops.

With the eastern frontier as secure as she could make it, Zenobia was free to turn her attention to other areas. During the course of 270 she emerged from the Palmyrene kingdom to take control of Arabia and Egypt, and tried to extend into northern and western Asia Minor. Zenobia's reasons for this sudden expansion have been variously interpreted, ranging from inordinate ambition, through ruthless opportunism, to economic necessity, or a permutation of any of these. Opinion is divided about her ultimate aims. After the death of Odenathus, it is suggested that she wanted to reinstate the territorial control that he had held, which is an acceptable supposition, except that as far as is known, Odenathus had influence in, but not absolute control of Egypt. She has been accused of harbouring secret plans to take over the entire Roman Empire from the moment that she took power in Palmyra,[2] or, with slightly more credibility, of seizing the opportunity, while the Romans were preoccupied with the Gothic invasions, of taking over as much as she could of the eastern Empire.[3] At the very least, she is declared guilty of establishing a secessionist state, a Palmyrene principality separate from Rome.[4]

Alternatively Zenobia's actions may have resulted from a perceived threat, or even an aggressive act, emanating from the soldier-Emperor Claudius. Drinkwater assumes that Zenobia felt the need to broaden her power base and her access to resources when Claudius became Emperor.[5] She probably did not feel that she could entrust the safety of her realm and the rest of the east to a Roman government that had shown itself to be extremely unstable internally, and stretched to the limit externally. Therefore she wished to take over the surrounding provinces in order to protect the whole area, to pre-empt a hostile confrontation with Rome and to be ready for attacks from other enemies, which the Romans could not be relied upon to prevent or defeat.

It is possible that the Romans had already made the first break with Palmyra. Potter suggests that the expedition of Heraclianus, ostensibly to round off Odenathus's abandoned Persian campaign, but in reality to establish control over Palmyra, dates to the reign of Claudius, perhaps after the battle of Naissus in 269 when troops could be released. In this case Zenobia's rapid empire building could be interpreted as a perfectly justifiable reaction to an aggressive act, so that she would be prepared for the next one. Whatever her reasons, her expansion of Palmyrene control over the east would be seen in Rome as a provocative or hostile act, and has been labelled as such by modern scholars.[6]

Unbridled ambition to rule the Roman Empire probably did not feature very largely in Zenobia's motives. It is more likely that her chief reasons for territorial expansion were to satisfy the dual needs of defence and economic stability. She was Queen of Palmyra, with a duty to protect her people and foster their interests. As part of that duty she had inherited an obligation to Rome to defend the eastern frontier, and to keep the peace among the nomads of the desert. She had probably also inherited the same obligations to protect the provinces of Syria and Mesopotamia, or if her kingdom was confined to the Palmyrene desert, she probably felt that she could protect it much more effectively by taking control of the eastern bloc from the Black Sea to Egypt. The attempt to absorb all these different areas did not necessarily spring from exactly the same motive. It is too simplistic to ascribe Zenobia's actions in 270 to a specific reason or a single desire. There were different advantages to be gained from ruling different provinces, including strategic positioning in response to perceived threat, extra resources in manpower and supplies, and if possible the facilitation of commerce. Each of the provinces that she took over may have answered some but not all of her needs.

ECONOMIC AND DEFENCE MOTIVES IN PALMYRENE EXPANSION

The commercial aspects of Zenobia's empire building are more credible than a simple megalomaniac desire to rule the world.[7] Profits from trade may not have been the sole driving force behind the march into Arabia and then Egypt, but the Nile province was renowned for its wealth, even in the depressed circumstances of the second half of the third century, and had potential that the Palmyrenes were probably eager to exploit, despite the fact that trade via the Euphrates had not entirely ceased.[8]

For two centuries at least the Palmyrenes had been responsible for defending the Euphrates frontier against the Parthians and then the Persians, and for patrolling the desert. Defence usually costs a lot of money, even if the troops employed are of low grade and the installations and bases are shabbily constructed, neither of which seems to have been the case with regard to the Palmyrene army. In exceptional circumstances when danger threatens, soldiers can sometimes be persuaded to perform their tasks without pay, purely for love of their country, but they still have to be clothed and fed, and if salaries are added to the total, the expense eats into resources which then require constant, reliable replenishment. Palmyra in the third century was hardly impoverished but the trade which injected taxes, tolls and profits into these resources had diminished. The caravans had not ceased altogether, but the dearth of inscriptions in the 260s, compared to those of previous decades, coupled with the general decline of commerce all over the east, points to a corresponding decline in revenues in Palmyra.

Lacking the fine details of Palmyrene state finance and that of the wealthy individuals who supported the city with their donations and gifts, it is impossible to estimate the total income, or to compare it with the likely expenditure on defence of the desert and eastern frontier. The Tariff of Palmyra attests that revenues were raised on goods carried into and out of the city and its environs, and the document fixes the rate of taxation on different types of goods, but there is no corroborative information about the volume of traffic and the revenues accrued from it, nor about what happened to the cash raised and what it was used for. Monetary assistance to defray the cost of defence from the Roman Emperors can probably be discounted, especially in the second half of the third century when Rome faced multiple problems including financial ones. The Palmyrenes were responsible for the maintenance of peace in the desert and along the Euphrates, and while they were assured of the generation of wealth from trade they easily accomplished their tasks. After 260 they still had to perform the same tasks, but at a time when trade was declining and resources were diminishing. They defended the frontier and the desert for the benefit of Rome, but this defence was also essential for their own security. The Palmyrenes therefore did not have the option of withdrawing their services to Rome, because to do so would be to endanger themselves.

There was no question of renouncing Rome and trying to ally with the Persians. Even if the Palmyrenes did so, their neutrality between the two powers would be severely compromised and then Rome would become the enemy. Another consideration was that an alliance with a Persian ruler would probably not be permanent. Circumstances would probably change dramatically with the accession of a new Persian king, who might break off friendly relations or even declare war, so Zenobia would then be truly isolated between two hostile powers, since the Romans would never tolerate an attempt to ally with their greatest enemy.

However great was the gap between her revenues and her expenditure, Zenobia had to continue in the time-honoured fashion, working with or on behalf of the Romans, steering a course between total subservience and complete autonomy. Obedience to Rome, especially in the straitened circumstances of the mid third century, could involve the requisition of manpower and supplies to fight wars elsewhere in the Empire, leaving the Palmyrenes short of resources that they needed for themselves. On the other hand, dependence on Rome for the defence of the eastern provinces was clearly not an option. The Emperors were preoccupied with the various tribesmen threatening the security of the northern provinces, with no time to spare for the problems of the east.

Zenobia did not want to see her people descend into abject poverty that would endanger her ability to defend her territory against nomads and Persians. In order to continue to discharge these vital tasks, which the Romans were in no position to undertake, she required secure boundaries, secure finances, and access to resources, including food and manpower. If she was to obtain all this, she also required mastery of her own fate and that of her people, and a wider power base via control of the neighbouring eastern provinces. It was a delicate balance, to achieve independence and extend her control without incurring the hostility of the Roman Emperor, but this is the path that Zenobia chose to take.

THE ROMAN WORLD IN 269–70

The expansion of the Palmyrenes into Arabia, Egypt and Asia Minor took place against the background of turmoil in the rest of the Empire. The Gothic wars, the death of Claudius, and then the short, sharp scramble for Imperial power that made Aurelian Emperor, all served to turn Roman attention away from the east, giving Zenobia the opportunity to take over Arabia and Egypt almost unhindered except by local commanders.

The chronology of this period is not fully established, though the researches of various scholars have established some fixed points, mostly from Egyptian papyri and from coins, which help to elucidate the history of the Empire and the sequence of Palmyrene activities. The victory of the Roman Emperor Claudius at Naissus in 269 brought the depredations of the Gothic tribes to a temporary halt. The Goths were bottled up in the mountains, and many of them surrendered, but before Claudius could follow up the victory and perhaps establish a lasting peace, plague broke out in his army, and he fell victim to it himself, at Sirmium, probably in August or September 270. The Senate in Rome declared his brother Quintillus Emperor, but the Danube armies preferred the general Lucius Domitius Aurelianus. The reign of Quintillus lasted for little more than a few weeks before the armies prevailed and Aurelian took power.

Previous generations of scholars placed the death of the Emperor Claudius at the beginning of the year 270, and dated the Palmyrene expansion to the spring of the same year. Thus Alföldi thought that around the same time, or just before the death of Claudius, the Palmyrenes invaded Egypt in February 270.[9] It is now considered that around this time, at the beginning of 270, the Palmyrene army was occupied in taking over Arabia. The invasion of Egypt is now usually dated to the late summer or even the autumn of the same year. From the evidence of various papyri it seems that there was a period of confusion in Egypt between September and November 270, when the regnal years of the Emperors, which according to Egyptian dating tradition began in August each year, was suspended in favour of consular dates, in line with the Roman calendar. The consuls, unfortunately, are not named, but it seems that the members of the Roman government in Egypt were uncertain about who was the legitimate Emperor,[10] and hedged their bets by refusing to acknowledge any of the contenders – Quintillus, Aurelian or the Palmyrene Vaballathus – until it was clear who was in the ascendancy and likely to remain there. By December 270, the use of regnal years resumed, with Aurelian listed as Augustus, and Vaballathus as *vir clarissimus rex consul Imperator Dux Romanorum.*[11]

This is paralleled by the coinage from the Antioch and Alexandrian mints from November 270, where Aurelian is recognized as Augustus and Vaballathus is named with his usual list of titles, but definitely given a lower rank, as on the Arabian milestones and the Egyptian papyri. It has been argued that since the mint mark appears on the same side as the portrait of Aurelian, this means that the Emperor is represented on the reverse side, while Vaballathus is shown in the superior position on the obverse, but this is unlikely to be the intention and probably was not interpreted as such by contemporaries. Aurelian is titled *Imperator* and wears the radiate crown, while Vaballathus has no such titles and wears the laurel, signifying his subordination to the Emperor.[12]

Modern chronological studies of the late 260s and early 270s provide a broad general outline for Zenobia's tenure of the eastern provinces. She timed the beginning of her expansion to coincide with the preoccupation of the Emperor Claudius with the Goths. In the spring of 270 the tribesmen had been defeated but had not yet been brought to terms. Zenobia could not have foreseen that the Emperor would die of plague some short time later, nor could she have predicted that the general Aurelian would come to power before the end of the year, but by the time that he was fully acknowledged as Emperor, she had claimed Arabia, and had established a firm hold on Egypt.

ARABIA

The Roman province of Arabia did not extend over the land that comprises the present-day Arabian peninsula, which remained outside the Roman Empire. The

Romans called this area Arabia Felix, maintaining some influence over it but not total control. The territory of the Roman province of Arabia was quite small in comparison to the rest of the peninsula, bordered on the north by Syria Phoenice, and on the west by Syria Palestina. The southern boundary is uncertain and rarely appears on maps of the provinces of the Roman Empire.

The strategic position of Arabia, on the land route to the Red Sea and the Nile delta, meant that the Palmyrenes required control of it before they advanced into Egypt. Some scholars place the invasion of Egypt before the Palmyrenes took control of Arabia, but it is more likely that Zenobia would secure this area before she advanced into Egypt, not least because it would leave a potentially hostile garrison in the rear of her armies in Egypt. More than one general had successfully invaded Egypt from this direction, so it would make more sense for Zenobia to ensure that she was in command to prevent such an occurrence.

In the opinion of the later ancient authors, notably Malalas and John of Antioch, Zenobia invaded Arabia to exact revenge for the murder of her husband.[13] Modern opinion is divided about the motives for Zenobia's invasion of Arabia, ranging from a desire to reconstitute the power base of Odenathus[14] to an overtly aggressive act against rule by Rome,[15] which is described by some as the first move in her long-term ambitions to usurp the Roman Emperor.[16]

Another reason for the presence of the Palmyrene army may have been the troublesome Arab nomads who had recently combined into a federation of tribes known as the Tanukh. These separate tribes were originally settled in the north-western sector of the Arabian peninsula, but they migrated or were displaced when the Sassanid Persians defeated and wiped out the Parthian Arsacid dynasty in the first half of the third century. From then onwards the tribesmen joined forces with the resident population of the desert west of the Euphrates from Hira to Hit, and the Tanukh confederation was born.[17] This federation was the only serious Arab rival to the power and influence of the Palmyrenes, and had begun to pose a threat to stability in the desert. Zenobia needed to curb the growing power of the Tanukh before she advanced beyond Syria and Arabia into Egypt, rather than leave such an enemy in the rear, where they could disrupt communications and impede or even defeat armies.

The Tanukh leader Jadhima was a contemporary of Zenobia, and according to Arab tradition she arranged a meeting with him and then treacherously murdered him. Removal of the chief would not by itself reduce the power of the Tanukh, so it is probable that there were battles and skirmishes and Jadhima may have been killed in one of them.[18] A new Arab dynasty arose after Jadhima's death. His nephew succeeded him and became the founding king of the Lakhmids. This was 'Amr ibn 'Adi, the son of Jadhima's sister.

The Arab legends are probably an amalgam of fact and fiction. The existence of the Tanukh federation is not in doubt, and the supposition that they were enemies of the Palmyrenes is probably historically accurate.[19] Their ruler Jadhima is attested as a historical personage by an inscription from Umm al-Jimal, south-west of Bostra, carved in Nabataean script and in Greek. This is a gravestone commemorating a man called Fihr, described in the text as the teacher of Jadhima, who is in turn expressly described as king of the Tanukh.[20] Amr ibn Adi is also attested on an early fourth-century inscription from Namara. It is in Arabic, written in Nabataean script, commemorating Amr's son, Imru al-Qais.

In Arab legend Amr is the sole victor in the war against Zenobia and the conqueror of Palmyra, with no mention whatsoever of any assistance from Aurelian and the Romans. For some scholars this rather important omission casts doubt on the authenticity of the story.[21] It is possible that Amr may have joined forces with the Romans when Aurelian marched on Palmyra. There is no evidence of a formal alliance between this Arab federation and the Emperor, but Aurelian did employ Arab troops in his eastern campaign, and it seems that after the demise of Palmyra it was the Lakhmids who succeeded the Palmyrenes as the guardians of the desert west of the Euphrates.[22]

All that can be ascertained from a distillation of legend and fact is that the Palmyrenes and the Tanukh were enemies and Zenobia launched an attack on them, probably in spring 270 when she moved into the Roman province of Arabia. Hostilities between the Palmyrenes and the Tanukh are not attested in the ancient classical literature or by abundant archaeological finds. The destruction of the ancient unwalled Nabataean city of Umm al-Jimal may have occurred when the Palmyrenes fought the desert tribesmen.[23]

Other evidence of military action bears no relation to a Palmyrene war with the Arab federation of the Tanukh, but derives from the rebuilding of the temple of Jupiter Ammon, the tutelary god of *legio III Cyrenaica* at Bostra. After Aurelian's victory over Zenobia, the temple was reconstructed, and a Latin inscription was set up on the lintel over the entrance recording its destruction by the Palmyrene enemy (*a Palmyrenis hostibus*).[24]

Bowersock suggested that for some time after the Persian invasions under Shapur, the governors of Arabia felt the need to establish fortifications to protect the province not only from the Persians but also against aggression on the part of the Palmyrenes, whose growing power was resented.[25] If so, Zenobia's troops seem to have experienced very little trouble in overcoming or circumventing these fortifications, which could just as easily have been established to protect the settlements against raids by desert tribes.

According to Malalas, the Palmyrenes killed the governor of Arabia, the *dux* Trassus. No other source records this event, or the governor Trassus, whose very existence has been doubted,[26] but taken together with the destruction of the temple of Jupiter Ammon at Bostra, this meagre evidence suggests a short, sharp battle, resulting in a complete and rapid Palmyrene takeover. When the governor was killed, the legion perhaps came over to Zenobia and cooperated with her until her defeat by Aurelian, at which point they could legitimately be termed 'enemies' when the rebuilding of the temple was begun.[27] Such a label would have been impossible while Zenobia ruled, but would be mandatory if Aurelian was to be appeased.

Palmyrene control of routes in Arabia is indicated by the presence of milestones with Latin inscriptions recording Vaballathus. The milestones set up by Zenobia in her own territory all displayed Greek or Palmyrene inscriptions, but outside her Palmyrene realm, she used the language of the Romans. She also adapted the titles of Vaballathus to suit Roman themes. His early titles, in Palmyrene and Greek, expressed eastern concepts, such as King of Kings, as Odenathus had styled himself. In Arabia, Vaballathus is presented as a Roman governor and commander with appropriate titles. The texts of the milestones in Arabia are sometimes incomplete or partially obliterated, but a comparison of all the milestones allows archaeologists and historians to restore the titles with confidence. Vaballathus appears as Lucius Julius Aurelius Septimius Vaballathus Athenodorus, *vir clarissimus rex consul Imperator Dux Romanorum*. These titles are paralleled in Egyptian papyri from December 270.[28] The adoption of the title consul for Vaballathus is problematic, because it is unlikely that he had been granted the office of consul, or that he had been given the rank and insignia without the office by the bestowal of *ornamenta consularis*, either by Gallienus or Claudius. His father Odenathus had held the rank, but in Roman tradition it was not passed down by inheritance. Zenobia perhaps ignored strictly traditional procedure in order to legitimize control of the provinces. Another more salient point is that when she took over Arabia and marched into Egypt, Zenobia did not yet choose to present Vaballathus as *Imperator Caesar* or as Augustus. The title *Imperator*, as used on these milestones, in the middle of a run of other titles, was a purely military title signifying a commander of troops, as was *Dux Romanorum*.[29]

EGYPT

There were probably several reasons why Zenobia desired to take over Egypt. Its strategic position, with access to the Red Sea ports and to the Mediterranean, its legendary wealth, even in the difficult times of the third century, and abundant food supplies all served to make it an attractive proposition to the Palmyrenes.

Egyptian trade had been fostered by the Ptolemies, who improved routes or established new ones connecting the Red Sea to the Nile. These routes were protected by fortifications and guards[30] to facilitate the passage of goods to and from ports in India and the Arabian peninsula across the eastern desert. In Roman times from the first century BC onwards, trading activities prospered. The Romans concentrated on the more important routes. One ran westwards from the Red Sea port at Quseir al-Qadim, which may be the ancient Myos Hormos, to Coptos on the Nile, and another road to Coptos ran north-westwards from Berenike (Foul Bay) much further south on the Red Sea coast.[31] Berenike was perhaps the largest and most important port, attested by the number and variety of archaeological finds from the site. In the *Periplus Maris Erythraei* all distances and sailing times to other ports were measured from Berenike.[32]

The Romans protected the routes by military patrols and by closely spaced stations with access to water, called appropriately *hydreumata*. There was usually a fortified enclosure surrounding the well, and space where men and animals could shelter. There may have been a local tax levied on the caravans to offset the expenses of the garrison and the maintenance of the *hydreumata*. An inscription known as the Coptos tariff lists the tolls to be levied on all road users.[33] Anyone travelling with an ass was charged two obols, and a covered wagon was charged four drachmas. Even funeral processions had to pay for use of the road, and the highest charge of all was for women for the purposes of prostitution, who paid an astronomical one hundred and eight drachmas.[34]

Coptos was an important warehousing centre on the River Nile for goods coming down the river and then overland to the Red Sea for export, and for imports being carried overland to the Nile and thence to Alexandria and the Mediterranean. It was not an emporium where buying and selling was carried out[35] but it seems that goods were stored and probably catalogued in the warehouses, to assess the local tax. When this was paid the goods were released for transport. The Romans levied a tax of twenty-five per cent (the *tetarte*) on all goods carried, but this was collected at Alexandria, so the records made at Coptos perhaps served to ensure that all goods were accounted for and nothing was sold at a profit en route, thus evading the tax.

The operation of trade in Egypt was similar to the Palmyrene system. Groups of people, including the wealthy and the not so wealthy, combined to set up a caravan, and may have employed their own guards to travel with it across the desert.[36] The scenario would be familiar to the Palmyrenes. When the wars between the Romans and the Parthians in the mid second century had made the normal Palmyrene trade routes more dangerous, some groups of merchants had established themselves in Egypt to take advantage of different routes to the Mediterranean, skirting the Arabian peninsula from India, and into Egypt via the Red Sea.[37] It seems that there was no monopoly on any trade goods[38] so from the middle of the second century the Palmyrenes had been able to carry on their commercial activities in Egypt without displacing the existing merchants.

The presence of Palmyrenes in Egypt, well before the invasion by Zenobia in 270, is attested by several inscriptions. At Berenike, a dedication was set up in 215 to Julia Domna and Caracalla, by a Palmyrene called Julius Aurelius Mokimos.[39] At Coptos, a Palmyrene, Zabdalos, son of Salmanos, paid from his own funds for the building of the *propylaea*, three *stoas* and the chambers. A group of Palmyrenes set up a dedicatory inscription in his honour, recording his contribution to the city. There is no date on the inscription, but since it is associated with pottery sherds from the mid second century, it is assumed that this is the context for the building of the chambers to which the inscription refers. It is possible that the Palmyrenes had recently arrived at Coptos, and the new buildings were their commercial headquarters. Surrounding the building there were twelve *stelae* with portraits in Palmyrene artistic style, but the carving was evidently done by Egyptians.[40] There were also Palmyrene shipowners (listed as *naukleroi* in Greek) operating on the Red Sea and the Nile, as attested by an inscription from Dendera.[41] A unit of Palmyrene archers was stationed at Coptos in 215, perhaps for the purpose of patrolling the routes to and from the Red Sea ports.[42] This would have been a task with which they were quite familiar, and the archers would have been experienced in dealing with raids by desert tribes.[43]

By the middle of the third century the insecurity of the routes caused by the raids of the bandits and desert tribesmen, already noticeable in the previous century, had reached endemic proportions and had a deleterious effect on trade.[44] It was no longer the tribesmen alone who raided caravans and made travelling unsafe. Whole villages had been deserted and the population had dispersed to avoid the periodic plagues, the Roman authorities and the crippling taxation, and having lost their livelihoods as farmers they turned to robbery.[45] Perhaps more serious were the attacks of the Blemmyes, a powerful tribe from the south, beyond the frontiers of Egypt. They captured and held Coptos from c.268 until 270.[46] It has been suggested that the Blemmyes were in league with Zenobia's army and helped the Palmyrenes to invade Egypt,[47] but it is also possible that the Palmyrene communities already settled in Egypt appealed to their compatriots to assist them in dealing with the bandits and tribes who threatened the routes.

Zenobia may have entertained plans for commercial regeneration through Egypt. The lack of monopolies on trade goods would allow the Palmyrenes to expand their use of Egyptian ports, adapting to the seasonal voyages to India as the other merchants did. Ships left Egypt in summer in June or July, taking advantage of the monsoon winds which brought them to India after a voyage of about three weeks. The return journey usually started six months later, when the north-easterly winds assisted the passage back to Egypt in December or January.[48] The Palmyrene merchants were already familiar with the Indian ports of Barygaza and Barbarikon, and would simply sail there from the Red Sea instead of the Persian Gulf. The use of these long-distance trade routes through Egypt, and the shorter ones from Arabia to the Red Sea, would liberate the Palmyrenes from dependence on good relations with the Persians. Hartmann points out that Palmyrene trade in Egypt pre-dated the conquest by Zenobia, but after the takeover the Palmyrenes were enabled to exploit the Red Sea trade at the same time as easy access to the Gulf was more restricted and the routes through the Persian Empire were more difficult.[49] It has been suggested that when they controlled Egypt, the Palmyrenes brought goods from Palmyra into Arabia and from there to the Red Sea and to Alexandria, but as Young points out this seems unnecessarily circuitous, especially for the goods normally brought from the Gulf via the Euphrates.[50] Even if they were carrying only home-produced Palmyrene articles for trade it would have been easier to transport them to the Mediterranean by the usual routes through Syria, which was under Zenobia's control.

Trade through the Egyptian ports had declined in the third century, as evidenced by the dearth of finds of the period at Berenike, compared to the first and second centuries, and to the fourth century when commerce resumed. The Roman Empire was afflicted not only by a lack of security but also by financial problems, which did not help trade to flourish. The drastic reduction in the silver and gold content of the coinage resulted in a lack of confidence in the monetary system, and the growth of barter systems. Inflation affected the markets for goods, because people could no longer afford to buy the luxury items on which the trade depended. Despite the problems with security and finance, trade had not ceased altogether, and it could be that among Zenobia's long-term plans was the revitalization of commerce by bringing in Palmyrene merchants to conduct trade and Palmyrene troops to ensure the safety of the routes.

The arrival of the general Zabdas and the Palmyrene army in Egypt coincided, probably by design, with the absence of the Prefect of Egypt, Tenagino Probus, who was commanding a naval expedition, following the orders of the Emperor Claudius to attack the Mediterranean pirates. The date of the invasion is not established beyond doubt. Zosimus places it after the Roman victory at Naissus and before the death of Claudius[51] so it was probably in mid- or late summer when Zabdas started the campaign. Some scholars opt for a somewhat later date for the invasion. Watson, for example, sets it in October, after the death of Claudius, claiming that Zosimus made a mistake in his dating, and claiming that Zenobia's decision was mostly based on opportunism.[52] The accusation that she was opportunistic is no doubt correct, but Zenobia's invasion of Egypt was scarcely based on a sudden whim. She made her plans, and watchfulness and a good intelligence service would trigger the mobilization. One potential argument against the October date for the Palmyrene invasion is that Tenagino Probus was more likely to take to the seas to combat the pirates in the summer months, to give himself enough time to round them up before autumn.

Tenagino Probus was a successful general. He had governed Numidia, and he had recently restored order in Cyrenaica. In the summer of 270 he was probably conducting naval operations around the islands of Crete, Cyprus and Rhodes,[53] and would be unaware for some time that in Egypt the troops were fighting against the Palmyrene army. Zosimus sets the size of the Palmyrene army at 70,000 men, and their opponents, the Roman and Egyptian troops, at 50,000, but these figures seem somewhat inflated.[54] The Palmyrenes seem to have had an easy victory in this first round of battles. According to Zosimus, Zabdas left 5,000 men in Egypt and returned to Syria,[55] then Tenagino Probus appeared, defeated the Palmyrene troops and their sympathizers, and established control of Alexandria. In turn, Zabdas marched back and defeated Probus and his Egyptian and Libyan troops. He was assisted by an officer called Timagenes, who was stationed with the Roman troops in the area. It has been suggested that Timagenes was a native Palmyrene, but there is no proof of his origins.[56] He clearly sympathized with the Palmyrenes, and was instrumental in bringing about the final victory of Zabdas. Probus has retreated southwards to the southern end of the Delta, and chosen some high ground to make a stand. Timagenes took some Palmyrene and probably some Roman troops round the rear of the defensive position, which soon became untenable against attacks from front and rear.[57] Probus was killed in the battle, or committed suicide, probably at about the same time as the Emperor Claudius died of plague at Sirmium, in late summer or early autumn 270.

The Palmyrenes had taken over Egypt in two successive stages, during which time there would be considerable turmoil while the contestants struggled for supremacy, until eventually it was clear who was really in command. The confusion of the Egyptian records, when regnal years of the Emperors was temporarily abandoned, have been mentioned above. The uncertainty in the documentation reflects the conflict during the brief reign of Claudius's brother Quintillus and the proclamation of Aurelian, but it also indicates that immediately after the invasion Zenobia was not yet strong enough to install Vaballathus as ruler of the eastern half of the Empire with authority over Egypt. It required an additional effort to establish control over the whole country, and especially over Alexandria, which she did not accomplish until the end of 270. Zosimus is the only source that implies that there were two Palmyrene invasions, which is not accepted by all scholars, who prefer to interpret the events as an initial invasion, with no withdrawal of armed forces, quickly followed by an influx of additional troops.[58] There may not have been two invasions, but there were at least two battles or series of battles before the Palmyrenes were fully in command of Egypt.

At the beginning of 271, Palmyrene control of Egypt was fully established and normal government was reinstated. Julius Marcellinus was made governor of the province, but he was not given the office of Prefect. Instead he was given the title *agens vice praefecti*, which meant that he acted on behalf of the governor. This was normal Roman procedure if a governor died or was killed while still in office and another man was appointed to replace him, usually for an interim period while a suitable candidate was appointed by the Emperor. Marcellinus held this post until spring 271. It has been argued that he was the official Imperial candidate, representing a short-lived attempt to regain control of Egypt,[59] but this seems unlikely. He was most likely Zenobia's choice,[60] and the fact that Marcellinus was not installed as Prefect, but held the office in place of the Prefect in strict accordance with Roman practice after the death of Tenagino Probus, may have been deliberate policy on the part of Zenobia to appease the Imperial government. Normally the provincial governors were appointed by the Emperors, and in Egypt, these governors were chosen from the equestrians rather than from the senatorial classes. The appointment of the Prefect of Egypt was regarded as the peak of the equestrian career. In the case of Arabia, Zenobia was not so strictly scrupulous about appointing governors, but Egypt had always been the special preserve of the Emperors and therefore much more sensitive, not least because much of Rome's grain supply was exported from there. It is not recorded that Zenobia tried to interrupt this supply and in 270 the corn ships left as usual, bound for the port of Rome at Ostia.

The next governor was Statilius Ammianus, who took office in spring 271, only a few months after Marcellinus was installed. Ammianus had governed Arabia in 264–5 and would therefore have been known to Odenathus. They presumably cooperated reasonably well, and Ammianus was probably loyal to Zenobia. He seems to have been made Prefect, which might indicate that Zenobia's choice of governor also met with the tacit approval of Aurelian, but there is no shred of evidence that the Roman Emperor and Zenobia had reached an understanding on her rule of the east. Ammianus remained in office until perhaps the end of 272, or even early 273, and he entered into negotiations with Aurelian when the Imperial recovery of Egypt began. This does not mean he was a turncoat, treacherous by turn to Aurelian and then to Zenobia, but he was perhaps imbued with the realisation that there was little to be gained by putting up a fight for Egypt in a cause that he considered already lost.[61]

The government of Egypt probably continued as before under the Emperors. Zenobia genuinely tried to foster the interest of the various groups of people that made up the population, especially in Alexandria, where so many different cultures met and not infrequently quarrelled. As Queen of Palmyra she was ruler of a predominantly Aramaic community, but she was also imbued with Hellenic ideals and traditions. She adopted Roman forms in her administration, but she was also open to alternative lifestyles, customs and religions. Her distinctive Palmyrene blend of Graeco-Roman, Hellenistic and Persian culture did not imply an automatic aversion to Jews and Christians in Egypt or anywhere else. She tried also to nuture the native population, and although the claim that she was descended from Cleopatra was a political fiction, invented either by herself in an effort to enhance her rule, or by her enemies to discredit her,[62] the revival of the legend may have helped to win over the Egyptians. The story was told that Callinicus, a philosopher and rhetor from Petra, wrote a history of Alexandria and dedicated it to her in the name of Cleopatra.[63] She restored some older traditions that dated back to the Ptolemies, and attended to ancient monuments that had fallen into disrepair.[64] One of the monuments that she repaired was a statue, presumed to be that of Memnon, conqueror of the ancient Persians, but actually of the Pharaoh Amenhotep III. It was badly cracked and perhaps in danger of falling down, but it was through these cracks that the statue emitted its famous sounds at sunrise, as the warm air outside met the cold air inside. Zenobia ordered its repair, and afterwards it never spoke again. This attention to pre-Roman administration and ancient buildings was not an attempt to stir up Egyptian nationalism, nor was it prompted by anti-Roman sentiments. It can be classified as part of a programme to win over as many different sectors of the provincial population as she could.

ASIA MINOR

Zenobia's attempted occupation of Asia Minor is not well documented, and has not been satisfactorily explained. According to Zosimus she had succeeded in taking control of the whole area as far as Ankara,[65] and after she had taken over Arabia and Egypt in 270 she started to extend her dominion over the rest of Asia Minor. She was ultimately unsuccessful because she had left it too late and was brought to a halt by the expedition of Aurelian. There is no evidence that Palmyrene troops settled down and occupied the provinces of western Asia Minor. No inscriptions mentioning either Zenobia or Vaballathus have been found, and the mints continued to issue coins for the Roman Emperors Claudius, Quintillus and then for Aurelian, but issued none for Vaballathus, not even on the reverse of coins of Aurelian, in sharp contrast to the mints at Antioch and Alexandria.[66] Since she clearly did not control the mints, it is questionable how far and how deep Zenobia's rule penetrated, even in the eastern provinces of Asia Minor, despite Zosimus's assertion that she held the territory as far as Ankara. Perhaps with more time she would have brought all the provinces of Asia Minor into her realm, but in 271 she had to abandon her plans, whatever they were, and stand against Aurelian.[67]

Whether she was successful or not in gaining control of the whole area, no light is shed on the reasons why Zenobia wanted to rule Asia Minor. It has been pointed out that although the absorption of Egypt may have been driven by commercial interests, the same cannot be said of Asia Minor, not noted for Palmyrene commercial activity, nor for trading on the same scale as the other eastern provinces.[68] Defence may have been Zenobia's perceived requirement. The Goths had made great inroads from the Black Sea and even after the Roman victory at Naissus there was no guarantee that the Emperors could always repel them successfully and permanently. Control of Cappadocia would help to protect the northern border of Syria by providing a forward zone to give warning of any attacks from the north, or from the east through Armenia. Control of the provinces of Asia, Lycia, Pamphylia and Cilicia would give access to the Mediterranean, and Bithynia-Pontus, which the Palmyrenes were trying to take over when Aurelian arrived,[69] would have provided access to the Black Sea coast, where the Palmyrenes could guard against Gothic inroads. Protection of this vast area would depend upon the cooperation of the local population and the Roman troops, and in this entire region, Zenobia failed to engender loyalty and enthusiasm from the military or the populace. The Palmyrenes were not welcome in Asia Minor, and when Aurelian arrived, the provincials looked to Rome for protection.

ZENOBIA'S RULE OF THE EAST

By 271 Zenobia had taken control of most of the east, with the exception of Asia Minor. She had gained far more territory than Odenathus had ruled,[70] at a time when Aurelian was powerless, either to defend the east or to prevent her expansion. It is not known whether she communicated with the Emperor. Throughout the year 271 he may have condoned her rule of the east, perhaps deliberately lulling her into a false sense of security, or it may have been that Zenobia interpreted his forced inaction as acquiescence.

Zenobia had been as conciliatory as possible while she extended her power base, consistently presenting Vaballathus as subordinate to Aurelian in documents, on inscriptions and on coins. His titles proclaimed his authority in the east, but not his supremacy in the Roman world. In this way Zenobia hoped to reach an agreement with Aurelian and retain her control of the east, but there is no record of any formal treaty or even of a tacit understanding between the Emperor and the Palmyrene Queen.[71] Despite the lack of evidence it has been suggested that either Gallienus or Claudius[72] had made an agreement with Zenobia, but Aurelian either refused to acknowledge it, or, even worse, played along with it and then duplicitously abandoned it when it suited him to do so.[73]

If Aurelian had been allowed the time and resources to turn against Palmyra he may have done so before 272, but throughout his first two years as Emperor he was forced to plug gaps and dash from crisis zone to crisis zone. In 270 he repulsed the first attempt of the Germanic tribes, principally the Iuthungi, to fight their way into Italy, and then spent a short time in Rome in the winter of 270 to 271. The Vandals attacked Pannonia in the spring of 271, and after dealing with them Aurelian hastened back to Italy, where the Iuthungi made another attempt to invade. He stopped them, in a battle that he nearly lost, at Placentia. His problems then shifted from external threats to internal strife. Three usurpers rebelled against him, the financial crisis came to a head in the revolt of the workers at the mint in Rome, and there were threats from disaffected senators and some of the military officers. Aurelian overcame all the opposition, and in the second half of 271 marched to Byzantium and then to the Balkans to face an invasion of the Goths. It may have been now that he made the momentous decision to abandon the province of Dacia, and bring the population across the Danube into Moesia, where they settled.

It had been a difficult and hectic year, but he had survived it intact. He decided to waste no time in reconstituting the Empire. The Gallic Empire in the west was still not under his control, but he was already in Byzantium with his armies, poised to march against Palmyra. In the winter of 271 to 272 he started to prepare for the campaign. There may have been negotiations, an ultimatum, or even a declaration of war, but the sources are completely silent on this point. With or without advance warning, Zenobia would learn of the impending mobilization and would not mistake its purpose.

When Aurelian marched against her, Zenobia had two choices. She could quietly give up the territory she had overrun and remain in Palmyra under the old arrangements for defence of the eastern frontier, or she could make a stand and hope to retain her power. Economically she may not have considered retreat to Palmyra and the *status quo ante* as a viable option. It may have been too late in any case. Her attempts at conciliation had not been interpreted as she had intended, and there was probably no escape now from harsh retribution.

Certain now that Aurelian would not tolerate her rule in the east, in spring 272 she claimed for herself and for Vaballathus the full Imperial titles that she had always assiduously avoided. Coins were issued from the Antioch mint showing only Vaballathus, wearing the radiate crown of the Roman Emperors, and with the legend *Imp. Caes. Vhabalathus (sic) Augustus*, spelling his name in Latin but as closely as possible to its Palmyrene form. In all other respects she adhered to *Romanitas*, choosing for the reverse sides of Vaballathus's coins the common ideology as represented by Roman gods with their symbols, and legends such as *Virtus Augusti, Aeternitas Augusti*, or *Victoria Augusti*.[74] She represented herself as a Roman Empress, Septimia Zenobia Augusta, or in Greek, Septimia Zenobia Sebaste. She portrayed herself with a hairstyle current in third-century Rome, resembling the Syrian Empresses, Julia Domna, Julia Mamaea and Julia Soaemias, and Salonina, the wife of Gallienus. On the reverse of several of her coins she portrayed the most important Roman goddess, Juno Regina, holding a *patera*, and accompanied by a peacock. Aurelian represented his wife Severina in similar style.

On milestones as well as coins she claimed Imperial titles. Four milestones from the *Via Nova Traiana* between Bostra and Philadelphia are dedicated to Vaballathus in the dative case as *Imp. Caes. L. Julio Aurelio Septimio Vaballatho Athenodoro*. His victory titles are usually included, though the reading in some cases is difficult, especially as the milestones were reused and different inscriptions were added.[75] Another milestone found near Byblos bears a Greek inscription naming Septimia Zenobia Sebaste as the mother of the *Imperator* Vaballathus.[76] The major problem with these inscriptions is that there is no firm dating evidence, but some scholars have argued that they are contemporary with Zenobia's coinage of 272 when she began to call herself Augusta. A particular difficulty arises with the Greek inscription naming Zenobia as the mother of the *Imperator* Vaballathus. The inscription has been damaged and the name of the reigning Emperor has been obliterated. This lack gives scholars free rein to restore the name according to their own theories, so some authors have suggested that it should be Claudius,[77] while others prefer to date the inscription to the reign of Aurelian.[78] If these alternative dates are correct, it would seem that Zenobia had already adopted the title Augusta before Aurelian began to mobilize against her.[79] A better and much more sensible interpretation is that the unknown Emperor on this milestone is actually Vaballathus himself, as Hartmann suggests.[80]

The chronology of this period is worse than vague, allowing some debate as to who was the first to open hostilities. Hartmann outlines three possible scenarios. While Aurelian was fighting the Iuthungi and was faced with many more difficulties, Zenobia may have chosen that moment to raise rebellion and try to usurp, but Hartmann points out that if Zenobia had been intent on usurpation, a better time to attempt it would have been when Gallienus was assassinated, or when Claudius died, and in each case there was a period of infighting among the Romans for supremacy.[81] A second possibility is that Aurelian's mobilization in Byzantium precipitated Zenobia's reaction and sudden declaration of Imperial power.[82] A third possibility, favoured by Hartmann, is that it was only after Aurelian's invasion and the first battle in the east, at Antioch, that Zenobia started to claim Imperial titles, a suggestion which smoothes the chronological difficulties.[83] Although such a scenario portrays her as conciliatory to the very last moment, it seems a little late in the day for Zenobia to spring into action and suddenly adopt Imperial titles, as though she had only just realized that she needed to ensure her command in order to meet the threat.

In reality she could not have failed to take notice of Aurelian's imminent mobilization and she probably made plans to counter the attack, part of which would be to award herself and Vaballathus suitable titles. If it was to be war with

Aurelian, it would be useless for Zenobia to continue to represent herself and her son as subordinates of the Emperor. That was not the way to rally the troops to her cause, whether they were Roman or Palmyrene. She needed full authority, just as other leaders such as Uranius Antoninus had discovered, and this authority was vested in Roman Imperial titles, with the right of command.

This was not a revolt, nor an attempt at usurpation, except in so far as Aurelian chose to interpret it as such.[84] Nor was it an attempt to set up a secessionist state like the Gallic Empire, where cooperation with the legitimate Emperor was entirely lacking. Zenobia did not envisage herself at the head of a separate state, or an Arab nationalist regime that imposed its customs, language and law on the rest of the east. She ruled strictly within Roman parameters, but like Cleopatra before her, she was an easy target for propaganda, as a foreign enemy intent on the destruction of Rome and all that it stood for.[85] With the Roman equivalent of a press release on those lines, Aurelian could portray himself as the heroic leader of a perfectly justifiable and righteous war, the unifier of the Empire and the eradicator of the deadly foe.

10. In Zenobia's time Palmyra was a prosperous and beautiful city, famous for its temples and public buildings. The merchants of Palmyra employed and displayed their wealth in beautifying their city and honouring leading citizens with statuary and inscriptions recording their services and achievements. This photo shows the temple of Baal-Shamin, originally founded in 17 BC and rebuilt in the second century AD. The entrance to the *cella* is fronted by six columns with pediments for statues that have since disappeared. Photo courtesy of David Reid.

11. The theatre at Palmyra showing the stage in very good preservation, and the seats of the auditorium. Photo courtesy of David Reid.

12. Among the main attractions of the ruins of Palmyra are the funerary towers, designed as the last resting place of entire families and their descendants. There were other types of tombs, ranging from simple graves each marked by a stone, to underground chambers designed and decorated like houses, and in the later period the elaborate temple tombs. Inside all these tombs there were niches for the bodies of the dead, some of which were mummified, each covered with a stone, often bearing a portrait of the individual. The tower tombs had several storeys and could accommodate a large number of the dead of a single family. An inscription shows that Odenathus founded one of these family tombs, but it is not known where it lay. Photo courtesy of David Reid.

13. Sculpture showing a Palmyrene man from the sculpture garden of the Syrian National Museum, Damascus. His right arm is shown in typical pose inside his cloak. Photo courtesy of David Reid.

14. Sculpture showing a Palmyrene woman from the sculpture garden of the Syrian National Museum, Damascus. She wears the elaborate headdress and veil typical of the Palmyrene nobility. Photo courtesy of David Reid.

15. When Zenobia took over from her husband she issued coins in the name of Vaballathus, but was careful to acknowledge the Emperor Aurelian, so she displayed both their heads. Aurelian wears the radiate crown, and is titled *Imp(erator) C(aesar) Aurelianus Aug(ustus)*, while Vaballathus wears a laurel wreath and makes no claim for supremacy as Augustus in his titles VCRIMDR, which have been interpreted as *V(ir) C(larissimus)* or more probably *C(onsularis) R(ex) IM(perator) D(ux) R(omanorum)*, indicating that he was of consular rank as was Odenathus, that he was king of the Palmyrenes, commander of the Palmyrene armies and military leader of the Romans. This coin, bearing the heads of both Vaballathus and the Roman Emperor, is one among many examples that circulated in the east as Zenobia tried to establish her rule as regent for Vaballathus alongside and subordinate to Aurelian. Drawn by Jacqui Taylor.

16. Antoninianus of 272 from the Antioch mint. Late in her reign Zenobia started to use the title Augusta, perhaps as part of a bid to retain control of the east, or perhaps in response to an unfavourable reception from Aurelian. In the expectation of war between herself and the Emperor she would need to ensure the loyalty of the Roman commanders and troops, so she appeared as a Roman ruler, depicting herself in the style of the Syrian Empresses, Julia Domna, Julia Mamaea and Julia Soaemias. Drawn by Jacqui Taylor.

17. Bronze As showing Aurelian's wife Severina. This coin post-dates Zenobia's rule of the east but Severina is portrayed in strikingly similar fashion to the coinage of Zenobia, honouring the same goddess, Juno Regina. Drawn by Jacqui Taylor.

18. Antoninianus of late 271 or early 272 from the Antioch mint, showing Vaballathus as Augustus, wearing the radiate crown. There is no mention of Aurelian on these late coins, indicating that Zenobia had renounced any attempt to reconcile the Emperor to her rule of the east. On the reverse Hercules is shown with his club and lion skin, a symbol of all-conquering power with appeal to both the Roman and the Greek citizens of the eastern provinces. Drawn by Jacqui Taylor.

19. Greek tetradrachm, showing Zenobia as Septim(ia) Zenobia Seb(aste), equivalent to the Latin Augusta. On the reverse the goddess Homonoia holds her usual symbol, the cornucopia. She was the goddess of concord and the union of minds, an appropriately hopeful message for the eastern provinces facing the advent of Aurelian. Drawn by Jacqui Taylor.

20. Aurelian reasserts himself and reminds his audience of his military power on this gold aureus from the Milan mint, proclaiming on the reverse *Concordia mil(itum)* or unity of the army. The goddess Concordia, seated, holds two military standards. Drawn by Jacqui Taylor.

21. After the defeat of Palmyra, Aurelian proclaimed himself *Restitutor Orientis*, the restorer of the east. On the reverse of this fine coin he showed the sun god, Sol, standing between two captives, signifying the end of Palmyrene rule. When he had subdued the Gallic Empire, Aurelian elevated himself to *Restitutor Orbis*, restorer of the world. Drawn by Jacqui Taylor.

22. Palmyrene male, hair curled and beard neatly trimmed. His right arm is held in the fold of his cloak, a characteristic pose for Palmyrene portraiture. Odenathus may have been portrayed in the same pose. Photo courtesy of Manchester Museum.

23. Portrait of an aristocratic Palmyrene lady, showing her elaborate headdress and jewellery, swept-back hairstyle and pendant earrings. Zenobia's portraits, which have not survived, may have represented her in this fashion. Photo courtesy of Manchester Museum.

6

Aurelian and the Roman Recovery

There is no surviving contemporary account of the war between the Palmyrenes and the Emperor Aurelian. Sparse and often conflicting accounts derive from Greek and Latin literary works dating from a much later period, the only common ground being their more or less universal bias against Zenobia. The two main narrative sources are the life of Aurelian in the *Historia Augusta*, and the historical account of Zosimus; of the two, Zosimus is the more reliable and remains the only dependable means of reconstructing what may have happened. Even so, information is very sparse and there are many unanswered questions, irreconcilable except by speculation.

THE ROMAN RECOVERY OF EGYPT

While Aurelian made his preparations to sail from Byzantium to attack the Palmyrenes from the north, tradition holds that he also prepared to attack from the south by sending his general Probus, the future Emperor, to wrest Egypt from Zenobia's control. This is questionable, and has been discounted by some scholars. The story derives from a single passage in the *Historia Augusta*, not in the life of Aurelian but in the biography of Probus.[1] It seems possible, but not certain, that the author confused the Emperor Probus with the Prefect of Egypt, Tenagino Probus, who died fighting the Palmyrenes in 270. After enumerating all the public works and buildings allegedly erected by the Emperor Probus in Egypt, the author goes on to describe how he fought against the Palmyrenes, who held Egypt in the name of Odenathus and Cleopatra, embedding the story in the realms of fantasy where Zenobia was supposedly equated with the Queen of Egypt. According to the story, Probus was so reckless in battle that he was nearly captured, but when he received reinforcements, he finally brought Egypt back under the control of Aurelian.

It sounds plausible, but scholars are divided over this vague reference without

place names or details of battles. It has been pointed out that Probus came from
the same part of the Roman world as Aurelian and was loyal to him,[2] which
lends some credibility to the theory that he was sent on this mission to recover
Egypt. It can be argued that it would make sense to attack the Palmyrenes from
the south through Arabia while Aurelian himself attacked from the north. It
was important to gain control of Egypt to ensure the continuity of the food
supply, and to protect the route into Syria. In order to put these projects into
effect, Aurelian would need a reliable and trusted officer, and who better, with
the benefit of hindsight, than a fellow countryman who was destined to become
Emperor? The story can neither be proved nor disproved on present evidence.
Apart from the mention of unspecified fighting in the *Historia Augusta*, there is
no information about battles or skirmishes, and as Hartmann points out, there
is not even a shred of evidence of a military invasion of Egypt under Probus or
any other general.[3]

Clearly, at some point Egypt was definitely recovered and brought under the
control of Aurelian, if not by Probus or an invading army, then by some other
means. Aurelian was awarded a *corona aurea* for his victory in Egypt,[4] which
may have been a peaceful one. The *corona aurea* is perhaps better interpreted
as a celebration of success rather than a military victory. Papyrus evidence
shows that by the second half of June 272 Aurelian was acknowledged in Egypt
as sole Emperor on official documents, with no mention of Vaballathus. It can
be assumed that Egypt was recovered some short time before the date of this
papyrus evidence, perhaps at the beginning of June or even at the end of May.
Hartmann suggests that Statilius Ammianus, who had been made Prefect of
Egypt by Zenobia, decided to negotiate with Aurelian, perhaps because news
had reached him of the Palmyrene defeat at Immae near Antioch.[5] This depends
on a synchronized chronology for events in Egypt and in Syria that cannot be
conclusively proved, but it is just possible that the battle of Immae was fought
at the end of May, and that the news reached Egypt leaving sufficient time for
Statilius Ammianus to declare for Aurelian in June, and to ensure that from that
moment onwards official documents and coins displayed only the Emperor's
name, at first using the previous system of regnal years which made this Aurelian's
second year.[6] Shortly afterwards, messages perhaps arrived from Aurelian,
confirming Ammianus as Prefect, and also apprising him of the fact that the
Emperor had backdated his reign to the death of Claudius in late summer 270.

Then the Alexandrian coinage could be amended, which may explain why a small number of coins were issued bearing the regnal year II and were quickly replaced with another issue bearing the year III.[7]

When the Romans arrived in Egypt to take control, it is possible that there were only a few Palmyrene sympathizers left in the country, because Zenobia may have already withdrawn her troops.[8] It may be significant that according to Zosimus[9] Zabdas had 70,000 troops when he invaded Egypt, and still commanded the same number[10] when he fought Aurelian near Emesa.[11] Estimates of the number of troops in any ancient account are notoriously unreliable, but this may be an indication that although Zenobia tried to maintain her administrative control of Egypt, she realized that Aurelian would focus on regaining this vital province as well as Arabia and the Syrian provinces, and therefore in preference to fighting on two fronts simultaneously, she chose to throw all her resources into the defence of territories that lay closer to Palmyra. If Palmyra was lost, a foothold in Egypt would have been of no use to her, but if she could retain control of the core of her territory, it might be possible to come to a peaceful arrangement with Aurelian which may yet include trading rights in Egypt and the possibility of profits for Palmyra.

AURELIAN'S MARCH TO SYRIA

It was probably in April 272 when Aurelian ferried his troops from Byzantium to Asia Minor. His army consisted principally of the Praetorian Guard, legionaries from the Danube provinces of Raetia, Noricum, Pannonia and Moesia, augmented by mounted units from Dalmatia, Moorish cavalry, and possibly some of the mobile cavalry units raised by Gallienus about a decade earlier. The continued existence of this cavalry as a separate body after 268 is disputed, but Aurelian may have assembled some of the horsemen for his campaign.[12]

Aurelian quickly made his way towards Ancyra, encountering little or no resistance from the provincials on the way there. The Palmyrene hold on the territory had never been strong, and Zenobia did not attempt to stop Aurelian's march by drawing up her army in Asia Minor. She may have ordered some of the cities to close their gates against him, but if she sent any such orders, none of them obeyed, except for Tyana, which opposed Aurelian for reasons which are obscure.[13] There seems to have been no Palmyrene garrison in the city or its vicinity, but there may have been some citizens who were sympathetic to the

Palmyrenes. Finding Tyana closed to him, Aurelian was allegedly so incensed that as he prepared to besiege the city, he declared that when he took it, he would not leave even a dog alive. It was a short-lived affair, never really amounting to a siege. Only one source, the life of Aurelian in the *Historia Augusta*, relates the story of the traitor Heraclammon, who showed the Emperor where there was a weak point in the city defences. The fate of Tyana was soon sealed, but Aurelian did not put the inhabitants to the sword. Instead he acted with studied clemency. The *Historia Augusta* carries the tale that he was influenced by the apparition of the long-dead philosopher, Apollonius of Tyana, who came to him to urge him to spare the city. The author of the *Historia Augusta* is somewhat obsessed with ghosts and shades and miraculous occurrences in the life of Aurelian, and the stories do not appear in other sources. There is no mention of such miracles in Zosimus's account, even though he was interested in religious matters and related phenomena.[14] It is just possible that these tales are not complete fabrications, but may contain some remnants of Aurelian's propaganda. He may have invented the story of the ghost of Apollonius, the most famous inhabitant of Tyana, as reinforcement for his political policy of *clementia*.[15] If he made it known that he intended to show mercy, even to a city that had opposed him, other cities whose loyalties might be a little uncertain would be encouraged and the citizens would probably receive him without a struggle. It would save a lot of time if he could make a rapid march to deal with the Palmyrenes without having to stop and lay siege to important cities on his route. It would probably also bring other benefits, if the grateful citizens whom he magnanimously spared could then be peacefully persuaded to supply his troops with food and fodder. These are practical considerations, but politically there would be another advantage in showing mercy to the cities of Asia Minor, because such a policy would perhaps enable him, when he entered the Palmyrene realm, to persuade Zenobia's Syrian allies to change their allegiance. Detaching an enemy's allies was as much a part of warfare as fighting battles.

The policy was sound. Potentially it would pay enormous dividends and it would also leave the reputation of Aurelian unstained, but it was a different matter for the soldiers poised around Tyana, ready for the assault. They would need to be handled carefully. They had been geared up to win the first victory in the campaign by taking the city, and were eager for a fight, anticipating the slaughter and plunder that sacking Tyana would entail. Now the Emperor wanted them to abandon the idea of heroics and portable wealth. Generals who tried to bring about such a reversal of fortunes sometimes paid with their lives. In the squabbling that broke out among the rival claimants for control of the Gallic Empire, the ruling Emperor Postumus had taken Mogontiacum (modern Mainz) and then tried to prevent the soldiers from sacking the city. They killed him and sacked it anyway. The Emperor Aurelian, however, enjoyed the favour of the gods and conversed with dead philosophers. He presented unassailable reasons why the city of Tyana should be spared, and managed to persuade the soldiers to obey him. They were still angry and reminded him that he had sworn that he would not leave a dog alive in the city, so Aurelian authorized them to kill all the dogs. The soldiers saw the joke and the justice of his instructions, and Aurelian survived intact, unlike the unfortunate canine population of Tyana.

THE BATTLE OF IMMAE

As he marched through the rest of Asia Minor, Aurelian was welcomed by the populace and did not have to stop to besiege any more cities, thus conserving energy and vital manpower, and also converting the population to friendly allies. Secure in the knowledge that there was no threat to the rear or to communications, he pressed onwards to find the Palmyrene army, probably travelling south to Tarsus, then eastwards along the coast by way of Adana, Issus and Alexandria ad Issum to the north-western border of Syria.[16]

Zenobia and Zabdas had brought their army to the vicinity of Antioch, an obvious objective for Aurelian. They could not afford to split up the Palmyrene army to watch and block the passes through the Taurus mountains, and had in-sufficient troops to meet Aurelian in battle at some point outside Syria, especially as this might give the Emperor the advantage of choosing his own battleground. Instead Zabdas preferred to await the arrival of the Romans, and chose his ground in the plain where he could use his heavy cavalry more effectively. He took up a position north of the city of Antioch, with Lake Antioch to the east, expecting Aurelian to approach from the north-west, but the Romans either anticipated his manoeuvres, or received intelligence of them, so Aurelian decided to circumvent the Palmyrenes, marching around the north of their position, and down the eastern side of Lake Antioch, to come at them from the east, which would cut off their retreat if they wished to withdraw towards Palmyra.

The battle of Immae was about to begin. There is a dearth of reliable details in the sources. The best account is provided by Zosimus,[17] but there are contradictions in other accounts. The author of the *Historia Augusta*[18] and Eutropius[19] conflate two separate events, combining details of the battle of Immae with Aurelian's attack on the Palmyrenes at Daphne, a short time after the main battle. A seminal paper by Downey[20] made sense of all the garbled sources and his conclusions have been generally accepted by other scholars.

Zabdas discovered the changed direction of Aurelian's march in time to move his cavalry to a new position a few miles to the east of the River Orontes, and met the Romans there.[21] When battle was joined, Aurelian stationed his light cavalry opposite the Palmyrene *clibanarii*, the heavy armoured horsemen. This probably encouraged the Palmyrenes to attack in anticipation of an easy victory over a more feeble enemy, an opinion that would be considerably reinforced when the Romans began to fall back and then flee. The Palmyrenes did not know that it was nothing but a ruse in accordance with Aurelian's orders, and in giving chase they exhausted themselves and their horses in the fiercely hot weather. When they were almost at the town of Immae, some miles east of Antioch, Aurelian ordered his troops to turn and attack. The Palmyrenes had little chance, being taken by surprise and faced with soldiers and horses more nimble than themselves, and not half as tired.[22]

Zabdas knew when he was defeated and withdrew. It is perhaps unlikely that Zenobia was present at the battle, but she was in Antioch, perhaps with Vaballathus, though the whereabouts of her son are unknown. When the news of the Palmyrene defeat arrived, probably brought by Zabdas himself, she decided at once that her position at Antioch was untenable. She probably needed no persuasion from Zabdas to escape. There was nothing to be gained for the Palmyrenes by walling themselves up and waiting for Aurelian to besiege them, and besides, the loyalty of the citizens was somewhat fragile. Aurelian's lenient treatment of Tyana and his policy of showing mercy to everyone who approached him would no doubt influence the citizens of Antioch, who had experienced much destruction at the hands of the Persians in the recent past and were probably still recovering from these economic disasters. They definitely would not want to see their livelihoods threatened once again by a victorious Roman army in pursuit of the defeated Palmyrenes.

For the time being, news of the Roman victory was suppressed, just long enough to enable Zenobia and Zabdas to leave the city. Like Cleopatra riding triumphantly into Alexandria after defeat at the battle of Actium, Zenobia showed firm presence of mind and calmed the people by pretending that her armies had won a great victory. She even spread the news that Zabdas had captured the Roman Emperor. This was a piece of pure theatre that Zenobia and Zabdas arranged, by dressing up a man who looked like Aurelian and parading him through the streets.[23] In the interval while the supposed triumphal procession was taking place, Zenobia prepared in secret to leave the city. Her resolution and courage in these dangerous circumstances cannot be doubted. The charade covered her escape with Zabdas so successfully that Aurelian did not know until the next day that the Queen and her general were no longer in the city.

The Romans camped a few miles outside Antioch, planning to attack the Palmyrene army from two sides at once, but when Aurelian learned that the Palmyrenes had fled, he marched peacefully into the city. The men who had been closely associated with the Palmyrenes hastily removed themselves, quite unnecessarily as it turned out, because Aurelian pardoned one and all, even those who had helped Zenobia. His policy seemed to put an end to hostilities at Antioch, and provided a valuable example to other cities, making it potentially more difficult for Zenobia to retain old allies or recruit new ones when Aurelian pursued her further into Syria.

The battle of Immae was interpreted at a later period as the turning point for Zenobia and Aurelian, and was presented as such in the epitomes or breviaries of the ancient historians, who ignore the later battles and place all the emphasis on Immae, as though it was absolutely decisive.[24] Not all modern scholars agree with this interpretation.[25] Immae was merely the first battle of three that Aurelian had to fight before he reached Palmyra itself, so it was not necessarily inevitable at this point that he would eventually win a complete victory. The fact that he emerged as the victor of the campaign no doubt influenced the ancient authors, who knew quite well what the final outcome had been and could therefore afford to gloss over the fact that after Immae, Aurelian's final victory was not necessarily assured. Zenobia still had a chance. Her army had been mauled but not annihilated, she had held onto most of her wealth and influence, and she had the advantage of knowing the terrain and how to survive in it. She knew as well as her generals that the combination of desert conditions, hostile nomads, lack of food and water, disease and illness, might well prove to be her greatest allies against the Romans. She would not view the battle of Immae as a turning point in her fortunes. It was certainly a disastrous setback, but she probably did not yet consider that it was a point of no return.

THE DEFEAT OF THE PALMYRENE GARRISON AT DAPHNE

The Palmyrene troops stationed at the fort at Daphne, to the south of Antioch, did not flee with Zenobia. This was perhaps only a small and insignificant force, but Aurelian was unwilling to leave any Palmyrenes who could threaten his rear when he marched after Zenobia, so he decided to take the place by force. The fort was situated on a steep hill, theoretically well protected by nature, but Aurelian ordered the legionaries to attack up the slopes, using the tortoise formation (*testudo*) with their shields over their heads to protect them from missiles. The Palmyrenes were eventually dislodged as more and more Romans gained the summit and entered the fort. Some Palmyrenes were forced over the cliff edge and fell to their deaths, but it seems that some soldiers escaped, possibly to join Zenobia later on.[26]

Aurelian did not pursue Zenobia immediately after the capture of the fort at Daphne, but remained in Antioch for a short time, to secure the city and attend to its government and that of Syria Coele. There was probably a great deal of traffic into and out of Antioch during the Emperor's stay there, as both he and the people of the province consolidated their position. This may be the context for the ejection of the heretical bishop, Paul of Samosata, who had enjoyed Zenobia's favour and support during the schism among the Christians of Syria.[27] There was also the question of control of the mint, which was apparently not a peaceful process for Aurelian. The most important factor of the Emperor's temporary residence at Antioch was that it enabled him to gather reinforcements for his army. The legions of the Upper Euphrates sent detachments, the city of Tyana provided levies, and from Palestine came auxiliary troops who fought with clubs.[28]

THE BATTLE OF EMESA

The delay in the pursuit of the Palmyrenes allowed Aurelian to rest and reinforce his army, but it also afforded some respite for Zenobia to do the same. She had taken up residence at Emesa, where she assembled the remnants of her army and brought in auxiliaries from her allies.[29] Her cavalry still outnumbered Aurelian's, and she had a moral advantage in that the Palmyrenes were now fighting for their homelands, which would be a sharp stimulant. Despite the ready acceptance by the later authors of the battle of Immae as the turning point in the campaign, it perhaps did not seem that the tide had turned to the Palmyrenes who camped at Emesa to await the arrival of Aurelian. Zabdas was a capable general and the Palmyrene heavy cavalry was still a formidable force. At this stage Zenobia's army still had a slight chance of defeating Aurelian in battle. If the Emperor could be effectively crushed he might be forced to come to terms, even if only temporarily while he reformed his army, and in addition there was every chance of further distractions that might divert his attention away from the east, in the form of tribal invasions across the Danube or into Italy, or revolts in the west, which would allow Zenobia enough time to recoup her losses and re-establish her influence. She was not beaten yet.

As at Antioch, Zabdas formed up the Palmyrene army on a flat plain near Emesa where he could deploy the cavalry. Aurelian accepted battle on the ground chosen by Zabdas, and attempted to repeat the stratagem he had employed at Immae, ordering his cavalry to pretend to flee. When the time came to put this manoeuvre into effect it was no longer a ruse. The Romans fled in deadly earnest as the Palmyrene heavy cavalry attacked furiously and repelled them. The Romans were slaughtered wholesale.[30] Aurelian was within an ace of losing this battle. Then the Palmyrene line started to waver and break up, and their loss of cohesion gave the Romans an opportunity to turn and attack the enemy flanks, ably assisted by the Palestinian clubmen, who wreaked havoc among the Palmyrenes. Zenobia's army was routed, and the soldiers killed many of their own men as they trampled them down in the scramble to get away.[31] With difficulty Zabdas and some of the troops managed to reach Zenobia at Emesa.

If she had entertained hopes of bringing the war to an end before she fought the battle at Emesa, Zenobia cannot have been so sanguine now that her army had been shattered. She had no choice now except to fall back on Palmyra, bringing the war to her own city, a scenario that she had doubtless wished to avoid. The flight from Emesa was clearly not so orderly as that from Antioch, since Zenobia left her treasury behind, a significant loss and indicative of tremendous haste.[32] Aurelian's troops were probably close behind Zabdas, so it would have been a choice between abandoning the treasury or risking capture. By the skin of her teeth, Zenobia got away.[33]

After the battle of Emesa, Zenobia's problems escalated. She had lost her treasury, much of her army, and the Romans were now closer than ever to Palmyra itself. Her allies now were the tribes who were still well disposed to her, and the geography and climate of the terrain surrounding Palmyra. In order to defeat her totally Aurelian would have to follow her to her own city, contending with hostile desert conditions, combined with attacks from unfriendly nomads.[34] Zenobia no doubt hoped that these difficulties might impede his progress or even bring him face to face with disaster.

The difficulties of the campaign are outlined in a letter, supposedly written by Aurelian to Mucapor, reported in the *Historia Augusta*. The context is after the battle of Emesa, when Aurelian had entered the city, allegedly astonished at the vast stores of weapons and military equipment that the Palmyrenes had left there. Great emphasis is laid on the enormous strength of the Palmyrene army, 'as though it were commanded by a man'.[35] This letter probably never existed, but provided a useful device for the author to present the problems that Aurelian had to overcome, which of course made his final victory all the greater and avoided the accusation that it was all supremely easy because he was fighting only a woman. Despite the hyperbole, Aurelian still needed all his skill, his expertise as a commander, his talents for diplomacy and, above all, luck, which happily did not desert him. At some point in the campaign against Zenobia, Aurelian received an arrow wound, reported in the *Historia Augusta* in the context of the so-called siege of Palmyra.[36] The wound fortunately healed without complications. King Richard I of England, nicknamed the Lionheart, did not fare so well in similar circumstances in France in the spring of 1199, when he received a crossbow bolt in the shoulder, survived the incident, but died when gangrene set in after the attentions of the surgeon.

THE SO-CALLED SIEGE OF PALMYRA

Aurelian's progress across the desert in pursuit of Zenobia was not an easy passage according to the *Historia Augusta*. He was harassed by attacks of *latrones*, literally meaning robbers or bandits, most likely Arab nomads who were either allied to Zenobia or who were merely antisocial opportunists allied to no particular group, taking advantage of the occasion to make raids on the vulnerable sections of the Roman army, with the enticing prospect of booty.[37] These tribesmen were presumably to be distinguished from the Tanukh, who were opposed to Zenobia's regime and fought on the side of the Romans. Without help from the Tanukh, Aurelian's army may have suffered even more hardships.

One of Aurelian's major problems concerned supplies, to ensure the survival of his troops in the vast desert that lay between him and Palmyra. Modern authors emphasize the distance that the army had to travel, about 150 miles through the desert between Emesa and Palmyra, a journey that would necessitate an enormous amount of food, fodder and water to sustain men and animals on the march.[38] If all the Arab and desert tribes had been hostile, Aurelian would perhaps have thought twice about attempting to reach Palmyra rapidly, but according to the sources he recruited some of the tribes to provide him with food, and Zenobia's allies deserted her when Aurelian approached, so he did not have to worry about attacks from them.[39]

Arriving at Palmyra, the sources state that Aurelian prepared for a siege of the city.[40] Aurelian had besieged Tyana, so it is to be expected that when he reached Zenobia's city, he would act in the same way. The difference is that Palmyra, unlike Tyana and many other eastern cities, was not enclosed in Zenobia's day by a defensive circuit of walls. To the authors and their readers of the later Roman Empire, when the accounts were produced, this would be the most readily acceptable method by which to mount an attack on a city. In the later Empire it would probably seem quite inconceivable that a city like Palmyra was not walled. In some parts of the Empire, from the second half of the third century onwards, tribal migrations and prolonged civil wars had shown that Roman peace and security could be easily threatened, and most cities had either inherited defensive walls, or the inhabitants had begun to think of erecting walls rather hastily to fend off attacks.

At Palmyra, a narrow wall had been built enclosing much of the territory of the city. The works date from the first century BC and the first century AD, and would have been standing in Zenobia's day, but it is unlikely that these walls provided a secure military fortification against Aurelian. One disadvantage was that there seem to have been undefended gaps. If the circuit of walls was ever completed, there is no evidence for it today, leaving archaeologists to conjecture where the missing parts of the wall may have run. Another problem for the defenders is that the walls lie some distance from the centre of the city, and there are no signs that towers or fortified gates were incorporated into the system. It is perhaps best interpreted as a deterrent to the nomadic tribes to hinder their free movement, and the walls perhaps also provided a customs barrier, rather than a defensive circuit.[41] Since the walls cannot be shown to join up all around the city, they could probably be easily penetrated, and even if they had ever been complete, it would have required truly enormous numbers of men to defend the whole work. Nonetheless, it has been suggested that Aurelian faced the Palmyrenes across this wall at some point, as though besieging the city.[42]

It is feasible that the Queen tried to erect some sort of defences or barricades at Palmyra during the time that it took for Aurelian to approach, and it has been suggested that the foundations of certain walls enveloping parts of the city probably date from this period. A couple of decades after the war with Zenobia, the Emperor Diocletian built a fortress in the north-west corner of Palmyra and surrounded most of the city with walls, complete with towers and defended gateways, but excluding some parts of the original settlement that lay to the south. This shrinkage of the city limits was not uncommon in the later Empire when defensive walls were built, one of the main reasons being that a shorter circuit enabled the inhabitants to economize on the manpower that would be necessary to defend the city. Two centuries later Justinian also attended to the defences of Palmyra, so there are two distinguishable phases of building in the fortifications. Attempts have been made to recognize an original first phase, pre-dating the Diocletianic defences, which can be ascribed to Zenobia's defensive activity, especially since the Diocletianic walls cut across the city, as though Zenobia had decided that she could defend only a limited area. Conclusive proof is lacking for this original primary building phase, and one of the most telling factors that weighs against the theory is that Zenobia would not have had sufficient time to build walls between her flight from Emesa and Aurelian's arrival at Palmyra, unless she had decided to defend the city as soon as she took over from Odenathus, for which there is no evidence. Another factor is the lack of proof that in the 270s there was a complete circuit even within the city boundaries, leaving no gaps and taking in vital parts of the city, including the spring that supplied it with water.[43]

A possible alternative is that Zenobia fortified a camp, placed her army inside it and Aurelian besieged her there, but nothing in the archaeological record supports this theory. The fortifications of other eastern settlements usually surround the city and the fortress as well,[44] and if Zenobia had chosen at this final moment to separate the military and civilian elements, it would have given Aurelian free entry into Palmyra while the Queen and her army looked on.

Though some modern authors accept the reality of the siege of Palmyra,[45] the evidence for it is purely literary, and it is not corroborated by archaeological means, except by hypotheses combining parts of the existing walls with supposed measures taken by Zenobia, none of which can be proven. The siege probably never happened in the conventional sense of a blockading army drawn up close to the walls, defenders posted on the top, and the two sides lobbing missiles at each other until one of them gave in.

If there was no siege in the conventional sense, the fall of Palmyra may have been brought about by a kind of blockade. The *Historia Augusta* states that Aurelian prevented armed contingents sent by Zenobia's allies from reaching her. These were allegedly from the Persians, the Saracens and the Armenians,[46] from whom, apart from the Persians, there is very little evidence that Zenobia had asked for troops, but it is possible that the author may have misunderstood which peoples or tribes sent assistance, or he may have used later anachronistic versions of the ethnic names. The point is still valid, in that from a military point of view it would be essential to prevent any more troops from joining the Queen, a process that would be assisted by using good intelligence services and sending out clouds of scouts to warn of the approach of enemy allies. There may have been only a few skirmishes between the Romans and these contingents. Instead, according to the *Historia Augusta*, Aurelian used his psychological techniques by winning over the allies of Zenobia, 'forcibly or by cunning' (*ad se modo ferociter modo subtiliter transtulit*).[47] The methods used are not explained in detail, but the scenario has a universal appeal. Soldiers throughout history have been persuaded to change their allegiance by various means, ranging from the simple promise of life and liberty, through to cartloads of ready cash. Aurelian's policy of *clementia* would by this time have been widely known, and since he had won two major battles, then marched as far as Palmyra, where he had arrived with his army intact, it would probably have seemed fairly certain to Zenobia's allies at this point that they were fighting for a lost cause.

Similarly, all routes into the city were probably patrolled to forestall the delivery of food supplies. A blockade can be achieved without building long lines all around a city and its territory, provided that the blockading army has sufficient manpower to watch routes, and it seems that Aurelian had gathered a large army, with the ranks swelled by the allies he had won over from Zenobia, and the cooperative Tanukh tribesmen. Zosimus says that Aurelian requisitioned food supplies of all kinds from the countryside around Palmyra, thus denying supplies to Zenobia and at the same time provisioning his own troops.[48]

Negotiations probably took place, but at which point in the proceedings and in what form is not known. The *Historia Augusta* relates the text of letters that supposedly winged their way between the two protagonists, though the contents of these letters may represent only the fact that negotiations were attempted and not what was actually said. According to the *Historia Augusta* Aurelian opened negotiations first, just after the battle of Emesa. He urged Zenobia to surrender and to give up all her possessions, promising to spare her life and that of her children, which implies that there may have been more offspring than just Vaballathus. The Emperor also promised to appoint a place where Zenobia could live in peace, and that he would respect the rights of the Palmyrenes.[49]

Zenobia's reply was allegedly arrogant in the extreme, but this may have been retrospective justification for Aurelian's war against her. She invoked Cleopatra, who had preferred to kill herself rather than be captured and paraded through the streets of Rome. Zenobia did not want to continue to live ignominiously at the mercy of the Romans. Giving the impression of supreme confidence, Zenobia declared her intention of continuing the struggle, with the help of her allies from the Arabs and from the Persians.[50]

This last point is contentious. Too literally interpreted it seems that Zenobia had made an alliance with Shapur and was about to bring the whole weight of the Persian army upon the Romans. If this was true, then the war between Palmyra and Rome would have instantly escalated into a frontier war of massive proportions. This can only be literary hyperbole. It is unlikely that Shapur, too old now for warfare on this scale, was so heavily involved with the Palmyrenes, or that he was anywhere near ready to mobilize. Zenobia may have been deluding herself that she could acquire assistance so rapidly, or she may have been bluffing, making empty threats by which she hoped to frighten the Romans into coming to terms in order to avoid a much more expensive frontier war. It is more likely that the story originated with Aurelian's propaganda machine, stirring up enmity against Zenobia, who was shown as courting Rome's greatest enemy in the east.

There may have been a grain of truth in the use of Persian troops, since both

Romans and Palmyrenes employed some of them in their armies. These may have been relatively small numbers of mercenaries, acting in their own interests, and not necessarily with the sanction of the Persian king. The Persian reinforcements coming to aid Zenobia were cut off by Aurelian[51] but this hardly involves a large army. The numbers of Persian troops employed by Aurelian himself at Palmyra were probably quite small. The story goes that one of them, an archer, asked permission to shoot a Palmyrene who repeatedly yelled insults from the city walls (wherever such walls may have been) and on receiving the consent of the Emperor, he took aim and felled the man with one shot.[52]

Facing Aurelian's army without sufficient food supplies, unable to break out and having lost her allies, Zenobia's position became less and less tenable. Her choices were limited. She could wait until the Palmyrenes were so weakened that they might possibly turn against her and one of the army officers or one of the nobles might try to arrange a peace with Aurelian. She could surrender and place herself at the mercy of the Roman Emperor, but perhaps did not trust his word that she and her city would be spared. She could gather the army and offer battle, but by now she may not have been able to command all her troops and probably did not want to risk another defeat. Or she could escape, possibly to fight another day. Instead of choosing to negotiate further with Aurelian, Zenobia chose to go to the Persians. This may have been a last-ditch attempt to persuade Shapur that the Persians and the Palmyrenes had a common enemy and that he should send troops to help her. Or it may simply have been a plea for sanctuary. She left the city after dark, with an escort. Zosimus says that she rode a female camel, the swiftest of the breed, and faster than any horse,[53] towards the Euphrates, but Aurelian's scouts learned of her flight from the city and his cavalry caught up with her before she was able to cross the river.[54]

Zenobia and presumably Vaballathus were now prisoners of the Emperor, and the resistance of Palmyra folded like a stack of cards. The leading Palmyrenes struggled with their consciences, some of them hoping to continue the fight against the Romans and others deciding that further fighting would benefit nobody. These people came out of the city to give themselves up to Aurelian, in ones and twos at first and then in larger numbers when it was known that the Emperor received everyone with free pardons. The examples that he had set all along the march from Asia Minor began to yield profit for him now, and it is to his eternal credit that at this point he did not exact a terrible revenge by burning Palmyra to the ground and selling the whole population into slavery. He limited the reparations to dismantling the city's capacity for aggressive action by destroying military equipment. He honoured his promise, if he had made one as reported in the *Historia Augusta*, of respecting the rights of the citizens.

From 272 onwards Aurelian celebrated his achievement and proclaimed to the world via his coinage that he had repossessed and pacified the eastern half of the Empire. The Antioch mint issued coins with the legend *Restitutor Orientis* (Restorer of the East), and other coins bear the legend *Pacator Orientis* (Pacifier of the East), and *Oriens Augustus*.[55] He wanted to ensure that the inhabitants of the Empire were in no doubt as to who now ruled the east.

Zenobia and probably Vaballathus were despatched to Emesa to stand trial. The Queen's courtiers and advisers were all eventually captured and likewise sent to Emesa. It is not known what happened to Zabdas, who disappears from the record, along with his colleague Zabbai. They were perhaps executed after trial, as was the philosopher Longinus, whose condemnation as chief instigator of Zenobia's ambition is reported by Zosimus and the author of the *Historia Augusta*.[56] Zenobia is now portrayed as an arrogant but craven woman, too cowardly to face punishment and hoping to evade it by claiming that none of the preceding events were her fault. She said that she had been wrongly advised by the immediate members of her court circle and led into ambitious projects because she had listened to them.[57]

If this complete renunciation of her responsibilities is true, it is a departure from her previous displays of courage from the first moments of her rule, for instance when, recently widowed, she assumed the authority of Odenathus as leader of the Palmyrenes and then set about ensuring the safety and prosperity of her people. The reversal of her fortunes after the series of defeats at Aurelian's hands may have broken her spirit, but the Queen who had turned her first defeat at Immae into a transient resounding victory was surely capable of assuming a noble dignity in the face of adversity. There are no contemporary sources to describe her actions, only hostile Roman ones that filtered into the later sources. Aurelian was an accomplished psychologist and could mould circumstances to his own advantage. It was in his own interest to cast Zenobia in the role of self-seeking coward and betrayer of her people. Such a manufactured scenario would spread indignation among her fellow Palmyrenes and make them lose faith in her rather more rapidly than allowing her to become a dignified martyr and a national heroine, cruelly treated by the Roman conquerors and crying out for revenge. It would be so much easier to discredit her, and thereby detach ardent supporters and faithful allies from Zenobia's cause, if they could be persuaded that she had been using them for her own personal gains and did not care a fig about them or their families when she had been defeated.

Perhaps in the end it was for the best. It was no doubt a cause of bitterness for Zenobia to witness how easily support for her melted away once she was led off into captivity, but if she knew that it had been brought about by clever propaganda she would have understood, and perhaps more readily accepted the compromise. If her reputation was in tatters, at least it may have been of some comfort to Zenobia that Aurelian had entered Palmyra without putting it to fire and sword, and the city itself and the population were intact. As Aurelian's prize she had sacrificed her life and ambition but not her people. A fight to the death that saw her city annihilated had been avoided. It was probably a small consolation as she emerged from the trials at Emesa and set off with her conquerors towards Rome.

7

Aftermath

During and after the campaign against Zenobia, Aurelian attended to the defence of the eastern frontiers and the control of the city of Palmyra. He did not occupy the city in force, but left a detachment of six hundred archers under their commander Sandarion to keep the peace.[1] It is not known what happened to the Palmyrene army or what was left of it. Presumably it was disbanded, and it is possible that the Palmyrenes were forbidden to recruit soldiers to use as caravan guards, since these men, with their considerable expertise in desert fighting, had formed the nucleus of the army.[2] It is significant that after the fall of the city in 273 no further caravan inscriptions are known from Palmyra. Trade may have declined for several reasons, but if it is true that Aurelian had deprived the Palmyrenes of any defensive potential, the insecurity of the trade routes along the Euphrates and through the desert would have forced merchants to seek alternative means of continuing their commercial activities.

Throughout the Empire the Romans usually ruled through local elites, specially chosen to ensure that their people were kept in order and that they remained friendly to Rome. Zosimus relates how the Roman victory had polarized the leading men of Palmyra, some opting for a continuation of the war, and others advocating submission to Aurelian.[3] It is possible that among the factions in the city who voted against the aggressive stance of the more warlike men, there was a chosen leader cultivated by Aurelian to fill the vacuum left by the removal of Zenobia and the family of Odenathus. This may have been Septimius Haddudan, who is known from a fragmentary inscription, in Palmyrene without a Greek translation, which informs us that he had helped the Roman Emperor, but does not elucidate any of the details as to how, why, and when.[4] From another inscription, it is known that Haddudan was a senator, the only man besides Odenathus to possess such a rank, and he held an important position in Palmyra, as Symposiarch of the college of priests of Bel in the period 272 to 273.[5]

The date when this honorary inscription for Haddudan was set up is uncertain, not least because the line giving the Seleucid year is damaged, but even if the date of the inscription could be established beyond doubt, it would not throw any further light on the period when Haddudan assisted the Emperor Aurelian. It is considered by some authors that Haddudan's collaboration with the Romans belongs to the context of the Palmyrene revolt which broke out in 273, while Aurelian was waging war against the Carpi in the Balkans.[6] It is highly probable that Haddudan did facilitate the restoration of law and order after the short-lived rebellion in 273, but it is also possible that the honorary inscription refers to his cooperation in 272 when Zenobia had been captured and her rule of Palmyra and the east had come to an end. There is no proof, but it is feasible that he was already Aurelian's choice of local leader or figurehead when the Romans departed in 272 with Zenobia and Vaballathus as the Emperor's prisoners, and it was necessary to place someone at the head of local administration.

As well as making arrangements for the control of Palmyra, Aurelian stabilized the frontiers of the east. He placed an officer called Marcellinus, possibly Aurelius Marcellinus,[7] in command of Mesopotamia, perhaps even before he fought the battle of Emesa, in order to ensure that no attacks through this area by the Persians should disrupt the Palmyrene campaign. The province may have been under threat from the Persians, who always sought to regain it, but this is just conjecture. Likewise there is no proof for the theory that Zenobia had renounced control of it and the Romans stepped in.[8] If he had not already attended to Mesopotamia during the course of the war with Zenobia, Aurelian could not leave the east without ensuring the safe government and protection of this sensitive area.

The responsibilities of Marcellinus may have extended over a wide territory besides Mesopotamia. It is possible that his title was *Rector Orientis*, as Zosimus says,[9] echoing that of Priscus, the brother of the Emperor Philip, three decades earlier. Another suggestion is that Marcellinus was governor of Mesopotamia and the whole of the east (*praefectus Mesopotamiae et totius orientis*).[10] It is significant that Aurelian placed an officer in command of the whole of the east as Philip had done, treating the eastern provinces as a distinct unit and foreshadowing the grouping of provinces into Dioceses, as in Diocletian's administrative reorganization a couple of decades later. The east was perhaps more readily governed as a unit than some of the western or Danubian provinces, an important factor being the presence of the Persians all along the extensive frontier. Odenathus and then Zenobia had assumed responsibility for the entire area, at a time when the Roman Emperors were compromised and could not attend to government or security of the east, with the advantage that economic, political and military matters were facilitated if there was unity of command and sharing of resources to meet the expense and effort of defending the eastern frontier.

The perceived threat from the Persians had not diminished when Palmyra fell to Aurelian, who now took steps to stabilize the potentially dangerous situation. Agreement seems to have been reached without much trouble. There may have been a demonstration of Roman military strength, or even some border skirmishing, but there is no evidence to support the theory that there was any military action, much less a major conflict, despite the fact that the Senate bestowed on Aurelian the victory title *Parthicus Maximus*. On a milestone found in Syria, the Emperor is designated *Persicus Maximus* and also *Arabicus Maximus*, which would seem to be unofficial versions of his titles.[11] The hyperbole in the *Historia Augusta* about Aurelian's victories over the Persians seems to support the adoption of these titles, but the author may simply have invented a military victory, because it was only to be expected from such a supremely successful Emperor.[12] There was more likely a negotiation by letter or by an exchange of embassies, but all that has survived in the historical record is that gifts were brought to Aurelian from the Persians, which presumably entailed expressions of mutual goodwill and promises of continued non-aggression. Among the sumptuous gifts was a magnificent purple cloak of unique dye not paralleled anywhere in the world, defying the attempts of Aurelian and other Emperors to find out where the dye came from and how it was made. The cloak was still visible in the temple of Jupiter on the Capitoline Hill in Rome many years later. The author of the *Historia Augusta* devotes many words to the description of this miraculous garment, and none at all to any political or military agreement that might have been reached between the Romans and the Persians.[13] Attention to the security of the frontier may have ended there, with the Persians exonerated from any association with Zenobia, and the Romans relieved of the necessity of mounting an expedition across the Euphrates. There is no record of any formal treaty between Romans and Persians. The protection of the Euphrates frontier that until now had been the responsibility of the Palmyrenes now passed to the Arab tribes who had assisted Aurelian, under the Lakhmids led by 'Amr ibn 'Adi.[14]

THE REBELLION OF THE PALMYRENES

Aurelian did not travel directly to Rome with his prisoners, but was diverted to the Balkans, to block the invading tribesmen of the Carpi, who had breached the Roman frontier probably at the end of 272 or the beginning of 273. Zosimus[15] relates that while Aurelian was preoccupied with fending off the invasion, in the east the governor Marcellinus was approached by some of the leading Palmyrenes, with a man called Apsaeus[16] at their head, offering to support him if he chose to declare himself Emperor. The story goes that Marcellinus had no intention of embroiling himself in their plot, but he used delaying tactics, pretending to be considering the idea so that he could send a message to the Emperor to warn him of impending trouble. During the interval Apsaeus and his Palmyrene supporters appointed Antiochus as Emperor.[17] This man was possibly Zenobia's father,[18] or, according to other scholars, her son. It is argued that Antiochus had been left behind in Palmyra, perhaps because he was considered harmless when the other notables were taken prisoner and sent for trial to Emesa. When the rebellion was crushed, Zosimus says that Aurelian did not punish Antiochus, on account of his obscure origins, which suggests that he had been the tool of the ringleaders rather than the original agitator.[19] A similar story appears in the *Historia Augusta*, except that the man who was made Emperor is called Achilleus, described as a kinsman of Zenobia's.[20] Some scholars have suggested that Achilleus has probably been confused with Antiochus[21] but Paschoud thinks that Achilleus is really Septimius Apsaeus, also related to Zenobia.[22] Others accept the story at face value, that Zenobia had yet another kinsman called Achilleus.[23] Potentially, then, there were three different men involved in the second Palmyrene rebellion, all connected somehow with Zenobia, possibly even related to her. This may be true, but it is perhaps wiser to leave Achilleus out of the equation altogether, and to concentrate on Apsaeus, who may have been the prime instigator, and Antiochus, who may have been the willing tool of Apsaeus and the figurehead of the movement, readily accepted because of his relationship to Zenobia.

One of the first moves, according to the *Historia Augusta*, was to massacre Sandarion and the six hundred archers whom Aurelian had left in the city. This would be a typical beginning to a rebellion, but it is not recorded how they achieved it, except that the rebellion is described as 'not of modest proportions' (*non mediocriter*), perhaps added as an afterthought when it is considered how long it would take to kill six hundred armed guards.[24] If true it implies that there were many men who were privy to the plot, and Aurelian's attempts to disarm the Palmyrenes had been ineffective.

It is not clear what the rebels hoped to achieve. If they did approach Marcellinus first, it would seem that they did not intend that it should be simply a Palmyrene affair, limited to the restoration of the previous semi-autonomy enjoyed by the city from the first century AD. The Palmyrenes presumably wanted to create an eastern Empire, or rather to recreate the sovereignty of Odenathus and Zenobia, possibly for economic reasons, where a unified and independent collection of provinces could foster trade and defend its own frontiers. It is less likely that they wished to take over the entire Roman Empire, but they perhaps hoped that they could come to some agreement with Aurelian. Possibly they overestimated the length of time it would take Aurelian to finish off the war in the Balkans. While the Emperor was engaged with the Carpi, the Palmyrenes may have planned to win over most of the eastern provinces and therefore gain sufficient strength to face him on equal terms. Perhaps also Aurelian's widely advertised clemency led them to imagine that they could negotiate their independence, or that he was weaker than he really was.

The news reached Aurelian at his headquarters in the Balkans, probably in spring 273. He departed for the east immediately, arriving in Antioch before the citizens had any inkling of his approach.[25] Speed was the most important factor, if the rebellion was to be nipped in the bud. His march to Palmyra and the second capture of the city were accomplished in a very short time, without much trouble and probably no fighting, or at least no battles are reported by Zosimus or the *Historia Augusta*.[26]

Both authors do report that Aurelian destroyed the city. Zosimus makes the laconic statement that Aurelian razed the city without opposition.[27] The account in the *Historia Augusta* is more elaborate. In the life of Aurelian, the author says that the city of Palmyra was destroyed because it deserved such a fate, and then goes on to describe the 'savage fury' of the Emperor, expressed in a letter to Cerronius Bassus,[28] who is otherwise unknown except for this reference. In this letter, Aurelian says that there had been great slaughter of the Palmyrenes, including women, children, old men and peasants, but he had put a stop to it eventually because the few ringleaders had learned their lesson. Aurelian then goes on to ask that the Temple of the Sun in Palmyra should be restored to its former glory, after being pillaged by the standard-bearers of the Third Legion. This was poetic justice for *legio III Cyrenaica*, whose temple at Bostra the Palmyrenes had destroyed when they overran Arabia, but it is not certain to which temple Aurelian referred in his letter. He was well known for his devotion to the sun god, Sol, so the author of the *Historia Augusta* may have inadvertently labelled the temple as such, not being well informed about the deities of Palmyra and their temples. The great Bel temple in Palmyra was not destroyed, though it may have been pillaged. Zosimus says that some of the statues and artefacts were taken to Rome for dedication to the sun god in Aurelian's new temple.[29]

At first sight, the accounts of the destruction of Palmyra and the massacre of its inhabitants seem quite plausible. Aurelian would have been perfectly justified in taking revenge on the rebellious Palmyrenes, especially as he had treated the city leniently after his first victory. But signs of widespread destruction within the city are not evident. The Great Colonnade and the temples remained unharmed. These magnificent buildings, still visible today, show no signs of repair after extensive damage, and there are no indications that any of the buildings were newly established during the period after Zenobia's reign and Aurelian's victories. They therefore survived the rebellion of 273, which casts doubt on the tales of Aurelian's terrible revenge, and on the report of the slaughter of the citizens.

Nothing is known of the fate of Apsaeus and his adherents, but according to Zosimus, Aurelian spared Antiochus, considering him unimportant.[30] This does not sound like an Emperor whose alleged savage fury led him to kill hundreds of Palmyrenes indiscriminately.

It cannot be denied that the city of Palmyra declined over the next two or three decades, but it was a slow process. During the reign of Diocletian, the city of Palmyra was fortified and became a relatively unimportant town, just one of the stations of the fortified route named after the Emperor, the *Strata Diocletiana*. In the fourth century, only the splendid buildings in the city reminded citizens and visitors of how wealthy it had once been. But the decline of Palmyra as a wealthy trade centre did not come about suddenly after Aurelian's second expedition and cannot be entirely blamed upon him. Palmyrene culture, customs and language were not obliterated at a stroke, and the city retained its legal status. Hartmann argues that there was no widespread destruction by Aurelian, and that the city declined from a combination of different factors;[31] Young accepts that there was probably some destruction but points out that the religious cults and Palmyrene institutions survived for some time after 273.[32] What was lacking after Zenobia's removal and the failure of the rebellion of 273 was the lifeblood of the city, long-distance trade. The periodic insecurity of the frontiers and the absence of the Palmyrene caravan guards dealt the final blow to the operation of trade, and in consequence the aristocrats and the financiers disappeared, perhaps migrating elsewhere to set up businesses at other trade centres. Routes through Syria and Mesopotamia were not disrupted, and though it could be argued that new routes and new trade centres were found when Palmyra ceased to function, it is more likely that they were contemporary with or even pre-dated the Palmyrene operations, and began to enjoy greater prosperity when trade through Palmyra came to an end.[33]

THE REVOLT OF FIRMUS IN EGYPT

The Palmyrene cause was not completely crushed when Aurelian had dealt with Palmyra. A rich merchant called Firmus started to agitate, perhaps in agreement with Palmyrene traders, though what he hoped to achieve is not clear. According to the *Historia Augusta* he claimed to rule Egypt, but did not adopt the Imperial title and insignia, as though he wished to proclaim an independent state.[34] In the life of Firmus himself, the author of the *Historia Augusta* waxes more lyrical, claiming that he was one of three men named Firmus, one of them being the Prefect of Egypt, another the proconsular commander of the African frontier, and the third being the one who tried to claim the rule of Egypt. This man was supposed to be one of Zenobia's allies,[35] and his purpose was said to be the defence of the remaining Palmyrenes of Zenobia's party.[36] He is accused of raising rebellion against Aurelian in alliance with barbarians,[37] and in another passage of negotiating with the Blemmyes,[38] implying that he had come to some agreement with the tribesmen to reinforce his following.

The rest of the life of Firmus ranges from the fantastic to the incredible, emphasizing his great wealth and gargantuan strength. The author clearly did not have very much information on Firmus. He says that Aurelian was in Thrace when he heard of the revolt, and immediately marched against Firmus and defeated him, whereas Zosimus describes how Aurelian marched, presumably straight from Palmyra, though this is not stated, to Alexandria where the inhabitants were divided among themselves and on the point of revolt.[39] Firmus is not named, and it sounds as though the trouble, whatever its nature, was limited to the city of Alexandria and did not concern a serious rebellion involving the whole of Egypt. The fate of the rebels is not elucidated. Firmus was probably strangled, the punishment associated with criminals, and his adherents were rounded up and probably put to death. The *Historia Augusta* maintains that Firmus had disrupted the corn supply, always an emotive issue for the Romans.[40]

Beyond these few facts, it is not clear what happened, nor why there was trouble involving the Palmyrenes in Egypt. The motives may have been economic rather than political, especially as the alleged instigator was a merchant, who evidently did not aim at Imperial rule. The very existence of Firmus has been doubted[41] but the movement, if such it was, presumably had a leader, who may or may not have been called Firmus. How far he was involved with Zenobia must remain conjectural, and it is not even known if the Queen herself ever heard of the revolt in Egypt.

THE FATE OF ZENOBIA

No one knows for certain what happened to Zenobia after her capture near the Euphrates and her trial at Emesa. The ancient authors tell conflicting stories. Zosimus says that she died on the journey to Rome, before the convoy of prisoners had even crossed the straits to Byzantium.[42] According to this version she either contracted a disease which killed her or she deliberately starved herself to death. Zonaras hedges his bets, employing the useful device of repeating what others have said, one version being that Zenobia arrived safely in Rome, but another version says that she died on the way there, worn out with grief.[43]

Only Malalas gives any details of the journey through the eastern provinces, where she was allegedly paraded through the streets of Antioch, riding on a camel and bound by chains, then installed on a special dais that Aurelian built in the city, where she remained in chains for three days.[44] Public humiliation is just about feasible, since as Emperor he would need to demonstrate, particularly to the eastern cities, that rebellion did not go unpunished, but Aurelian probably stopped short of executing Zenobia and Vaballathus, not simply because it would stain his hands with the blood of a woman and an adolescent boy, but also because an execution would negate his carefully orchestrated *clementia*.[45] He still had to resolve the problem of the Gallic Empire, and perhaps hoped that negotiation with the Emperor Tetricus might prove as effective as fighting. If he allowed the Gallic Emperor to reach the conclusion that he had no hope of survival, he might decide to fight to the death and make it that much more difficult, and a much more lengthy process, to reintegrate the whole Empire under Aurelian's control.

The campaign against Tetricus and his followers in the Gallic Empire began in the later summer of 273, or early in the year 274.[46] Esuvius Tetricus was the fifth man to be declared Emperor of the *Imperium Galliarum* by the armies, and he was also the last. The Gallic Empire had remained independent since the crisis of 260, when the armies of the Rhine declared Marcus Cassianus Latinius Postumus as Augustus. He took control of the German provinces, Gaul, Spain and Britain, denying to Gallienus access to these provinces and to the revenues from them. Postumus was successful in defending the Gallic Empire from invasions across the Rhine, and enjoyed the support of the soldiers and the civil population. He survived for about nine years, but then was assassinated by the troops. Three Emperors were created within a short time, but were removed almost as quickly. Ulpius Cornelius Laelianus took power for about four months, followed by Marcus Aurelius Marius, who lasted barely eight weeks. Marcus Piavonius Victorinus fared somewhat better, ruling for nearly eighteen months, but then he fell victim to one of his officers. Tetricus was declared Emperor in his place, probably late in 270 or in spring 271.

During the Palmyrene wars, Tetricus had made no move to invade Italy, perhaps because he had no desire to take over the whole Empire, or because he had not enough troops to embark on such a project. Aurelian had placed troops on the lower reaches of the Rhône, and he ensured that the passes through the Alps were guarded.[47] Another factor that may have contributed to Tetricus's reluctance to invade Italy was the presence of the Germanic tribesmen across the Rhine, united under the confederation of the Franks. So far Tetricus and the Rhine legions had managed to repulse incursions and keep the Franks out of Roman territory, but the Gallic Empire was beginning to experience financial problems, and the loyalty of the troops was perhaps not as ardent as it had been. When it was known that Aurelian had defeated Zenobia, and then the Carpi on the Danube, it was clear that sooner or later he would be able to turn his attention to the west.

Tetricus had set up headquarters at Trier on the River Moselle, close enough to the Rhine to deal with incursions of tribesmen. When Aurelian crossed the Alps and marched towards Lyon, which fell to him without a significant struggle, Tetricus mobilized to meet him. The two armies met at Châlons-sur-Marne, where the terrible battle of the Catalaunian Fields decided the issue. The troops of the Gallic Empire started to waver when they heard that Tetricus had been captured, and they never recovered the initiative. Aurelian's practised legions soon overpowered them. The result was more like a massacre than a battle.[48] Tetricus was spared, to march in Aurelian's triumph in the autumn of 274. It was rumoured that there had been some double dealing, and that Tetricus had betrayed his troops and had made a personal appeal to Aurelian for mercy, quoting a line from Virgil's *Aeneid*, asking the unconquered hero to rescue him from his troubles.[49] The rumours probably started because Aurelian did not have Tetricus put to death, an unexpected outcome that was attributed to subterfuge rather than Aurelian's deliberate policy.

When the Empire was reunited, Aurelian claimed with some justification to have restored the world, or at least the Roman version of the world, and he used his titles and the legends on the coinage to advertise his achievement. Superlative epithets such as *Victoriossimus* (most victorious), *Gloriosissimus* (most glorious) and *Fortissimus* (most strong) appear on inscriptions.[50] Other inscriptions label him *Restitutor Orbis* (restorer of the world),[51] echoed on his coins, where he is also *Pacator Orbis* (pacifier of the world).[52] The ultimate accolade was the elevation of Aurelian from a mere mortal to a divine being, declared in his titles *Dominus et Deus* (lord and god). Very soon, his divinity and sovereignty were backdated to his birth, expressed as *deus et dominus natus*.[53] In keeping with his new-found status, Aurelian started to wear a diadem and cloth of gold, and demanded that his subjects bow down to him. He had probably learned from the customs of the easterners and the Persians. He was Rome's foremost general, statesman, politician, psychologist, and a supreme actor, and he had developed a sense of his own importance in ruling the Empire.[54]

With all his battles fought and won, and the Empire reunited under one Emperor, Aurelian held a magnificent triumph in the autumn of 274. According to the account in the *Historia Augusta*[55] Aurelian displayed three Royal chariots, one of them a gift from the king of the Persians, another that had belonged to Odenathus, and the third one Zenobia's own chariot. Various animals such as elephants, giraffes and tigers, and tamed beasts from Libya and Palestine, were paraded through the streets. Eight hundred pairs of gladiators preceded the captives. From the east came the Blemmyes and Egyptians, Arabs from Arabia Felix, Indians, Bactrians, Saracens, Persians and Palmyrenes, even though most of these prisoners were said to have drowned when the ship carrying them to Byzantium sank in a storm, and only Vaballathus was rescued.[56] From the west were the tribesmen: Goths, Alans, Roxolani, Sarmatians, Franks, Suebi, Vandals and Germans. Allowance must be made for exaggeration, and for the anachronistic use of tribal names, but even when all the elaboration is swept away, the triumph would have been a spectacular event, befitting the Emperor who became a god in his own lifetime.

Apart from Zosimus, who says that Zenobia died before leaving the east, most of the ancient authors agree that Zenobia was displayed to the Roman public in Aurelian's triumph, along with the defeated Gallic Emperor Tetricus.[57] In the life of Zenobia, the *Historia Augusta* devotes several lines to Zenobia's appearance, richly adorned with jewels and bound with golden chains so heavy that she kept stopping because she could not bear the weight of them.[58] In the description of the triumph from Aurelian's point of view, Zenobia is presented as just one among many marvels, the weight of her golden chains being carried by other people.[59]

Zenobia's appearance in Aurelian's triumph is generally accepted by modern scholars, who reject the account of Zosimus that she died before reaching Rome.[60] Among many other questions, two queries arise from the sparse information about her eventual fate: where was Zenobia between her capture in 272 and Aurelian's triumph in 274, and what happened to her afterwards? She may have been kept under house arrest in Rome while Aurelian waged war against Tetricus, but she is not mentioned in the sources until she was paraded in the triumphal procession to the temple of Jupiter on the Capitol Hill. After the triumph, Malalas says that she was beheaded.[61] He is the only source that relays this information, and such a fate is unlikely. Other ancient authors insist that her life was spared. Aurelian's policy seems to have been consistent. The wars were over; the Empire was reunited; he had been acknowledged as sole Emperor, and lord and god. He did not need to make any further demonstrations of strength and power. He did not execute Tetricus after the triumph, but gave him a post in the government, making him *corrector*, probably of the district of Lucania in Italy. The accounts of the lives of Tetricus and Aurelian in the *Historia Augusta* are contradictory.

In the biography of Tetricus it is said that he was made *corrector Lucaniae*, but in the life of Aurelian, Tetricus is said to have been *corrector totius Italiae*, giving him control of all of Italy, obviously a more wide-ranging and more important post than governor of Lucania. Opinion among modern scholars is divided as to which post Tetricus took up. There is epigraphic evidence for *correctores* of the whole of Italy that pre-dates the appointment of Tetricus, whereas the evidence for *correctores* of a single region is not found until *c*.283, a decade after Aurelian's selection of his former rival for such a post. On this basis, David Magie, the editor of the Loeb edition of the *Historia Augusta*, opted for Tetricus's appointment as *corrector* of the whole of Italy.[62] Watson on the other hand favours the lesser appointment in charge of Lucania.[63]

The most important point, with reference to Zenobia, is that Aurelian most likely did spare her life, just as he did for Tetricus. It would detract from his policy of *clementia* to treat his former enemies differently, and it would have made Zenobia into a female martyr, in which state she might have been more dangerous to him than she was as a deposed Queen living in ease and probably luxury in Italy. According to the *Historia Augusta* Aurelian provided Zenobia with a fine villa at Tibur (modern Tivoli), not far from the more famous villa of Hadrian.[64] This marries up very well with another passage in the *Historia Augusta*, allegedly reproducing the text of a letter that the Emperor wrote to Zenobia as he was about to march on Palmyra, in which he promised that he would spare her life and in agreement with the senate would allow her to live freely in a place appointed by him, if only she would give up the struggle and surrender.[65] The author may have been tying up loose ends and making his stories match in each of the biographical sketches, but since contradictions scarcely bothered him in other instances, there may be some truth in the statement that Zenobia lived on after the triumph in Italy.

It is probable that Vaballathus lived with her, though he is not actually named in the sources. She lived with her children, according to the *Historia Augusta*,[66] but they are not named, and Zonaras indicates that Zenobia had more than two daughters, though he does not say how many there were.[67] One of them was supposed to have married Aurelian, which is pure fantasy, and the others married noble Romans. Syncellus says that Zenobia herself was married to a Roman senator.[68] Eutropius and Jerome say that Zenobia's descendants still lived in Rome.[69] Another indication that there were descendants of Zenobia and

Odenathus in Italy is found in the late fourth-century letters of Libanius. Writing to Anatolius, he refers to a descendant of Odenathus, whose very name struck fear into the Persians. A short time later Libanius wrote to Eusebius, asking for the oration on Odenathus by Longinus.[70]

ZENOBIA: REBEL AND USURPER, OR HEROINE AND PATRIOT?

It is hard to know Zenobia in any of the roles that have been ascribed to her. Even after exploring her origins and background in Palmyra, and her probable fate, she remains elusive. With no authenticated likeness of her, save for the idealized, Roman-style coin portraits, it is not even possible to form an opinion of her character based on her physiognomy or the mode of her portrayal. Such interpretations may be of little value, but the portraits of other leaders contemporary with Zenobia at least afford a clue about how they saw themselves and how they willingly presented themselves to their own populace and to the rest of the world. The Persian King Shapur I is shown on his rock-carved portraits as a conquering hero, and the third-century Roman Emperors with their close-cropped hair and concerned frowns demonstrate how they shouldered the burdensome responsibilities on behalf of the people of the Empire. Nothing has yet been discovered that shows the physical form in which Zenobia represented herself to her own people and the inhabitants of the eastern cities. Her rule was short and eventful, focused on other matters than the choice of sculpted portraits. Besides, Palmyrene portrait sculpture tended towards depersonalized forms, so it is doubtful whether any facet of her character would have been revealed in her statues that once stood in the Great Colonnade in her native city.

The problem as already stated is in the dearth of reliable source material, exacerbated by the confusing contradictions and the pronounced Roman or Arab bias in the sources that do still exist. The consequence is that there is considerable latitude for alternative theories. We know some scant details of what Zenobia did, but there are few clues as to her reasons. There are gaps too in our knowledge of how the Romans dealt with her. For nearly four years she was granted virtual independence, which implies that the Romans were either content with her rule, or stunningly indifferent. When Odenathus was assassinated, Zenobia took control and assumed his responsibilities, conveniently preventing any other candidate from stepping in to fill the power vacuum. It was not an act of open rebellion but a continuation of the status quo. As an immediate reaction to the removal of the man who ruled the eastern provinces it is not surprising that Zenobia's actions went unchallenged by the Roman Emperors, but if her assumption of power was viewed at this early stage as rebellion or an attempt at usurpation, it is surprising that the situation was allowed to endure. The ancient authors, who knew what the final outcome had been under Aurelian, solved this particular conundrum by assuming that Zenobia meant to usurp power, and then throwing all the blame for her continued survival upon Gallienus, condemned for his inefficiency and laxity.

The Roman provincial governors made no recorded move to oust Zenobia or to declare for any candidate of their own as Emperor. On the contrary they seem to have acquiesced in Zenobia's rule and even to have assisted her, without any declaration on her part or on theirs of an intention to usurp. The central government cannot have been as apathetic as the hostile sources suggest. The preoccupation of the Romans with rebellions on the Rhine and Danube and with tribal pressure on the frontiers is not sufficient reason for the apparent inactivity with regard to Zenobia, if she was perceived as a threat. The expedition of Heraclianus may be a fictionalized account, more a narrative of what ought to have happened than a documented event, but it was a half-hearted affair at best because there was no follow-up or any discernible consequence. It did not lead to a state of war between Rome and Palmyra, nor is there any record of a formal agreement, though some modern scholars have suggested that Claudius acknowledged Zenobia and Vaballathus. If any such agreement were ever made, it would have been in Aurelian's interest to suppress knowledge of it, so that when the time came to reintegrate the eastern half of the Empire under his control, Zenobia could be properly labelled a rebel and the war against her as a just one. In Roman eyes, even if there had been some authorization for Zenobia to continue as the successor of Odenathus with a brief over the whole of the east, she overstepped the boundaries in more ways than one when she extended her territorial control to Asia Minor, Arabia and Egypt.

This is the watershed where the opinions of modern scholars diverge. If Zenobia had stayed at home, as Palmyrene successor of Odenathus, protecting the frontiers, keeping order in the desert, creating a court circle and a literary salon, she would probably have been tolerated by the Romans and acceptable to historians, who could then have devoted their speculations to the extent of Palmyrene control, Zenobia's relationship with the governors of neighbouring provinces, her policy with regard to Mesopotamia and the relations between Palmyra and the Persians. But she extended her control for reasons which remain obscure.

On several counts her expansion is perplexing. The timing looks suspiciously like opportunism, giving rise to further speculation that Zenobia had until this point successfully concealed a congenital ambition to rule the world. Did she act in accordance with an agreement made with Claudius, or did she make her first move only after he was dead? The chronology remains debatable. Did she hope to be able to reconcile her extension of territorial control with the Roman government, and if so, how? Why did she feel that she needed her armies to take control of Arabia and Egypt? Political and military considerations may have necessitated a wider power base, and economic needs may have been the driving force behind her occupation of Egypt. Would she have been able to open up more trading ventures in Egypt without an army, or was the problem there one of internal security that the Emperors could not deal with directly, giving her the advantage of establishing Palmyrene trade through the country to compensate for the increasing difficulties of the Euphrates route?

To march into another province with her army was bound to be seen as an aggressive act at Rome, but Egypt was particularly sensitive, not least because of the all-important corn supply and the revenues, and the fear that any usurper who seized Egypt could cripple Rome. It could be argued that if Zenobia was prepared to take such a step with its inherent risks, there must have been pressures which, if ignored, would incur even greater risks. These need not be tangible threats still detectable at a remove of nearly two thousand years. Perception probably has more influence on the action of political leaders than reality, and in Zenobia's case we know only a very little about the reality and nothing at all about her perceptions.

What were her options? She could have refused to take control after the death of her husband and left the situation ripe for usurpation by someone else. She could have abdicated after order was restored following the assassination, and handed over to one of her generals or one of the Roman governors. She could have appealed to the Emperor and then sat back to wait upon events. Or she could take her inherited responsibilities seriously and try to fulfil them in the most effective manner.

A strong Roman government with a clear mandate for the east, carried out by designated personnel, would have obviated the need for Zenobia or anyone else to take control, but the circumstances of the second half of the third century were extraordinary and Zenobia took extraordinary measures to deal with them. In this book it is suggested that these extraordinary measures comprised Zenobia's attempts to secure the defence of the east and economic stability for the people for whom she was responsible, and that she was no rebel but a queen who was committed to these broader ends, as well as preserving her city from attack and from financial ruin. Other interpretations are equally valid, and the reader may draw his or her own conclusions about who and what Zenobia was.

Glossary

Ala milliaria	auxiliary cavalry unit of *c.*1,000 men.
Ala quingenaria	auxiliary cavalry unit of *c.*500 men.
Archemporos	the organizer and leader of a trading caravan, possibly synonymous with, or a later term for, the *synodiarch* (q.v.).
Argapet	a Persian term for the governor of a city. Septimius Vorodes, one of the most influential men in Palmyra after Odenathus and perhaps his deputy, held this title from *c.*265, though there is debate concerning the precise powers this title bestowed on him.
Auctoritas	a measure of the reputation and social and political standing of Roman senators and politicians. The literal translation 'authority' does not convey its true meaning. *Auctoritas* could be earned and increased by political or military achievements and lost after disgraceful conduct.
Aureus	Roman gold coin, worth twenty-five *denarii* (q.v.).
Auxilia	literally 'help troops', the term used by the Romans to describe the units recruited from non-Romans, organized as *alae* and cohorts during the Empire.
Ballista	artillery engine firing either arrows or stone projectiles.
Cataphractarii	heavy cavalry, with both horse and rider being protected by armour, and the cavalrymen perhaps armed with lance and shield. See also *clibanarii*.
Centuria	a century, or a division of a cohort, nominally of

	100 men, but in practice, from the late Republic and throughout the Empire, a century comprised 80 men.
Centurion	commander of a century, or *centuria* (q.v.).
Clibanarii	slang term for heavy armoured cavalry, derived from *clibanus*, meaning oven. It is not certain whether these troops were the same as *cataphractarii* (q.v.) or whether they were armed and fought in a different way.
Cohors	a cohort, which had two meanings, the first a division of a legion containing six centuries, and the second denoting an auxiliary infantry unit, either 500 (*quingenaria*) or 1,000 (*milliaria*) strong.
Cohors equitata	part-mounted auxiliary unit, either c.500 strong (*quingenaria*) or c.1,000 strong (*milliaria*).
Colonia	literally a colony, originally a settlement of Romans outside Rome, or a city founded for army veterans; during the early and later Empire this was the highest status that a provincial city could attain, conferred by the Emperors on various cities throughout the Empire.
Constitutio Antoniniana	act passed by Caracalla in AD 212, making all freeborn inhabitants of the Empire Roman citizens.
Consul	the consuls were the most senior magistrates of the Republic, elected annually in pairs, responsible for civil duties and command of the armies. During the Empire the consuls were still elected annually, but with reduced military responsibilities and subordinate to the Emperor.
Consul ordinarius	during the Empire there were often more than two consuls in the year. The *ordinarii* were the officially elected consuls, who might hold office for a month or two, giving way to the *consules suffecti*

(q.v.), who were appointed to gain experience of government and to acquire the rank of consul. The *ordinarii* were the eponymous consuls, giving their name to the year.

Consul suffectus
the suffect consuls were those who held office after the *ordinarii*, gaining experience and rank before going on to other appointments.

Corrector
Roman officials with the title *corrector* were appointed from the reign of Trajan to attend to the affairs of free cities which did not come under the jurisdiction of the provincial governors. *Correctores* held military and civil powers and their responsibilities were not totally restricted to the free cities in a province. It used to be thought that Odenathus was appointed *corrector totius orientis*, which would give him command of the whole of the east, a reasonable assumption on the basis of the duties of these officials, but the evidence for his appointment and this title is now questioned. See also *epanorthotes*.

Curiales
members of the city councils.

Denarius
Roman silver coin worth four *sestertii* (q.v.).

Diocese
administrative grouping of several provinces, instituted by Diocletian. Each Diocese was governed by a *vicarius* (q.v.).

Diploma
literally, a letter folded in two; the term is used by modern scholars to describe the pair of bronze tablets issued to discharged auxiliaries and the men of the fleets. It is not the term that the soldiers would have used for the tablets.

Dromedarius
camel rider. The Romans recruited units of Palmyrene *dromedarii* and employed them in desert conditions in the east and in Africa.

Dux (plural Duces)
literally, leader; the term used for equestrian military officers in command of troops in the

	frontier regions, usually with the title *Dux Limitis*. Their commands sometimes covered more than one province. *Duces* were raised to senatorial status by Valentinian.
Epanorthotes	Greek term (an alternative title was *diothotes*) used in Greece of Roman senatorial officials with the Latin title *corrector* (q.v.), usually sent out to regulate the administration and finances of the free cities. In Palmyra, epigraphic evidence shows that Vaballathus held this title, transliterated into Palmyrene script. This lent support to the theory that *epanorthotes* should be equated with the Latin title *corrector*, as in Greece, and that therefore Odenathus must have held the title, but some doubt has now been cast on this association.
Equestrian, equestrians, in Latin *eques*, plural *equites*	Roman middle classes, originally named for their association with the cavalry in the early history of Rome. The equestrians were aristocrats, but ranked below the senators. They pursued careers as businessmen, as officers in the army, and served in a variety of administrative posts throughout the Empire. Equestrians could achieve senatorial status if they accrued sufficient wealth or could be promoted by the Emperors.
Equites legionis	cavalry of a legion, initially thought to number 120 men, but increased by the Emperor Gallienus to over 700 men.
Equites singulares	cavalrymen usually seconded from the *alae*, acting as bodyguards to a provincial governor, usually in units 500 strong. The *equites singulares Augusti* were the cavalrymen guarding the Emperor.
Exploratores	scouts; initially *exploratores* were individuals or small groups of men sent out to reconnoitre. In the later Empire *exploratores* were formed into specific units, equated with the *numeri* (q.v.).

Gladius	short thrusting sword, probably originating in Spain. It was used by the Roman army from the third century BC to the third century AD.
Hydreumata	fortified posts on desert routes in Egypt with accommodation for groups of travellers and for housing troops. The walls enclosed the all-important wells to supply caravans and other travellers with water.
Legion	the term *legio* originally meant the choosing, or the levy, and was eventually applied to the main unit of the Roman army. Around 5,000 strong, the legion was an infantry unit, but also contained some cavalry, the *equites legionis* (q.v.). Legions of the late Empire were smaller, newly raised units being only about 1,000 strong.
Limes (plural *limites*)	frontier. In the Roman Empire frontiers were delineated by various means, ranging from a simple road equipped with watchtowers to a physical barrier like Hadrian's Wall in Britain. The frontier between the Roman province of Syria and the Persian Empire was marked for most of its length by the River Euphrates, and the desert zone between Palmyra and the river was patrolled by the Palmyrene army.
Naukleroi	traders who owned, or chartered, sea-going ships.
Numerus	meaning 'unit' in a very general sense, but from the late first or early second century applied to small, so-called ethnic units commonly found on the German and Dacian frontiers and in Africa.
Ornamenta consularis	the insignia of a consul, awarded by the Emperors to distinguished individuals, conferring the rank of consul on the recipient without the actual office.
Ornamenta triumphalia	insignia of a triumph (q.v.) awarded to Roman generals, signifying a victory or a significant

achievement, without holding an actual triumph in Rome, which was reserved for the Emperors alone.

Portoria — Roman customs dues raised originally at harbours, but during the Empire the system was extended and these duties were levied on goods carried on major routes. The percentage rate was not uniform throughout the provinces, but depended on local or regional economies.

Praefectus — prefect, a title given to several different officials and military officers of widely different ranks; most commonly a governor of a province, or a commander of an auxiliary *ala* or cohort. The summit of an equestrian (q.v.) career was to be appointed to one of the four great prefectures: *Praefectus Annonae* (the Prefect of the *Annona*, in charge of military supplies), *Praefectus Vigilum* (the Prefect of the *Vigiles*, the fire brigade in Rome), the Praetorian Prefect (q.v.), or the Prefect of Egypt.

Praefectus castrorum — camp prefect, third in command of a legion during the Empire.

Praepositus — title given to an officer temporarily in command of troops, such as the *numeri* of the German and Dacian frontiers, or vexillations of troops brought together for a war. It is not strictly a rank, and soldiers of different grades could be appointed as *praepositi* for very varied tasks of high or low importance.

Praeses (plural *praesides*) — provincial governor of equestrian rank. *Praesides* were more common from Severan times onwards.

Praetor — the praetorship had a long history. Originally the praetors were the chief magistrates in early Republican Rome, but were eventually superseded by the consuls. When the consuls were absent the praetor was in charge of the courts, acted as president of the Senate, and had the right to command armies.

Praetorian Prefect

The Praetorians derived from the armed escorts of the military commanders of the Republic. In 2 BC Augustus created a permanent Praetorian Guard, and placed two Prefects of equestrian status in command of it, though on occasion one Praetorian Prefect managed to gain ascendancy over the other and sometimes eradicate him. The Praetorian Prefects were important and powerful men, serving on the advisory council of the Emperors and adding civil and judicial responsibilities to their military duties.

Primus pilus

the most senior centurion in a legion, commanding the first century of the first cohort.

Quaestor

originally the lowest-ranking magistrates of the Republic, appointed to assist the consuls in financial matters. The office was held by young men at the start of their career, before they had entered the Senate. As the Empire expanded more quaestors were created to deal with provincial administration. Quaestors acted as deputies to consular governors, and could hold commands in the army. Sometimes in modern versions of ancient works, quaestor is translated as quartermaster, which is not strictly accurate.

Sagittarius

archer. The Romans raised units of Palmyrene horse archers, and some *dromedarii* were armed with bows and arrows.

Sestertius

Roman silver coin; four *sestertii* equalled one *denarius* (q.v.).

Signifer

standard bearer, carrying the *signum*.

Stipendium

military pay, also applied to a period of service.

Strategos

Greek term meaning general, used in Palmyra of

the two military officers in command against the nomads and in charge of keeping the peace in the city. In the case of Odenathus, it may equate with the Roman title *Dux*.

Synodiarch   organizer, leader and protector of a caravan, and probably the financier as well. See also *archemporos*.

Testudo   literally, tortoise or turtle, a formation where soldiers raised their shields above their heads and overlapped them at the front and the sides to advance in almost complete protection.

Tetarte   a tax of 25 per cent levied on goods carried through Egypt, levied at Alexandria.

Triumph   a triumph was granted by the Senate to victorious generals, who valued this opportunity to show off their captives and the spoils of war by processing along the Via Sacra in Rome, to the Temple of Jupiter. The *triumphator* rode in a chariot with his face painted red, and was supposed to approach the Temple on his knees to dedicate the spoils, with a slave at his side constantly reminding him that he was mortal. Augustus recognized the inflammatory nature of the triumph and took steps to limit it to members of the Imperial family. Other generals were denied the procession, and were granted triumphal ornaments instead (*ornamenta triumphalia*).

Vexillatio   a detachment of troops, often drawn from different units to fulfil a temporary purpose.

Vexillationes   late Roman cavalry units, possibly instituted by Gallienus. Their strength is disputed, perhaps consisting of 500 men, but some scholars argue for *c.*1000.

Vicarius   governor of a Diocese (q.v.), answerable to the Praetorian Prefects.

Notes

Notes to Chapter 1: Zenobia in history and legend

1 Beattie and Pepper (2001: 284).
2 *HA* (Thirty Pretenders 27.1; 30.2; Claudius 1.1).
3 For Arab and Manichaean sources see Ball (2000: 78; 462 n.181); the name *sptymy'btzby* appears on a milestone on the road from Palmyra to Emesa (*CIS* II 3971); Hartmann (2001: 205).
4 Hartmann (2001: 205); Equini Schneider (1993: 32) opts for 240; Stoneman (1992: 2) says Zenobia was born in 241.
5 An inscription dated to 242–3 attests Julius Aurelius Zenobius Zabdilah as *strategos* during the visit of Severus Alexander in 231–2 (*Inv.* III 22 = *OGIS* II 640 = *CIS* II 3932 = *IGR* III 1033); Hartmann (2001: 59 n.61; 117 n.208) and Sartre (2005a: 551 n.105) dismiss Zenobius as the father of Zenobia.
6 Hartmann (2001: 59 n.60).
7 Sartre (2005a: 355; 550–1 n.96) argues that Odenathus gave the name Septimius to his associates, and suggests that this may be how Zenobia became Septimia; for discussion see Hartmann (2001: 117 n.208).
8 For the inscriptions see *CIS* II 3971 = *IGR* III 1029 = *OGIS* 651. Dodgeon and Lieu (1991: 371 n.20) refer to Ingholt (1976: 137) to suggest the connection with Antiochus IV, or possibly with Antiochus VII Sidetes; Stoneman (1992: 2; 112) opts for Antiochus IV Epiphanes. Hartmann (2001: 120 n.214) and Sartre (2005a: 551 n.105) discount the Royal descent.
9 Hartmann (2001: 121).
10 Hartmann (2001: 122–3 n.220) lists the authors who think that the usurper Antiochus was Zenobia's father, including Equini Schneider (1993: 25).
11 Hartmann (2001: 118 n.209); inscriptions: *IGR* III 1029; Kalinka (1900 nos 11 and 12).
12 Hartmann (2001: 121 n.217); Février (1931: 102) says that Antiochus was Zenobia's son, named for his grandfather; Kotula (1997: 142) agrees that Antiochus was her son and is also to be identified as the usurper; Paschoud (1996: 155) thinks he was her son, but not the usurper.
13 Hartmann (2001: 121 n.215) discusses adoption.
14 Hartmann (2001: 118–19 nn.210–11).
15 Septimius Hairan/Haeranes is named on three inscriptions: *CIS* II 3944 = *Inv.* III 16 in Dodgeon and Lieu (1991: 69–70 no. 4.1.4); Seyrig (1963: 161–2) in Dodgeon and Lieu (1991: 69–70 no. 4.2.2); Seyrig (1963: 161 n.134) in Dodgeon and Lieu (1991: 69–70 no. 4.2.5).

16 Gawlikowski (1985: 257 no. 13) in Dodgeon and Lieu (1991: 68 no. 4.1.5). For the sepulchral inscription see Dodgeon and Lieu (1991: 68 no. 4.1.2 = CIS II 4202 = Inv. VII B 55).

17 As Sartre (2005a: 352) points out, the revised family tree for Odenathus is not only the most simple solution, but it also solves all the previous problems. Hartmann (2001: 108–11) outlines by means of useful tables all the different suggestions for Odenathus's family tree.

18 HA (Thirty Pretenders 16.1).

19 HA (Thirty Pretenders 17.2); see also note 26 below.

20 HA (Thirty Pretenders 15.2).

21 HA (Gallienus 13.1; Thirty Pretenders 15.5).

22 Potter (2004: 641 n.1) prefers this solution, separating Hairan from Herodianus.

23 Hartmann (2001: 112–16).

24 Ball (2000: 78; 462 n.181).

25 HA (Thirty Pretenders 30.27).

26 Zonaras (12.27) in Dodgeon and Lieu (1991: 109 no. 4.11.1); Hartmann (2001:127).

27 HA (Gallienus 13.2; Thirty Pretenders 14.4; 15.2; 17.2; 24.4; 27.1; 30.2); Hartmann (2001: 125).

28 HA (Thirty Pretenders 17.2); the text hints at the plot without elucidating what exactly was planned.

29 HA (Thirty Pretenders 30.1).

30 HA (Aurelian 22.1).

31 HA (Aurelian 38.1).

32 Hartmann (2001: 125).

33 The suggestion is dismissed by Hartmann (2001: 125). Kienast (1996: 239) suggests that Herannianus is Hairan/ Haeranes, and that Timolaus is actually Vaballathus.

34 Potter (2004: 641 n.1); see also Potter (1990: 387–8); Seyrig (1963).

35 Hartmann (2001: 118 n.209); IGR III 1029; Kalinka (1900: nos 11 and 12).

36 Hartmann (2001: 120–1) discusses adoption.

37 HA (Thirty Pretenders 30).

38 HA (Thirty Pretenders 31).

39 HA (Thirty Pretenders 31.7; Claudius 1.1).

40 HA (Claudius 1.3).

41 HA (Thirty Pretenders 30.11).

42 HA (Aurelian 28.3).

43 Equini Schneider (2001: 24).

44 Stoneman (1992: 90).

45 Stoneman (1992: 11).

46 Equini Schneider (2001: 25); al-Tabari Annals 1.618–21.

47 Stoneman (1992: 156–7).

48 Stoneman (1992: 7).

49 Gilet (2001).

50 Lanavère (2001).

51 Libanius (Epistles 1078) in Dodgeon and Lieu (1991: 110 no. 4.11.5); Hartmann (2001: 303 n.167) discusses the date when the oration was composed, and lists the opinions of other scholars: Février (1931: 106) considered that the oration was composed during the lifetime

of Odenathus; Equini Schneider (1993: 19) says it was a funeral speech; Will (1992: 202) says it was a panegyric. Potter (2004: 261; 641 n.210) suggests that Longinus was at the court of Odenathus and the speech was intended to upgrade the image of the Palmyrene leader among the other eastern cities.

52 Lanavère (2001: 139); Equini Schneider (2001: 24).

53 Moliterno (2001).

54 Roland-Michel (2001); George Knox, 'Giambattista Tiepolo: Queen Zenobia and Ca' Zenobio: 'una della prime sue fatture' *Burlington Magazine* 121, 1979.

55 Sajous-d'Orion (2001).

56 Stoneman (1992: 7).

57 Pucci (2001: 173).

Notes to Chapter 2: Palmyra and Rome

1 Josephus (*Jewish Antiquities* 8.153–4); Hartmann (2001: 45–6 n.4).

2 Teixidor (1977: 107–8); Ball (2000: 74); the only source for the 'Amalaqi or 'Amlaqi is the Arab historian al-Tabari (Ball 2000: 462 n.165).

3 There are several inscriptions from the Bel Temple before its restoration in the first century AD: *Inv.* XI 86–100; *Inv.* XI 100 (44 BC) is the oldest securely dated inscription: Hartmann (2001: 46 n.6); Gawlikowski (1973: 53ff.).

4 Appian (*Civil Wars* 5.9).

5 Young (2001: 229–30 nos. 1 and 3) lists the inscriptions in honour of So'adu son of Bolyada, who helped to protect the merchants of two caravans, in AD 132 and 144, and on each occasion the text specifically states that four statues were set up in each of the four temples.

6 Millar (1981: 117); Stoneman (1992: 27); Hartmann (2001: 49 n.17) quoting the milestone inscription in Seyrig (1932: 276 no. 2).

7 Stoneman (1992: 29; 209 n.47) quoting Isaac (1990).

8 Pliny (*Natural History* 5.21 = 5.88 in the 1906 Teubner edition by Karl Mayhoff); Young (2001: 143); Hartmann (2001: 48 n.16).

9 Hartmann (2001: 49 n.19).

10 Hartmann (2001: 49 n.19) summarizes the theories about the date of the annexation. The majority of scholars argue for annexation under Tiberius, including Seyrig (1932; 1941: 171); Jones (1971: 266); Bowersock (1983: 136); Teixidor (1984: 10). Others pinpoint the date more closely, to the visit of Germanicus: Will (1985: 267; 1992: 36); Sartre (1991: 318); Millar (1993: 34).

11 Hartmann (2001: 49 n.17); the information derives from an inscription dated to the reign of Antoninus Pius (*IGLS* V 2550).

12 See *Inv.* IX 2 for the Latin inscription of Minucius Rufus, in Seyrig (1932: 274 no.1).

13 Tacitus (*Annals* 2.56).

14 Dio (57.17).

15 Tacitus (*Annals* 2.64). Sartre (2005a: 69–70) opts for 19 as the date of annexation and says that the presence of Germanicus in Palmyra is more easily explained if it was part of the Empire.

16 Tacitus (*Annals* 2.69–72).

17 Southern (2006: 160); Watson (1969: 128; 130).

18 One of the tax gatherers, Lucius Spedius Chrysanthus, is known by name from his gravestone dated AD 58, with text in Latin, Greek and Palmyrene (*Inv.* VIII 57= *CIS* II 4235). See also Stoneman (1992: 58). Hartmann (2001: 50 n.22) quotes other instances of tax gatherers (*publicani*): *CIS* II 3913; *Inv.* X 29 and 113.

19 Stoneman (1992: 27; 209 n.42) points out that earlier authors such as the German scholar Theodore Mommsen thought that Palmyra was already part of the Empire in the reign of Augustus; see also Gawlikowski (1983).

20 Hartmann (2001: 46).

21 Young (2001: 167–70) stresses the significance of the caravan trade for Palmyra.

22 For Julianus see *Inv.* IX 22 = *ILS* 8869; for *ala I Ulpia singularium* see Seyrig (1933: 161 nos. 4–5) = *AE* (1933: nos. 210–11). Hartmann (2001: 51 n.30) lists the attested Roman units and the evidence for them; significantly most of them first appear in the early third century. *Inv.* X 128 names Tiberius Claudius, prefect of *ala I Ulpia dromedariorum Palmyrenorum*. Hartmann (2001: 56 n.49) points out that it is not certain whether this unit was stationed in Palmyra, or whether the inscription was set up in his honour while he was based elsewhere.

23 Hartmann (2001: 61 n.69) quoting Isaac (1990: 325).

24 Hartmann (2001: 54 n.41).

25 Stoneman (1992: 28; 209 n.50) quoting Kennedy (1981: 193).

26 Young (2001: 165) argues that no Palmyrene troops were stationed at Dura before the campaigns of Lucius Verus. Hartmann (2001: 55 n.44) says that Palmyrenes are attested at Dura from 33 BC, but it is not clear whether these are permanent troops. The archers stationed at Dura in the mid second century were converted into a regular unit of the Roman army, probably at the beginning of the third century; see Hartmann (2001: 55 n.44); Isaac (1990: 144); Millar (1993: 131); Mann (1985: 218).

27 Young (2001: 229 nos. 5 and 6) from *Excavations at Dura Preliminary Report* VII/VIII 83 no. 845 dated to 169 and no. 846 dated to 171.

28 Young (2001: 148; 158; 270 n.49); Hartmann (2001: 55 n.45).

29 Young (2001: 158–9).

30 Hartmann (2001: 55–6 n.46) lists possible military posts along the trade routes.

31 Young (2001: 158–9) says that these posts were closely associated with the caravan routes.

32 Hartmann (2001: 54 n.42) lists the authors who support the theory that the Palmyrenes protected the desert frontier: Teixidor (1984: 93); Isaac (1990: 146f.); Kennedy and Riley (1990: 237); Will (1992: 52f.); Millar (1993: 122f.; 133); Gawlikowski (1997: 44). Sartre (2005a: 69–70) says that although the names of Roman auxiliary units are known, it is not understood where they were located, so it is impossible to discern whether they were ranged against the Persians or the nomads, or whether their brief was to control the city.

33 Hartmann (2001: 56).

34 Hartmann (2001: 53 n.37); Young (2001: 151; 221 no. 1; 271 n.63 = Dunant 1971 no. 45); Gawlikowski (1994: 27–33, esp. 32 no. 15).

35 For the text of the inscription see *CIS* II 3913, and for discussion see Teixidor (1984);

Matthews (1984); Stoneman (1992: 57–9; 212 n.24); Andreau (2001: 103–5), with photos. The Tariff combines the measures put in place by Germanicus in AD 17–18 and the additions by the edict of the legate Mucianus, AD 67 to 69.

36 Young (2001: 167); Matthews (1984: 171–3).

37 Young (2001: 138).

38 Young (2001: 18–23; 138; 188–90).

39 Stoneman (1992: 45; 211 n.65); Seyrig (1936: 397–402; 1941: 44–8); see also Stoneman (1992: plates 14; 16; 17), showing camels, one ridden by the god Arsu, and the other led by a merchant, and depicting a ship with full sail and details of rigging.

40 Young (2001: 144; 189; 270 n.35); *Inv.* X 38 for Tylos; *Inv.* X 112 for Phorath.

41 Young (2001: 149–51; 270–1 nn.55–7) quoting the theories of Will (1957), who differentiated between caravan leader, patron and financial backer.

42 Young (2001: 155; 271 n.72).

43 Young (2001: 154–6).

44 Young (2001: 155; 271 n.74); *Inv.* X 44.

45 Young (2001: 155; 271 n.71); *Inv.* III 13 = *CIS* II 3936; Hartmann (2001: 53 n.38; 77 n.52); Will (1992: 60f.).

46 Young (2001: 153; 271 n.70); *Inv.* X 107.

47 Young (2001: 151–3 nn.64–6); *Inv.* X 29 for Antioch; *Inv.* X 112 for Phorath; *Inv.* X 81 for centurion. On the Palmyrene origin of the archon of Phorath see Young (2001: 144; 270 n.35).

48 Appian (*Civil Wars* 5.9).

49 Stoneman (1992: 28; 31; 38–9; 195–8) on luxury goods and the Roman market; Young (2001: 142) points out that Chinese silk has been found in the tombs in Palmyra, as reported by Gawlikowski (1994: 32–3); see also Young (2001: 195–7) on the impossibility of a Parthian monopoly, and the journey of Maes Titianus.

50 *Periplus Maris Erythraei* 39 for Barbarikon and 49 for Barygaza; on silk available at Indian ports see Young (2001: 5; 197; 276 n.39).

51 Young (2001: 142).

52 Ball (2000: 74) accepts the theory that the decline of the city of Emesa and the fall-off of Nabataean trade boosted Palmyrene commerce, but points out that the Palmyrenes flourished not so much as a result of the decline of trade in other areas, but the corresponding rise in the importance of the port of Antioch; Young (2001: 138) disagrees with the concept that the state of commerce in other places affected the Palmyrenes.

53 Young (2001: 5).

54 Young (2001: 7).

55 Young (2001: 140); Gawlikowski (1994; 32–3); Hartmann (2001: 57 n.51); *Inv.* IX 6 for Seleucia; *Inv.* IX 11 for Babylon.

56 Young (2001: 140; 146; 153–4).

57 Chaumont (1974: 77ff.); Young (2001: 140; 269 n.20); Hartmann (2001: 57 n.53) says that Vologesias was opposite Ctesiphon on the Tigris and gives a list of references for the Euphrates/Tigris theories; Maricq (1959: 264ff.), Oppenheimer (1983: 456ff.) and Teixidor (1984: 31) place Vologesias on the Tigris; alternatively Gawlikowski (1988: 167ff.), Will (1992: 64) and Young (2001: 140) opt for the Euphrates.

58   Stoneman (1992: 45) refers to epigraphic evidence in Cantineau (1931: 25 no. 34) and Drexhage (1988: 24 no. 3) attesting the presence of a Palmyrene at Charax in the first century; Hartmann (2001: 57–8 n.55) gives a list of inscriptions attesting caravans to and from Charax, among them *Inv.* X 38 dated 131; *Inv.* X 81 dated 135; *Inv.* X 114 dated 138; *Inv.* X 111 dated 156; *Inv.* X 29 dated 161; see also Young (2001: 140).

59   Stoneman (1992: 45).

60   Young (2001: 145–7; 270 n.38) referring to Nodelman (1960: 111).

61   Young (2001: 144; 146; 270 n.36); Milik (1972: 12–14); Hartmann (2001: 57).

62   Young (2001: 147).

63   Hartmann (2001: 53).

64   Young (2001: 148).

65   Young (2001: 148; 193).

66   Young (2001: 149).

67   *Inv.* X 29; Young (2001: 149; 152; 193; 270 n.52; 271 n.66; 276 n.26).

68   Hartmann (2001: 56).

69   Pliny *Natural History* (5.21 = 5.88 Teubner edition); Young (2001: 143; 270 n.32).

70   Young (2001: 147; 270 n.47) suggests that commerce ceased when wars broke out; see Teixidor (1984: 49–54).

71   Hartmann (2001: 90 n.107) lists the Palmyrene Septimii. Inscriptions dated within the lifetime of Odenathus attest Septimius Malchus (*Inv.* III 8); Septimius Iades (*Inv.* III 9); and Septimius Vorodes; the Aurelius Vorodes of *Inv.* III 12 is probably the same as Septimius Vorodes in *Inv.* III 6–11; see Equini Schneider (1993: 17 n.22). Odenathus gave the name Septimius to his close associates, probably after 257. The other Septimii appear on inscriptions after the death of Odenathus: Septimius Zabdas; Septimius Zabbai; Septimius Apsaeus; Septimius Haddudan. See also Hartmann (2001: 86 n.87; 203–4 nn.151–2); Millar (1993: 123).

72   The name Julius Aurelius was adopted in honour of Julia Domna: Hartmann (2001: 59); see also Hartmann (2001: 90 n.107), quoting Schlumberger (1943), where he says that apart from the Septimii, all other families used the names Julius Aurelius.

73   Birley (1988: 117).

74   Dio (76.10); Birley (1988: 131–3).

75   Birley (1988: 132).

76   Dio (75.3.2–3 = pages 198–9 in the Loeb edition).

77   Southern (2001: 228 n.2); Millar (1993: 141–2).

78   Young (2001: 174); Hartmann (2001: 60 nn.65) quoting *Inv.* X 44 for Ogelus 'Ogeilu *Strategos* Against the Nomads first attested in 199.

79   *AE* (1933: no. 206) for *Strategos* of the Peace first attested in 198. Hartmann (2001: 60 n.66) points out that the phrase 'Strategos who makes peace within the boundaries of the city' appears only in the Palmyrene section of the inscription, but the Greek version can be safely reconstructed.

80   Hartmann (2001: 59 n.59) quotes *Digest* (50.15.1.4–5) on Caracalla bestowing colonial status on Emesa and Palmyra.

81   Hartmann (2001: 77 n.53).

82   Maricq (1958).

83 *RIC* (IV.3 79 no. 69).
84 *CIL* III 141495.5 = *ILS* 9005, dedication to Priscus by the *primus pilus* Trebonius Sosianus;
    Zosimus (1.19.2); Millar (1993: 156) says that this is the first attested appearance of the
    title, and in fact may actually be the first time that it was used.
85 Christol (1997: 99–100).
86 *IGR* III 1201; 1202 for Priscus under Gordian III; Hartmann (2001: 159 n.111) for debate
    on whether Priscus held *imperium maius*, giving him command over several provinces and
    their governors.
87 Christol (1997: 100; 116 n.3); Feissel and Gascou (1995: 71–94).
88 Zosimus (1.20.2).
89 Young (2001: 174).
90 Hartmann (2001: 76–7 n.50) for the last inscriptions from Volgesias: *Inv.* III 29, dated
    March 211; *Inv.* III 21 = *CIS* II 3933, dated April 247.
91 Hartmann (2001: 77 n.52); *Inv.* III 13 = *CIS* II 3936.
92 On alternative routes see Young (2001: 175; 188–9); Hartmann (2001: 78 nn.56–7).
    Aurelius Maccaeus: *CIS* II 3910; Aurelius Belacabus: *IGR* I 1169.
93 Young (2001: 233; 279 nn.12–14).
94 Odenathus is described as 'most illustrious senator' (*lamprotatos* in Greek, the equivalent of
    Latin *clarissimus*) on an undated inscription in Palmyrene and Greek, on his tomb which he
    set up in readiness for himself and his family: Dodgeon and Lieu (1991: 68 no. 4.1.2 = *CIS*
    II 4202 = *Inv.* VIIB 55). His son is also described as senator on an inscription: Dodgeon and
    Lieu (1991: 69 no. 4.1.4 = *CIS* II 3944 = *Inv.* III 16); Young (2001: 232; 279 n.12) points out
    that these two inscriptions also use the specific term *synkletikos*. Septimius Haddudan was
    made a senator probably after Aurelian had suppressed the rebellion: Hartmann (2001: 86).
95 Odenathus is designated Ras Tadmor on an inscription dated 252: Dodgeon and Lieu
    (1991: 68 no. 4.1.5) referring to Gawlikowski (1985: 257 no. 13); Hartmann (2001: 90
    n.112). Haeranes is attested with the same titles in 251: Dodgeon and Lieu (1991: 69 no.
    4.1.4 = *CIS* II 3944 = *Inv.* III 16); Hartmann (2001: 90 n.114).
96 An undated inscription names Odenathus as senator but not Ras Tadmor: Dodgeon and
    Lieu (1991: 68 no. 4.1.2 = *Inv.* VIIB 55 = *CIS* II 4202). Starcky and Gawlikowski (1985: 58)
    and Kienast (1996: 239) argue that Odenathus's senatorial status pre-dates his position as
    exarch or Ras Tadmor.
97 Hartmann (2001: 91 n.116; 92 nn.118–19) concludes that Odenathus was made Ras
    Tadmor in the 240s after the death of Gordian III, and was not made a senator until after
    250, basing this conclusion on a speculative date of 250 for an undated inscription. Sartre
    (2005a: 353) speculates that Odenathus became Ras Tadmor in the year 251, possibly as
    part of a bid for independence after the Emperor Decius died in the same year.
98 Hartmann (2001: 92; 93 n.122) says the title is unknown before these inscriptions appear,
    but there is evidence of *rs syr* for leader of a caravan. See also Young (2001: 232–3; 279 n.11).
99 Young (2001: 232; 279 n.10); Millar (1993: 165) points out that the only dedications are
    by merchants and a soldier, so he argues that this signifies that Odenathus's powers were
    limited to patronage and did not involve military command. Hartmann (2001: 102–3
    nn.158–60) describes a statue dated to 257–8: *Inv.* III 17 = *CIS* II 3945, where the word
    used to describe Odenathus is uncertain but related to *Patronus*.

100   The inscription recording the gift of a throne is fragmentary and bears no date: Hartmann
      (2001: 91 n.116) refers to Cantineau (1931: 138 no. 17) and Gawlikowski (1985: 253 no. 1)
      and says that it probably dates to c.250; see also Dodgeon and Lieu (1991: 68 no. 4.1.1). The
      Palmyrene and Greek inscription is securely dated in the month of Nisan in the (Seleucid)
      year 569, which is April AD 258: Dodgeon and Lieu (1991: 70 no. 4.2.3); Young (2001:
      235).

101   Hartmann (2001: 93–4 n.123) argues that Odenathus commanded the Palmyrene
      military forces and lists the opposing views: Ingholt (1976: 123) described Odenathus as
      commander in chief of the Palmyrene militia. Others see him as head of state, including
      Strobel (1993: 249); Potter (1990: 389); Stoneman (1992: 77ff.); Will (1992: 173f.); Equini
      Schneider (1993: 11).

102   Hartmann (2001: 92–3 n.122).

103   Hartmann (2001: 102) maintains that as exarch, Odenathus had full military powers to
      ensure the safety of Palmyra and the surrounding area, and he was supported by Rome.
      Kettenhofen (1982: 72ff.) argues that the Romans placed great reliance upon Odenathus
      for the defence of Palmyra and the desert.

104   Young (2001: 232; 279 n.9) disagrees with Ingholt (1976: 127–8), who claimed that
      Odenathus commanded the Palmyrene army in the 250s in the war against Shapur.
      Hartmann (2001: 100 n.147) admits that there is no evidence that Odenathus was involved
      in any military action before 260.

105   Hartmann (2001: 99).

106   Hartmann (2001: 99 n.142); Dixon and Southern (1992: 42 fig. 10) for the graffito from
      Dura believed to depict a *clibanarius*; see Zosimus (1.50.3) on heavy cavalry in Zenobia's
      army.

107   Hartmann (2001: 106).

108   Hartmann (2001: 54; 98 n.136) says that sanction by Rome testifies to the special position
      of Palmyra, in its role in frontier defence and control of the desert nomads.

109   Dodgeon and Lieu (1991: 50 no. 3.1.4; 360 n.1) on the date.

110   Dodgeon and Lieu (1991: 50).

111   Zosimus (1.27.2) places the raids on Syria in the reign of Gallus; see Dodgeon and Lieu
      (1991: 51 no. 3.1.4; 363 n.20). Hartmann (2001: 71) places the opening stages of Shapur's
      campaign in spring 253.

112   Dodgeon and Lieu (1991: 50 no. 3.1.4, *RGDS* Greek version line 11).

113   Dodgeon and Lieu (1991: 50 no. 3.1.4, *RGDS* Greek version lines 11–19).

114   Dodgeon and Lieu (1991: 360 n.1).

115   Zosimus (1.32.2).

116   Southern (2001: 78; 309 n.99).

117   Zosimus (1.12.2); Syncellus 437 in Dodgeon and Lieu (1991: 28 no. 1.3.3); Christol (1997:
      129–30); Potter (1990: 20–1); Kienast (1996: 220).

118   Millar (1993: 160–1; 308–9) and Christol (1997: 129) point out that the date of the coinage
      of 253 does not necessarily signify the first time that Uranius Antoninus took command.

119   F. Hartmann (1982: 140 n.3; 141 n.2) concludes that Uranius did not intend to usurp the
      Roman Emperor, but seized power to protect his territory in a time of great danger; see
      also Baldus (1971: 158; 162; 178); Christol (1997: 129; 168 n.15) says that this Uranius may

have been confused with an earlier potential usurper of the same name from the reign of Severus Alexander; Hartmann (2001: 75) points out that the Greek bronze and silver coins for local circulation bear the full Imperial title, whereas the gold coins with legends in Latin, and meant for wider circulation, did not include the whole panoply of Imperial titles, so Uranius had the power of Augustus in Syria but did not represent a challenge to the legitimate Emperor.

120   Hartmann (2001: 75 n.46); Baldus (1971: 143) suggested that Uranius retired into private life when Valerian arrived in Syria.

121   Kettenhofen (1982: 72; 133) suggests that Odenathus was active on Rome's behalf as early as 253; Hartmann (2001: 100 n.148) disagrees.

122   Dodgeon and Lieu (1991: 360–1 n.7).

123   Hartmann (2001: 104); Young (2001: 234).

124   CIS II 3945; 3926; 4202; Young (2001: 234; 279 n.16); Gawlikowski (1985: 254–5); Dodgeon and Lieu (1991: 70 nos. 4.2.2 and 4.2.3).

125   Young (2001: 234; 279 n.19), quoting Teixidor (1989), compares Abgar, King of Edessa; Potter (1996; 2004: 259; 640 n.196) says consular rank was awarded to client kings; Hartmann (2001: 107) for elevation to consular rank, and delegation of defence to rulers of other states, in special circumstances.

126   Hartmann (2001: 104–5; 108) considers the evidence and concludes that Odenathus was suffect consul *in absentia*, quoting other examples of elevation to the consulship to enable chosen men to govern upgraded praetorian provinces.

127   Hartmann (2001: 106 n.174).

128   Christol (1997: 148).

129   Hartmann (2001: 105 nn.170–3).

130   The date of the capture of Valerian is disputed, with estimates ranging from 258 to 260. Périn and Feffer (1987 vol. 1: 31) place the event in 258, simultaneous with the first incursions of the German tribes across the Rhine; de Blois (1975: 10–11; 1976: 2–3) consistently opts for 259, but Christol (1997: 139; 179 nn.4 & 7) points to papyrus evidence from Egypt: *P. Oxy.* 2186, dating to August 260, acknowledges the reigning Emperors Valerian, Gallienus and Gallienus's son Saloninus, but by October 260, *P. Oxy.* 1476 acknowledges the two sons of Macrianus, who took power after the Persian defeat of the Romans and the capture of Valerian, so the battle presumably took place in summer 260.

Notes to Chapter 3: Septimius Odenathus: restorer of the east

1   Sartre (2005a: 549 n.81) points out that title of Count of the Holy Benefactions allotted to Macrianus is anachronistic, but he agrees that Macrianus held some senior post under Valerian.

2   In *HA* (Gallienus 1.2) it is stated that as the Imperial power was about to collapse, there was a need to appoint an Emperor. The author sets this in the consulship of Gallienus and Volusianus, in 261, but Macrianus would not be able to wait that long, so the date would more likely be summer 260.

3   Hartmann (2001: 105 nn.170–3).

4   Zonaras (12.23); Eutropius (9.10); Festus *Breviarum* (23); Hartmann (2001: 139 n.52).

5 *HA* (Thirty Pretenders 12.12) says Macrianus took with him 45,000 men from the army of the east.

6 *HA* (Thirty Pretenders 14.1; 15.4).

7 *HA* (Gallienus 2.2); Zonaras (12.24).

8 Sartre (2005a: 354; 548–50 n.83).

9 Petrus Patricius says that Odenathus tried to make a treaty with the Persians, but gives no date (frg. 10 = *FHG* 4 p.187); Malalas (12) mentions the Saracen Enathus, which probably refers to Odenathus. By the time that Malalas wrote his history all the Arab tribes were termed Saracens; Hartmann (2001: 137 n.42). Drinkwater (2005: 45) sets the attempt in 253 and attributes it to Odenathus's opportunistic zeal for power. Hartmann (2001: 136 n.7) lists other authors who opt for the invasion of 253 for Odenathus's attempt to make a treaty.

10 Hartmann (2001: 136 n.38) refers to authors who suggest that Odenathus tried to make a treaty in 260.

11 Bauzou (2001: 33).

12 Hartmann (2001: 115) says that the titles were achieved successively.

13 *HA* (Gallienus 1.1) says that Odenathus seized power (*cepisset imperium*); *HA* (Thirty Pretenders 15.1) says that he assumed it (*sumpsisset imperium*).

14 *HA* (Gallienus 3.3).

15 Hartmann (2001: 184 n.184) lists and discredits these suggestions.

16 Sartre (2005a: 356; 551 n.107) points out that there was a delay between the death of Odenathus and the proclamation of Vaballathus as *Imperator*, as evidenced on inscriptions which call him King of Kings in Palmyrene, and *basileus* in Greek, but without any mention of *Imperator*; Hartmann (2001: 184) says that *Imperator* appears only in autumn 270, on coins, inscriptions and papyri, which dates to the period after the Palmyrene conquest of Egypt.

17 *HA* (Gallienus 10.1).

18 *HA* (Gallienus 13.1; Thirty Pretenders 15.5). Sartre (2005a: 354–5) says Odenathus never held the title Augustus and it is highly unlikely that Gallienus would grant him *imperium maius*.

19 Zonaras (12.23).

20 Sartre (2005a: 355) points out that there is no evidence whatsoever for the assumption that Odenathus was *dux*, disagreeing with Will (1992: 179), who says that he did hold the title as well as Vaballathus.

21 Hartmann (2001: 147).

22 Hartmann (2001: 154 n.100).

23 *HA* (Gallienus 1.1; Thirty Pretenders 15.1).

24 Hartmann (2001: 144) says that title *dux* followed the repulse of Shapur in 260.

25 Syncellus (466) in Dodgeon and Lieu (1991: 76 no. 4.3.2); Zonaras (12.23); Hartmann (2001: 151–2) says that the original source was probably Dexippus, a contemporary of Odenathus who organized the defence of Athens against the Heruli in 267–8, and wrote a history of the period.

26 *HA* (Thirty Pretenders 11.1–14).

27 Harl (1978: 460) says that Odenathus commanded the frontier regions.

28   *HA* (Gallienus 3.3).

29   Dodgeon and Lieu (1991: 88 no. 4.7.2).

30   *Inv.* III 19 = *CIS* II 3946 in Dodgeon and Lieu (1991: 88 no. 4.7.2); Young (2001: 238); Hartmann (2001: 147).

31   MacMullen (1963: 177; 1976: 33).

32   Sartre (2005a: 354) says it is nothing more than a formulaic title; see Swain (1993).

33   *CIS* II 3971; Young (2001: 178; 238; 274 n.161); Hartmann (2001: 148–9).

34   Hartmann (2001: 149–50); Potter (1990: 392–3).

35   Sartre (2005a: 550 n.90), referring to Swain (1993), who concluded that *epanorthotes* is not the exact equivalent of *corrector*.

36   Sartre (2005a: 355); Potter (2004: 260; 640 n.20); Hartmann (2001: 191–3) on the known governors and the evidence for them.

37   Hartmann (2001: 158–9 n.117), quoting Millar (1971: 8).

38   Hartmann (2001: 159) describes lead seals of Herodian and Zenobia, dating to the lifetime of Odenathus.

39   Hartmann (2001: 160).

40   Hartmann (2001: 159–60) argues for *imperium maius*; Sartre (2005a: 354–5) says it is highly unlikely that Gallienus would grant *imperium maius*, despite the precedents of Avidius Cassius under Marcus Aurelius and Priscus under Philip the Arab; see Potter (1996).

41   Sartre (2005a: 355) accepts the two campaigns without argument.

42   Zosimus (1.39.2) in Dodgeon and Lieu (1991: 75 no. 4.3.2).

43   Hartmann (2001: 165–6) interprets the vague references in the *Sybilline Oracles* (13.164–70) to the 'horned swift moving stag' and the 'greatest beast' as an indication that Odenathus defeated first Shapur, and then the Persians, implying that he made two campaigns, but Dodgeon and Lieu (1991: 71 no. 4.3.2) think that 'the swift moving stag' refers to Quietus.

44   *HA* (Gallienus 10.8).

45   Zosimus (1.39.1) in Dodgeon and Lieu (1991: 75 no. 4.3.2), translated as Gallienus *ordered* Odenathus to help to keep the peace in the east, which has more ramifications than *asked* him to keep the peace.

46   Hartmann (2001: 163) argues against Will (1992: 181).

47   Orosius (*Adversus Paganos* 7.22.12) describes Odenathus's troops as *collecta agresti*, and Jordanes (*Historia Romana* 290) uses the phrase *collecta rusticorum*; see Dodgeon and Lieu (1991: 75 no. 4.3.2).

48   Zosimus (1.39.1) in Dodgeon and Lieu (1991: 75 no. 4.3.2).

49   *HA* (Gallienus 10.6–7).

50   *HA* (Gallienus 10.4; 12.1; Thirty Pretenders 15.4).

51   De Blois (1975: 7) says there was a treaty in 264; Hartmann (2001: 173) disagrees.

52   *HA* (Gallienus 12) attests the two cities and Mesopotamia; (Thirty Pretenders 15.3) mentions Nisibis and Mesopotamia; Zosimus (1.39) mentions Nisibis; Jordanes (*Historia Romana* 290) in Dodgeon and Lieu (1991: 75 no. 4.3.2) says that Odenathus expelled the Persians from Mesopotamia and retook it; see Hartmann (2001: 164 n.8).

53   *HA* (Gallienus 10.5); Hartmann (2001: 167–8).

54 On the date of 263 see Hartmann (2001: 177; 178 n.59), quoting two inscriptions, by Nebuza in March 263 in which Odenathus is *vir consularis*, and the other by Vorodes during his term as *duumvir* which expired in February 264, for Herodianus, who is called King of Kings (*IGR* III 1032 in Greek); see Dodgeon and Lieu (1991: 77 no. 4.3.4); the text says that Herodianus received royalty, presumably in an official ceremony, near the River Orontes, on which Antioch stands.

55 *Inv*. III 19 = *CIS* II 3946 in Dodgeon and Lieu (1991: 88 no. 4.7.2).

56 *IGR* III 1032 in Dodgeon and Lieu (1991: 77 no. 4.3.4).

57 Hartmann (2001: 179) describes the inscription on the rim of a *krater* from the temple of Abgal; *HA* (Gallienus 10.1) calls Odenathus *Rex Palmyrenorum*.

58 Hartmann (2001: 179 n.63) refers to scholars who argue that Odenathus was merely king, or that Zenobia invented the title King of Kings as a posthumous honour for her husband on the inscription set up in 271.

59 Ball (2000: 76).

60 Young (2001: 177); Potter (2004: 260); Hartmann (2001: 182).

61 Hartmann (2001: 183) points out that all the inscriptions are from Palmyra or its immediate vicinity.

62 *HA* (Thirty Pretenders 15.7–8).

63 Hartmann (2001: 187) points out that the army of Syria stood firmly behind Zenobia and the Palmyrenes when Odenathus was murdered.

64 *HA* (Thirty Pretenders 15.2; Aurelian 27.2).

65 Hartmann (2001: 179) presumes that Zenobia took the title Queen at the same time as Odenathus became King of Kings. She is not attested as such until *c.*268–70 by the inscription on a milestone (*CIS* II 3971) in Palmyrene and Greek, referring to Zenobia in terms equivalent to the Latin *clarissima regina* (Hartmann 2001; 242–3 n.2). See also Dodgeon and Lieu (1991: 88).

66 Equini Schneider (1993: 33) considers that Zenobia took the title Queen at this time.

67 *HA* (Thirty Pretenders 15.1; 15.5; 15.7).

68 See note 45, above; Zosimus (1.39.1) in Dodgeon and Lieu (1991: 75 no. 4.3.2); Eutropius (9.11.1) relates that Odenathus worked on behalf of Gallienus; Sartre (2005a: 354) says that Gallienus regarded Odenathus as an ally, and adopted the title *Persicus Maximus* just as he would have done if one of his own generals had won victories on his behalf.

69 Sartre (2005a: 354) points out that the titles were not Roman, and did not infringe Imperial authority.

70 Sartre (2005a: 355).

71 *CIS* II 3938–3943 = *Inv*. III 6–11 in reverse order in Dodgeon and Lieu (1991: 78–9 no. 4.4.1).

72 Dodgeon and Lieu (1991: 370–1 n.18).

73 *CIS* II 3938 = *Inv*. III 11.

74 *CIS* II 3939 = *Inv*. III 10; *CIS* II 3940 = *Inv*. III 9.

75 Dodgeon and Lieu (1991: 78–9 no. 4.4.1); Hartmann (2001: 208).

76 Hartmann (2001: 211).

77 *CIS* II 3942 = *Inv*. III 7.

78 Dodgeon and Lieu (1991: 370–1 n.18).

79 Hartmann (2001: 208 n.165).

80 Equini Schneider (1993: 18).

81 Hartmann (2001: 209).

82 Bauzou (2001: 37).

83 Dodgeon and Lieu (1991: 370 n.18) referring to Schlumberger (1972: 339–41).

84 Bauzou (2001: 37).

85 Hartmann (2001: 208).

86 Hartmann (2001: 191–3).

87 *HA* (Gallienus 12.6).

88 Hartmann (2001: 212).

89 *HA* (Gallienus12.6).

90 *HA* (Gallienus 10.2–8); Hartmann (2001: 215 n.179).

91 Syncellus (467) in Dodgeon and Lieu (1991: 82 no. 4.5.1).

92 Zosimus (1.39.2) in Dodgeon and Lieu (1991: 81 no. 4.5.1); Bauzou (2001: 33) and Sartre (2005a: 355) accept the statement of Zosimus and place the murder at Emesa. Watson (1999: 59; 237 n.9) points out that Odenathus could have fought the Goths in 267–8, and after the campaign was concluded, he could then have visited Emesa.

93 Hartmann (2001: 213 n.177; 238–41) discusses the evidence and gives useful tables setting out the parallel reigns of Claudius, Quintillus, Aurelian and Vaballathus; see also Christol (1997: 159). Watson (1999: 223; 279 n.40) points out that although the papyrus evidence has been generally accepted without dispute, some scholars still date the assassination of Odenathus to 266 or 267.

94 Hartmann (2001: 215); Watson (1999: 59) says that there may have been several invasions of the Heruli which Syncellus perhaps conflated, thus compromising the use of this dating evidence for the murder of Odenathus (Syncellus 467) in Dodgeon and Lieu (1991: 82 no. 4.5.1).

95 Sartre (2005a: 355) says that none of the sources can be substantiated.

96 *HA* (Gallienus 13.1; Thirty Pretenders 15.5–6; 17.1–3).

97 Zonaras (12.24) in Dodgeon and Lieu (1991: 82 no. 4.5.1).

98 Syncellus (467) in Dodgeon and Lieu (1991: 82 no. 4.5.1).

99 Zosimus (1.39.2).

100 Anonymous Continuator of Dio (*FHG* IV, p. 194) in Dodgeon and Lieu (1991: 81 no. 4.5.1).

101 John of Antioch (frag. 152.2, *FHG* IV, p. 599) in Dodgeon and Lieu (1991: 81 no. 4.5.1).

102 Hartmann (2001: 225).

103 Hartmann (2001: 242) thinks that Gallienus may have been behind the alleged plot of Rufinus; Sartre (2005a: 355) favours the same theory. See also Gawlikowski (1985: 259).

104 Sartre (2005a: 355 n.98), referring to Potter (1996), says that Odenathus displayed signs of great ambition to rule the east if not the Empire.

105 Hartmann (2001: 159 n.117).

106 Sartre (2005a: 551 n.102) says that most authors support the family feud theory; Yon (2002: 97–113) points out that among the dominant families there were probably political battles that have not been recorded.

107 Hartmann (2001: 210).

108 *CIS* II 3942 = *Inv.* III 7.

Notes to Chapter 4: Zenobia widowed

1 Bauzou (2001: 35).

2 Christol (1997: 156), discounted by Hartmann (2001: 242).

3 Sartre (2005a: 356).

4 *CIS* II 3971.

5 Swain (1993) questions the interpretation of *pnrtt'* and *epanorthotes*; Sartre (2005a: 354; 550 n.90).

6 For the inscription see *Inv.* III 19 = *CIS* II 3946; Dodgeon and Lieu (1991: 88 no. 4.7.2) translate Odenathus's titles as King of Kings and *Restitutor* of all the Orient; for discussion see Hartmann (2001: 147–9) and Young (2001: 238).

7 Hartmann (2001: 243).

8 Hartmann (2001: 299).

9 Hartmann (2001: 315).

10 Hartmann (2001: 319).

11 Hartmann (2001: 322).

12 Millar (1971: 9); Hartmann (2001: 263).

13 Hartmann (2001: 244) says that Zenobia controlled Palmyra, the Syrian provinces and Mesopotamia as Odenathus had done.

14 Alföldi (1939: 179) argued that the extension of Zenobia's control over Syria can be dated to 270, using as supporting evidence the fact that the Antioch mint issued coins for Claudius, but none for the so-called usurper Quintillus, then ceasing to issue anything until Zenobia reopened the mint and struck coins for Aurelian and Vaballathus. It is implied that Zenobia did not control the city and then suddenly decided to take over the whole of the east. Watson (1999: 63) represents this with more credibility as a tightening up of her control of northern Syria at the same time as she invaded Arabia, but this suggestion takes no account of the drastically changed circumstances when Quintillus was declared Emperor and the armies chose Aurelian instead. Hartmann (2001: 265) points out that the fact that coins from the Antioch mint were issued bearing only portraits of the legitimate Emperors does not constitute firm proof that Zenobia did not control the city. It could indicate that she intentionally minted coins with the portrait of the legitimate Emperor, to make her loyalties clear.

15 Zosimus (1.50.2; 1.51.1) says that Zenobia was staying at Antioch. Eutropius (*Breviarum* 9.13.2) and *HA* (Gallienus 13.5) indicate that she took over all her husband's territories; see Dodgeon and Lieu (1991: 92–3 no. 4.8.2).

16 Hartmann (2001: 192); Rey-Coquais (1978: 58 n.216; 67).

17 Hartmann (2001: 298 n.148).

18 Watson (1999: 168).

19 Martin (2000: 402).

20 *HA* (Claudius 4.4).

21 *HA* (Thirty Pretenders 30.7).

22 *HA* (Aurelian 33.4).

23 Zosimus (1.51.2; 1.52.3; 1.54.2); see Dodgeon and Lieu (1991: 93–5 no. 4.8.2).

24 Hartmann (2001: 300 n.154).

25 Hartmann (2001: 265).

26 *HA* (Gallienus 13.4–5).

27 Christol (1997: 156).

28 Sartre (2005b: 514).

29 Hartmann (2001: 261).

30 Potter (2004: 266).

31 Hartmann (2001: 263).

32 *HA* (Thirty Pretenders 30.11).

33 Procopius (*On Buildings* 2.8.8).

34 Hartmann (2001: 269).

35 Gaborit (2001: 121–2).

36 Procopius (*On Buildings* 2.8.16–17).

37 Hartmann (2001: 271).

38 Gaborit (2001: 121).

39 *HA* (Aurelian 27.4).

40 *HA* (Aurelian 33.4).

41 *HA* (Thirty Pretenders 30.14; 30.18).

42 *CIL* VIII 4876 = *ILS* 571.

43 Hartmann (2001: 267–8).

44 Hartmann (2001: 299).

45 *HA* (Thirty Pretenders 27.2; 30.2).

46 Stoneman (1992: 120).

47 Fraser (2002: 121–2).

48 Saffrey (2001: 61–2).

49 Fraser (2002: 122) says that there were at least two dozen of them from the tenth to the fourth centuries BC.

50 Stoneman (1992: 120).

51 Hartmann (2001: 301 n.158) lists the authors who portray Zenobia as a warrior queen.

52 *HA* (Gallienus 13.5).

53 Zosimus (1.39.2).

54 *HA* (Thirty Pretenders 30.2).

55 Bauzou (2001: 35).

56 Hartmann (2001: 301–2 n.160).

57 Hartmann (2001: 301 n.159); Zosimus (1.44.1; 1.51.1–2) in Dodgeon and Lieu (1991: 87 no. 4.6.5; 93–4 no. 4.8.2).

58 *HA* (Claudius 11.1).

59 *HA* (Aurelian 25.1).

60 *CIS* II 3946; 3947 in Dodgeon and Lieu (1991: 88 no. 4.7.2).

61 Eunapius (*Lives of the Sophists* 456).

62 Hartmann (2001: 302 n.162).

63 Balty (2001: 63).

64 Hartmann (2001: 303).

65 Février (1931: 106), Watson (1999: 66) and Potter (2004: 261) suggest that Longinus had left Athens before the attack by the Heruli in 267 and was already a member of Odenathus's

court circle before the latter was assassinated.

66   Hartmann (2001: 303 n.167) lists the opinions: Février (1931: 106) considers that the oration was composed during the lifetime of Odenathus; Equini Schneider (1993: 19) interprets the work as a funeral speech. Will (1992: 202) says it was a panegyric. Potter (2004: 261) suggests that Longinus was at the court of Odenathus and Longinus's speech was part of the attempt to upgrade the image of the Palmyrene leader among the other eastern cities.

67   Libanius (*Epistles* 1078) in Dodgeon and Lieu (1991: 110 no. 4.11.5).

68   Hartmann (2001: 303 n.165).

69   Balty (2001: 63).

70   Ball (2000: 79) says that Longinus was not the first philosopher to be seduced by money and the promise of an easy life.

71   Equini Schneider (1993: 119).

72   Stoneman (1992: 131).

73   *HA* (Aurelian 30.3).

74   Hartmann (2001: 305).

75   *HA* (Aurelian 27.6); Hartmann (2001: 307).

76   Hartmann (2001: 306–7).

77   Hartmann 2001: 305–6 n.173; the theory that Callinicus dedicated the work to Zenobia was first propounded by Stein (1923) and has been accepted by several other historians.

78   Ball (2000: 79; 462 n.186).

79   Stoneman (1992: 129–38).

80   Stoneman (1992: 130; 218 n.3); Porphyry (*Life of Plotinus* 19).

81   *HA* (Thirty Pretenders 30.22).

Notes to Chapter 5: Septimia Zenobia Augusta

1   See above, Notes to Chapter 4, notes 13 and 14.

2   Sartre (2005a: 356) says that Zenobia intended to take over the whole Roman Empire; Saunders (1992: 155) thinks that this was part of her long-term plan.

3   Ball (2000: 79).

4   The title of Hartmann's book (2001) presents Palmyra as a separate kingdom.

5   Drinkwater (2005: 50).

6   Hartmann (2001: 278 n.89), referring to Damerau (1934: 51).

7   Schwarz (1960; 1976) consistently argues that Zenobia wanted to protect the commercial interests of Palmyra.

8   Watson (1999: 62) argues that the economic motive for Zenobia's expansion ignores the trade that was still operating through the normal channels. However, this in turn ignores the attested decline in Palmyrene trade, and takes no account of the impoverishment that surely would result in Palmyra if the situation did not improve.

9   Alföldi (1939: 179).

10   Christol (1997: 159); Hartmann (2001: 287).

11   Hartmann (2001: 249).

12 Hartmann (2001: 250–1).

13 Hartmann (2001: 278 n.89); Malalas (12) and John of Antioch (frg. 152.2) in Dodgeon and Lieu (1991: 86 no. 4.6.4).

14 Hartmann (2001: 278); Watson (1999: 61).

15 Hartmann (2001: 278 n.89) referring to Damerau (1934: 51).

16 Hartmann (2001: 278 n.89); Saunders (1992: 155) insists that Zenobia planned to rule the world.

17 Hartmann (2001: 347).

18 Hartmann (2001: 350).

19 Young (2001: 175); Bowersock (1983: 132) says that the Tanukh were the enemies of Palmyra.

20 Hartmann (2001: 343 n.290); Young (2001: 174; nn.147–9); Bowersock (1983: 133 n.44) says that the inscription is not wholly literate in either the Greek or the Nabataean versions.

21 Young (2001: 174).

22 Bowersock (1983: 137).

23 Hartmann (2001: 280–1 n.100; 343); Equini Schneider (1993: 68–70).

24 Dodgeon and Lieu (1991: 88–9 no. 4.7.3 = *IGLS* 9107 = *AE* 1947, no. 165); Speidel (1977: 723); Dodgeon and Lieu (1991: 371 n.24) suggest that it may have been the standard-bearers and the hornblowers of *III Cyrenaica* who ransacked the temple of Bel in Palmyra, to avenge the destruction of their own temple at Bostra.

25 Bowersock (1983: 131), referring to the inscriptions collected in Pflaum (1952).

26 Hartmann (2001: 279–80 n.94); Barnes (1973: 153).

27 Hartmann (2001: 281) says that the existence of the milestones on the Via Nova Traiana, with their Latin inscriptions, suggests that the legion cooperated with Zenobia.

28 Hartmann (2001: 249).

29 Hartmann (2001: 245–6); Potter (2004: 267).

30 Young (2001: 27).

31 Young (2001: 44).

32 Young (2001: 44); Casson (1989: 97).

33 Young (2001: 250 n.145); *OGIS* 674 = *IGR* 1.1183.

34 Young (2001: 48–50; 250 n.144).

35 Young (2001: 47; 51).

36 Young (2001: 64).

37 Young (2001: 173–5).

38 Young (2001: 37).

39 Young (2001: 81; 256 n.285).

40 Young (2001: 80–1; 256 n.278); for the inscription of Zabdalos see Bingen (1984).

41 Young (2001: 81; 256 n.279); *CIS* II 3910.

42 Young (2001: 81; 256 n.284).

43 Speidel (1984: 221–4).

44 Young (2001: 71–2; 85–7) says that the Blemmyes seriously disrupted trade in Egypt.

45 Alston (1995: 83–4).

46 Alston (1995: 70–1); Hartmann (2001: 284); Young (2001: 71).

47   Young (2001: 85–5).

48   Young (2001: 27–8).

49   Hartmann (2001: 78).

50   Raschke (1978: 644) suggests that the Palmyrenes used the overland route through Arabia. Young (2001: 81) considers this overland route too complicated.

51   Zosimus (1.44).

52   Watson (1999: 62; 238 n.19) dates the invasion to October, dismissing Zosimus (1.44.1) and *HA* (Claudius 11.1–2), even though both authors say that the Palmyrenes invaded Egypt while Claudius was still alive. Watson emphasizes the hints in the works of Zonaras and Syncellus, who imply that Claudius was already dead; see Dodgeon and Lieu (1991: 86–7 no. 4.6.5).

53   Crete was threatened by Scythians, according to the *Historia Augusta*, which presumably means pirates (*HA* Claudius 12.1).

54   Zosimus (1.44); Hartmann (2001: 284).

55   Zosimus (1.44.1–2) in Dodgeon and Lieu (1991: 87 no. 4.6.5).

56   Graf (1989: 144), dismissed by Watson (1999: 238 n.18).

57   Watson (1999: 63); *HA* (Claudius 11.1–2) says that Probatus, meaning Probus, was killed by a trick of Timagenes, but at the same time insists that the Palmyrenes were defeated by the Egyptians, who swore allegiance to Claudius.

58   Hartmann (2001: 286) referring to Strobel (1993: 264).

59   Christol (1997: 159).

60   Hartmann (2001: 193 n.115; 287 n.117); Potter (2004: 267) lists Marcellinus among the Roman officials who were willing to serve Zenobia.

61   Potter (2004: 270) says that Aemilianus was one of the officials who could move between two camps.

62   Hartmann (2001: 285) points out that there is no other corroborative evidence for the contemporary equation of Zenobia and Cleopatra, in the papyri, the coins or in any other ancient literature.

63   Watson (1999: 65); Potter (2004: 267); Hartman (2001: 285 n.112) lists the authors who have accepted the story, but doubts its veracity.

64   Watson (1999: 65); Potter (2004: 268).

65   Zosimus (1.50.1) in Dodgeon and Lieu (1991: 91 no. 4.7.4); Hartmann (2001: 294).

66   Hartmann (2001: 295–6).

67   Hartmann (2001: 294–6) describes her lack of success; Equini Schneider (1993: 75) says there was no Palmyrene occupation, merely a demonstration of power.

68   Young (2001: 180); Stoneman (1992: 161).

69   Zosimus (1.50.1–2) in Dodgeon and Lieu (1991: 91 no. 4.7.4).

70   Watson (1999: 67).

71   Cizek (1994: 103) is certain that Aurelian recognized Vaballathus as the successor of Odenathus, implying that he probably ratified his titles.

72   Graf (1989: 145) suggests that just after the death of Odenathus, Gallienus made terms with Zenobia. Mattingly (1936: 101–13) prefers Claudius as the Emperor who made an agreement, and says that Aurelian ignored it; in another work (1939: 301) he says that conciliation was a one-sided offer from the Palmyrenes.

73 Watson (1999: 67; 239 n.32).

74 Hartmann (2001: 357).

75 Hartmann (2001: 355 n.10); the best preserved with full text is *ILS* 8924.

76 *IGR* III 1027 = 1065 (duplicate entry) = *OGIS* 647.

77 Hartmann (2001: 356 n.11) referring among others to Potter (1990: 393) and Swain (1993: 162).

78 Watson (1999: 69; 240 n.41).

79 Equini Schneider (1993: 76).

80 Hartmann (2001: 356).

81 Hartmann (2001: 361).

82 Hartmann (2001: 360 n.22); Watson (1999: 69).

83 Hartmann (2001: 362).

84 Young (2001: 179) says that it was Aurelian's reaction to Zenobia's policies that portrayed her actions as a revolt; Bowersock (1987: 21) and Graf (1989: 159) prefer to label Zenobia a usurper.

85 Watson (1999: 66).

Notes to Chapter 6: Aurelian and the Roman recovery

1 *HA* (Probus 9.5).

2 Watson (1999: 70).

3 Hartmann (2001: 372).

4 Hartmann (2001: 372–3 n.54).

5 Hartmann (2001: 372).

6 Watson (1999: 223–4), referring to the last known papyrus to bear the joint names of Aurelian and Vaballathus (*P. Oxy.* XL 2904) and the first with the name of Aurelian alone (*P. Oxy.* XL 2902).

7 Watson (1999: 223–4).

8 Hartmann (2001: 372).

9 Zosimus (1.44).

10 Zosimus (1.52).

11 Hartmann (2001: 285 n.113).

12 Zosimus (1.52) describes Aurelian's army; see also Hartmann (2001: 205). Stoneman (1992: 166–8) speculates on the legions from which Aurelian could have drawn troops, and reconstructs the order of march, based on evidence from other campaigns and the accounts in the ancient military manuals.

13 Hartmann (2001: 365); Watson (1999: 71–2).

14 Hartmann (2001: 366).

15 Hartmann (2001: 388) documents the occasions when Aurelian showed mercy, advertising his *clementia* as a political device to win over his enemies and their allies. He also extended the policy to include the defeated Gallic Emperor Tetricus in 274.

16 Hartmann (2001: 368); Watson (1999: 72).

17 Zosimus (1.50–1.56).

18   *HA* (Aurelian 25.1).

19   Eutropius (9.13).

20   Downey (1950).

21   Cizek (1994: 260 n.4) says that Zosimus places the battle near the Orontes, whereas it was closer to another river called Oinoparas.

22   Zosimus (1.50–1.51) in Dodgeon and Lieu (1991: 93–4 no. 4.8.2); Downey (1950: 64–6).

23   Zosimus (1.51).

24   Watson (1999: 74; 241 n.12); Dodgeon and Lieu (1991: 92–5 no. 4.8.2). Eutropius (9.13.2) labels Immae as a battle of no great importance, and says that Zenobia was captured there. Festus (*Breviarum* 24) also says that Aurelian captured Zenobia at Immae; see Dodgeon and Lieu (1991: 92 no. 4.8.2). Neither of these authors mentions Emesa. Jordanes (*Historia Romana* 291) implies and Syncellus (470) states that the Palmyrenes were destroyed at Immae; see Dodgeon and Lieu (1991: 95 no. 4.8.2).

25   Cizek (1994: 260 n.4) favours the battle of Emesa as the real turning point.

26   Zosimus (1.52.1–2); *HA* (Aurelian 25.1) implies that the battle for Daphne took place before the Emperor had entered the city of Antioch.

27   Hartmann (2001: 370–1).

28   Zosimus (1.52.4) in Dodgeon and Lieu (1991: 94 no. 4.8.2); Watson (1999: 75; 241 n.19).

29   Zosimus (1.52.3); Hartmann (2001: 371 n.48); Watson (1999: 74; 241 n.12).

30   *HA* (Aurelian 25.2–3) says that the Roman cavalry were tired after their long march.

31   Zosimus (1.53).

32   *HA* (Aurelian 25.2–3); Zosimus (1.53).

33   Zosimus (1.54) in Dodgeon and Lieu (1991: 95 no. 4.8.2).

34   *HA* (Aurelian 26.1).

35   *HA* (Aurelian 26.3–6).

36   *HA* (Aurelian 26.1).

37   *HA* (Aurelian 26.1).

38   Stoneman (1992: 172–3); Cizek (1994: 111); Hartmann (2001: 382).

39   *HA* (Aurelian 28.2).

40   *HA* (Aurelian 28.1); Zosimus (1.54.2) says that Aurelian surrounded the city on all sides.

41   Hartmann (2001: 377–8).

42   Hartmann (2001: 376 n.67) discusses the views of modern authors who accept that there was a siege.

43   Hartmann (2001: 381).

44   Hartmann (2001: 380).

45   Hartmann (2001: 377–81) discusses the literary and archaeological sources and concludes that the siege of Palmyra is not historical fact. He lists authors for and against the siege (2001: 377 n.68). Among the more recent authors who accept the reality of the siege are Potter (1990: 61); Stoneman (1992: 173–6); Cizek (1994: 111–12); Watson (1999: 76–8). Other scholars express some doubt: Equini Schneider (1993: 81); van Berchem (1952: 4 n.2; 1954: 259); Gawlikowski (1974: 241).

46   *HA* (Aurelian 28.2).

47   *HA* (Aurelian 28.2).

48 Zosimus (1.54.2) in Dodgeon and Lieu (1991: 98 no. 4.8.4).

49 *HA* (Aurelian 26.7–9).

50 *HA* (Aurelian 27.1–5).

51 *HA* (Aurelian 28.1).

52 Zosimus (1.54.2–3).

53 Zosimus (1.55.1–2) in Dodgeon and Lieu (1991: 98–9 no. 4.8.4).

54 *HA* (Aurelian 28.3); Zosimus (1.55.3).

55 Hartmann (2001: 390 n.101); *RIC* V 1.280 nos. 140–1; *RIC* V 1.290 no. 231.

56 Zosimus (1.56.2) in Dodgeon and Lieu (1991: 100 no. 4.9.1); *HA* (Aurelian 30.3).

57 Zosimus (1.56.2–3).

Notes to Chapter 7: Aftermath

1 *HA* (Aurelian 31.2).

2 Young (2001: 184).

3 Zosimus (1.56.1) in Dodgeon and Lieu (1991: 99 no. 4.8.4).

4 The inscription was published by Gawlikowski (1971: 420); for discussion see Hartmann (2001: 383–5 n.86).

5 *Inv.* IX 28.

6 Gawlikowski (1971: 420); Equini Schneider (1993: 85). Dodgeon and Lieu (1991: 103 no. 4.10.1) date the inscription to the period 273 to 274.

7 Hartmann (2001: 373; 393).

8 Hartmann (2001: 373 n.56) refers to the suggestion by Février (1931).

9 Zosimus (1.60.1) in Dodgeon and Lieu (1991: 102 no. 4.9.4).

10 Hartmann (2001: 393 n.107) refers to the authors who opt for the title *Rector Orientis*, among them Paschoud (1971: 169); Equini Schneider (1993: 85); Watson (1999: 67); Stoneman (1992: 177). Instead of *Rector*, Peachin (1990: 175) suggests that Marcellinus was *praefectus Mesopotamiae et totius orientis*.

11 Hartmann (2001: 390–1).

12 *HA* (Aurelian 35.4; 41.9); Watson (1999: 242 n.32) says that similar tales are significantly absent in the account of Festus (24).

13 *HA* (Aurelian 28.5–29.1–3); Watson (1999: 242 n.31) says it can be assumed that there was some parleying between Aurelian and Shapur.

14 Bowersock (1983: 137; 138–40).

15 Zosimus (1.60) in Dodgeon and Lieu (1991: 102 no. 4.9.4).

16 An undated inscription from Palmyra, in Greek, names Septimius Apsaeus as citizen and protector (*Inv.* III 18 = *IGR* III 1049; Dodgeon and Lieu (1991: 103 no. 4.9.5); Hartmann 2001: 395 n.3). Presumably this is the same person as the Apsaios of Zosimus's work.

17 Zosimus (1.60.1–2) in Dodgeon and Lieu (1991: 103 no. 4.9.4).

18 Hartmann (2001: 396).

19 Zosimus (1.61); Dodgeon and Lieu (1991: 103 no. 4.9.4).

20 *HA* (Aurelian 31.1–2).

21 Hartmann (2001: 396 n.6).

22   Paschoud (1996: 155).

23   Ball (2000: 81).

24   *HA* (Aurelian 31.2).

25   Zosimus (1.61) in Dodgeon and Lieu (1991: 103 no. 4.9.4).

26   Hartmann (2001: 398).

27   Zosimus (1.61.1) in Dodgeon and Lieu (1991: 103 no. 4.9.4).

28   *HA* (Aurelian 31.5–10).

29   Zosimus (1.62.) in Dodgeon and Lieu (1991: 107 no. 4.10.3).

30   Zosimus (1.61.1) in Dodgeon and Lieu (1991: 103 no. 4.9.4).

31   Hartmann (2001: 400–2).

32   Young (2001: 182–4).

33   Young (2001: 182–3).

34   *HA* (Aurelian 31.2–3).

35   *HA* (Firmus 3.1).

36   *HA* (Firmus 5.1).

37   *HA* (Firmus 5.3).

38   *HA* (Firmus 3.3).

39   Zosimus (1.61.1) in Dodgeon and Lieu (1991: 105 no. 4.10.2).

40   *HA* (Firmus 5.4).

41   Watson (1999: 82).

42   Zosimus (1.59) in Dodgeon and Lieu (1991: 102 no. 4.9.4).

43   Zonaras (12.24) in Dodgeon and Lieu (1991: 109 no. 4.11.1).

44   Malalas (12.30) in Dodgeon and Lieu (1991: 101 no. 4.9.2).

45   Hartmann (2001: 392); *HA* (Aurelian 30.2) says that Aurelian thought it unseemly to execute a woman.

46   The date is disputed. Watson (1999: 93) says the campaign started in late summer 274; Cizek (1994: 121) points out that up to the end of February 274, the mint at Lyons issued coins for Tetricus, but by March, coins were being issued for Aurelian.

47   Watson (1999: 91).

48   Watson (1999: 93; 246 n.13) says that the sources make it clear that the slaughter was mostly by Aurelian's troops.

49   The story that Tetricus asked for mercy is repeated in several sources: *HA* (Thirty Pretenders 24.3); Aurelius Victor (*de Caes.* 35.4); Eutropius (9.13.2); Orosius (7.23).

50   *ILS* 578; 579.

51   *CIL* VI 1112, probably dating from late 274; *CIL* XII 5456 = *ILS* 577, probably dated to 275; *CIL* XII 5561 = *CIL* XVII 172; *CIL* VIII 10217 = *ILS* 578.

52   Hartmann (2001: 412 n.7); *Restitutor Orbis* (*RIC* V.1.271); *Pacator Orbis* (*RIC* V.1.265).

53   *CIL* VIII 25820; *CIL* II 3832; *CIL* VIII 4877 = *ILS* 585; *AE* 1938 no. 24. These inscriptions date from Aurelian's own lifetime.

54   Southern (2001: 122; 325 n.57); Cizek (1994: 186).

55   *HA* (Aurelian 33–4).

56   The story of the shipwreck derives from Zosimus (1.59); Watson (1999: 80) says that it may be a fabrication.

57   Dodgeon and Lieu (1991:105 no. 4.10.3).

58 *HA* (Thirty Pretenders 30.24–6).
59 *HA* (Aurelian 34.3).
60 Cizek (1994: 113); Watson (1999: 79); Hartmann (2001: 412).
61 Malalas 12.20; Dodgeon and Lieu (1991: 101 no. 4.9.2).
62 *HA* Thirty Pretenders 24.5; pp. 124–5 n.6 in the Loeb edition.
63 Watson (1999: 95).
64 *HA* (Thirty Pretenders 30.27).
65 *HA* (Aurelian 26.8).
66 *HA* (Thirty Pretenders 30.27).
67 Zonaras (12.27).
68 Dodgeon and Lieu (1991: 109 no. 4.11.1).
69 Eutropius (12.13.2); Jerome (*Chronicle* 274); Dodgeon and Lieu (1991: 108 no. 4.11.1).
70 Libanius (*Epistles* 1006; 1078); Dodgeon and Lieu (1991: 109–10 nos. 4.11.4 and 4.11.5).

Bibliography

ABBREVIATIONS

AAS *Annales Archéologiques Arabes Syriennes.*

AE *L'Année Épigraphique.*

ANRW *Aufstieg und Niedergang des Römischen Welt.* Ed. H. Temporini *et al.* (Berlin 1972–).

BASP *Bulletin of the American Society of Papyrologists.*

BÉO *Bulletin des Études Orientales.*

CE *Chronique d'Égypte.*

CIL *Corpus Inscriptionum Latinarum* (Berlin, 1863–).

CIS *Corpus Inscriptionum Semiticarum* (Paris, 1881–).

CSHB *Corpus Scriptorum Historiae Byzantinae* (Bonn, 1828–1878). 49 vols.

FHG *Fragmenta Historicorum Graecorum.* Ed. C. Müller (Paris, 1841–70). 5 vols.

GCS *Die Griechischen Christlichen Schriftsteller der Ersten Drei Jahrhunderte* (Leipzig and Berlin 1897 to date).

HA *Historia Augusta.*

IGLS *Inscriptions Grecques et Latines de la Syrie.* Ed. L. Jalabert *et al.* (Paris, 1929–).

IGR *Inscriptiones Graecae ad Res Romanas Pertinentes.* Eds R. Cagnat and G. Lafaye (Paris, 1906–27).

ILS *Inscriptiones Latinae Selectae.* Ed. H. Dessau (Berlin, 1892–1916).

Inv. *Inventaire des Inscriptions de Palmyre.* Eds J. Cantineau *et al.* Fascicules 1–11 (Beirut, 1920–65).

JÖAI *Jahreshefte des Österreichischen Archäologischen Instituts.*

JRS	*Journal of Roman Studies.*
JS	*Journal des Savants.*
MGH	*Monumenta Germania Historica* (Berlin 1877–1919).
OGIS	*Orientis Graeci Inscriptiones Selectae.*
P. Oxy.	*The Oxyrhynchus Papyri.* Eds. B.P. Grenfell *et al.* (London, 1898–).
RGDS	*Res Gestae Divi Saporis* = A. Maricq, (1958), 'Inscription of Shapur at the Kaaba of Zoroastre' *Syria* 35, 245–60.
RIC	*Roman Imperial Coinage.* Eds. H. Mattingly and E. A. Sydenham *et al.* (London, 1923–).
TAPhA	*Transactions of the American Philological Association.*
ZPE	*Zeitschrift für Papyrologie und Epigrafik.*

ANCIENT SOURCES

al-Tabari *Annals*. Selections edited by M. J. de Goeje. Leiden: Brill.

Appian *Civil Wars*. Trans. H. White, (Loeb). 4 vols.

Aurelius Victor *De Caesaribus*. Ed. F. Pichlmayr, rev. R Gruendel (Berlin, 1970).

Digest of Justinian. Eds. Th. Mommsen and Paul Krueger; English translation by Alan Watson. Philadelphia: Philadelphia University Press. 4 vols.

Dio *Roman History*. Trans. E. Cary and H. B. Foster (Loeb). 9 vols.

Eunapius *Lives of the Sophists* in *Philostratus* vol. 4 = Philostratus *Lives of the Sophists* and Eunapius *Lives of the Philosophers and the Sophists*. Trans. W. C. Wright (Loeb). 4 vols.

Eutropius *Breviarum Ab Urbe Condita Eutropii*. Ed. C. Santini (Leipzig: Teubner, 1979).

Festus *Breviarum*. Ed. J. W. Eadie (London, 1967).

Herodian. Trans. C. R. Whittaker (Loeb). 2 vols.

Historia Augusta = *Scriptores Historia Augusta* (Loeb). 3 vols.

Jerome *Chronicle*. Ed. R. Helm, *GCS* 1956.

John of Antioch. Ed. C. Müller, *FHG* IV, 535–622.

Jordanes *Historia Romana*. Ed. T. Mommsen, *MGH*, 1882.

Josephus *Jewish Antiquities* in *Josephus* vols 5–13. Trans. R. Marcus, A. Wikgren, L. H. Feldman (Loeb). 13 vols.

Libanius *Epistles* in *Libanii Opera*. Ed. R. Förster (Leipzig: Teubner, 1909–27).

Malalas *Chronographia*. Ed. L. Dindorf (*CSHB* 1831).

Orosius *Adversum Paganos* = *Pauli Orosii Historiarum Adversum Paganos*. Ed. C. Zangemeister (Leipzig: Teubner, 1889).

Periplus Maris Erythraei = *The Periplus Maris Erythraei: Text Translation and Commentary*. Trans. and ed. L. Casson (Princeton, NJ: Princeton University Press, 1989).

Petrus Patricius. Ed. C. Müller, *FHG* IV, 181–91.

Pliny *Natural History*. Trans. H. Rackham *et al.* (Loeb). 10 vols.

Porphyry *Life of Plotinus* in *Plotinus: Porphyry on the Life of Plotinus, and the Enneads*. Ed. A. H. Armstrong (Loeb). 4 vols.

Procopius *On Buildings* in *Procopius* vol. 7. Trans. H. B. Dewing and G. Downey (Loeb). 7 vols.

Syncellus. Ed. A. A. Mosshammer (Leipzig: Teubner 1984).

Tacitus *Annals*. Trans. C. H. Moore and J. Jackson (Loeb). 3 vols.

Zonaras. Eds. M. Pinder and T. Büttner-Wobst, *CSHB*, 1841–97.

Zosimus *New History* = *Histoire Nouvelle*. Ed. F. Paschoud (Paris, 1971).

MODERN WORKS

Alföldi, A. (1939), 'The crisis of the Empire AD 249–270', in S. A. Cook, F. E. Adcock, M. P. Charlesworth and M. H. Baynes (eds.) *Cambridge Ancient History Vol XII: The Imperial Crisis and Recovery*. Cambridge: Cambridge University Press, pp. 165–231.

Alston, R. (1995), *Soldier and Society in Roman Egypt*. London: Routledge.

Andreau, J. (2001), 'Le Tarif de Palmyre', in J. Charles-Gaffiot, H. Lafange, J. -M. Hofman (eds.), *Moi, Zénobie, Reine de Palmyre 18 septembre– 16 décembre 2001, Centre Culturel du Pantheon, Paris*. Milan: Skira Editore, pp. 103–5.

Baldus, H. R. (1971), *Uranius Antoninus: Münzprägung und Geschichte*. Bonn: Antiquitas, Reihe III, no. 11.

Ball, W. (2000), *Rome in the East: the Transformation of an Empire*. London: Routledge.

Balty, J. (2001), 'Longin à Palmyre', in J. Charles-Gaffiot, H. Lafange, J. -M. Hofman (eds.), *Moi, Zénobie, Reine de Palmyre 18 septembre –16 décembre 2001, Centre Culturel du Pantheon, Paris*. Milan: Skira Editore, pp. 63–6.

Barnes, T. D. (1973), 'More missing names (AD 260–395)', *Phoenix* 27, 135–55.

Bauzou. T. (2001), 'Zénobie : la dernière des princesses syriennes', in J. Charles-Gaffiot, H. Lafange, J. -M. Hofman (eds.), *Moi, Zénobie, Reine de Palmyre 18 septembre –16 décembre 2001, Centre Culturel du Pantheon, Paris*. Milan: Skira Editore, pp. 27–42.

Beattie, A. and Pepper, T. (2001), *The Rough Guide to Syria*. London: Rough Guides.

Bingen, J. (1984), 'Une dédicace de marchands palmyréniens à Coptos', *CE* 59, 355–8.

Birley. A. R. (1988), *The African Emperor: Septimius Severus*. 2nd edn. London: Batsford.

Bowersock, G. W. (1983), *Roman Arabia*. Cambridge, MA: Harvard University Press.

Bowersock, G. W. (1987), 'The Hellenism of Zenobia', in J. T. A. Koumoulides, (ed.) *Greek Connections: Essays on Cultural Diplomacy (Stephen J. Sr. and Beatrice Brademas Lectures 1976–1986)*. Notre Dame, IN: University of Notre Dame Press, pp. 19–27.

Butcher, K. (2003), *Roman Syria and the Near East*. London: British Museum Press.

Cantineau, J. (1931), 'Textes palmyréniens provenant de la fouille du Temple de Bêl', *Syria*, 12, 116–41.

Capelle, A. G. von (1817), 'Disputatio Inauguralis de Zenobia Palmyrenorum Augusta'. Unpublished dissertation, University of Utrecht.

Casson, L. (1989), *The Periplus Maris Erythraei: Text Translation and Commentary*. Princeton, NJ: Princeton University Press.

Chaumont, M. -L. (1974), 'Études d'histoire Parthe 3: les villes fondées par Vologèse', *Syria*, 51, 75–89.

Christol, M. (1997), *L'Empire Romain du IIIe Siècle: Histoire Politique 192–325 après J. -C*. Paris: Editions Errance.

Cizek, E. (1994), *L'Empereur Aurélien et son temps*. Paris: Les Belles Lettres.

Damerau, P. (1934), *Kaiser Claudius II Gothicus*. Leipzig: Klio Beiheft 33.

de Blois, L. (1975), 'Odaenathus and the Roman-Persian wars of 252–264 AD', *Talanta*, 6, 7–23.

de Blois, L. (1976), *The Policy of the Emperor Gallienus*. Leiden: Brill.

Dixon, K. R. and Southern, P. (1992), *The Roman Cavalry From the First to the Third Centuries AD*. London: Batsford.

Dodgeon, M. H. and Lieu, S. N. C. (1991), *The Roman Eastern Frontier and the Persian Wars AD 226–362: A Documentary History*. London: Routledge.

Downey, G. (1950), 'Aurelian's victory over Zenobia at Immae', *TAPhA* 81, 57–68.

Drexhage, R. (1988), *Untersuchungen zum Römischen Osthandel*. Bonn: R. Habelt.

Drinkwater, J. (2005), 'Maximinus to Diocletian and the crisis', in A. K. Bowman, P. Garnsey and A. Cameron (eds.), *Cambridge Ancient History Vol. 12: The Crisis of Empire AD 193–337*. 2nd edn. Cambridge: Cambridge University Press, pp. 28–66.

Dunant, C. (1971), *Le Sanctuaire de Baalshamin à Palmyre III: Les Inscriptions*. Rome: Institut Suisse.

Equini Schneider, E. (1993), *Septimia Zenobia Sebaste*. Rome: L'Erma di Bretschneider.

Equini Schneider, E. (2001), 'Un portrait de *Zénobie* et son temps', in J. Charles-Gaffiot, H. Lafange, J. -M. Hofman (eds.), *Moi, Zénobie, Reine de Palmyre 18 septembre –16 décembre 2001, Centre Culturel du Pantheon, Paris*. Milan: Skira Editore, pp. 23–5.

Feissel, D. and Gascou, J. (1995), 'Documents d'archives romains inédits du Moyen Euphrate', *JS* 1995, 65–119.

Février, J. G. (1931), *Essai Sur l'Histoire Politique et Economique de Palmyre*. Paris: J. Vrin.

Fraser, A. (2002), *The Warrior Queens: Boadicea's Chariot*. London: Phoenix Press. (First published by Weidenfeld and Nicolson, 1988).

Gaborit, J. (2001), 'Zénobia, forteresse sur l'Euphrate', in J. Charles-Gaffiot, H. Lafange, J. -M. Hofman (eds.), *Moi, Zénobie, Reine de Palmyre 18 septembre –16 décembre 2001, Centre Culturel du Pantheon, Paris*. Milan: Skira Editore, pp. 121–2.

Gawlikowski, M. (1971), 'Inscriptions de Palmyre', *Syria*, 48, 407–26.

Gawlikowski, M. (1973), *Le Temple Palmyrénien: Étude d'Épigraphie et de Topographie Historique*. Warsaw: PWN–Editions Scientifiques de Pologne.

Gawlikowski, M. (1974), 'Les defenses de Palmyre', *Syria*, 51, 231–42.

Gawlikowski, M. (1983), 'Palmyre et l'Euphrate', *Syria*, 60, 53–68.

Gawlikowski, M. (1985), 'Les princes de Palmyre', *Syria*, 62, 251–61.

Gawlikowski, M. (1988), 'Le commerce de Palmyre sur terre et sur eau', in J. -F. Salles (ed.), *L'Arabie et Ses Mers Bordières. Vol 1: Itinéraires et Voisinages: Séminaire de Recherche 1985–1986*. Lyon: GS–Maison de l'Orient, pp. 163–72.

Gawlikowski, M. (1994), 'Palmyra as a trading centre', *Iraq*, 56, 27–33.

Gawlikowski, M. (1997), 'The Syrian desert under the Romans', in S. E. Alcock (ed.), *The Early Roman Empire in the East*. Oxford: Oxbow Monographs, pp. 37–54.

Gawlikowski, M. (1998), 'Deux publicains et leur tombeau', *Syria*, 75, 145–51.

Gilet, A. (2001), 'Le voyage de L.F. Cassas (1756–1827) à Palmyre en 1785: la mort au temps de Zénobie et l'Orient vivant', in J. Charles-Gaffiot, H. Lafange, J. -M. Hofman (eds.), *Moi, Zénobie, Reine de Palmyre 18 septembre –16 décembre 2001, Centre Culturel du Pantheon, Paris*. Milan: Skira Editore, pp. 149–51.

Graf, D. F. (1989), 'Zenobia and the Arabs', in D. A. French and C. S. Lightfoot (eds.), *The Eastern Frontier of the Roman Empire*. Vol. 1. Oxford: B.A.R. Int. Series 553, pp. 143–67.

Harl, K. W. (1978), *Political Attitudes of Rome's Eastern Provinces in the Third Century AD*. Ann Arbor: University of Michigan Press.

Hartmann, F. (1982), *Herrscherwechsel und Reichskrise: Untersuchungen zu den Ursachen und Konsequenzender Herrscherwechsel im Imperium Romanum der Soldaten Kaiserzeit*. Frankfurt am Main: Peter Lang.

Hartmann, U. (2001), *Das Palmyrenische Teilreich*. Stuttgart: Franz Steiner Verlag.

Hoyns, G. (1852), *Geschichte der Sogenannten Dreissig Tyranen, Hauptsächlich des Odenathus und der Zenobia*. Göttingen.

Ingholt, H. (1976), 'Varia Tadmorea: II The Odeinat family', in *Palmyre: Bilan et Perspectives: Colloque de Strasbourg 18–20 Octobre 1973*. Strasbourg: Association pour l'Étude de la Civilisation Romaine, pp. 115–37.

Isaac, B. (1990), *The Limits of Empire: The Roman Army in the East*. Oxford: Clarendon Press.

Jameson, A. (1831), *Memoirs of Celebrated Female Sovereigns*. London: H. Colburn.

Jones, A. H. M. (1971), *The Cities of the Eastern Roman Provinces*. Oxford: Clarendon Press.

Jouve, J. (1758), *Histoire de Zénobie, Impératrice-reine de Palmyre*. Paris: Chez les Frères Estienne.

Kalinka, E. (1900), 'Inschriften aus Syrien', *JÖAI*, 3, Beiheft 19–36.

Kennedy, D. (1981), 'Auxilia and Numeri Raised in the Roman Province of Syria'. PhD dissertation: Oxford University.

Kennedy, D. and Riley, D. (1990), *Rome's Desert Frontier From the Air*. London: Batsford.

Kettenhofen, E. (1982), *Die Römisch-Persischen Krieg des 3. Jahrhunderts nach Christi nach der Inschrift Shapuhrs I an der Ka'be-Ye Zartost (SKZ)*. Beihefte zum Tubinger Atlas des Vorderen Orients no. 55. Wiesbaden: Dr Ludwig Reichert Verlag.

Kienast, D. (1996), *Römische Kaisertabelle: Grundzüge eine Römische Kaiserchronologie*. 2nd rev. edn. Darmstadt: Wissenschaftliche Buchgesellschaft.

Kotula, T. (1997), *Kryzys III Wieku w Zachodnich Prowincjach Cesarstwa Rzymskiego*. Wrocław: Wydawn, Uniwersytetu Wrocławskeigo.

Lanavère, A. (2001), 'Zénobie, personage du XVIIe siècle?', in J. Charles-Gaffiot, H. Lafange, J. -M. Hofman (eds.), *Moi, Zénobie, Reine de Palmyre 18 septembre –16 décembre 2001, Centre Culturel du Pantheon, Paris*. Milan: Skira Editore, pp. 139–42.

MacMullen, R. (1963), *Soldier and Civilian in the Roman Empire*. Cambridge, MA: Harvard University Press.

MacMullen, R. (1976), *The Roman Government's Response to Crisis AD 235–337*. New Haven: Yale University Press.

Mann, J. C. (1985), 'The Palmyrene diplomas', in M. Roxan, *Roman Diplomas 1978–1984*. London: Institute of Archaeology, Occasional Publication no. 9, pp. 212–19.

Maricq, A. (1958), 'Classica et Orientalia: 5. Res Gestae Divi Saporis', *Syria*, 35, 295–360.

Maricq, A. (1959), 'Classica et Orientalia: 7. Vologésias, l'emporium de Ctésiphon', *Syria*, 36, 264–76.

Martin, A. (2000), '*P.Mich.* Inv. 5478a et le préfet d'Égypte Statilius Ammianus', *Latomus* 59, 399–402.

Matthews, J. F. (1984), 'The tax law of Palmyra', *JRS*, 74, 157–80.

Mattingly, H. (1936), 'The Palmyrene princes and the mints of Antioch and Alexandria', *Numismatic Chronicle* series 5, no. 16, 89–114.

Mattingly, H. (1939), 'The Imperial Recovery', in S. A. Cook, F. E. Adcock, M. P. Charlesworth and M. H. Baynes (eds.), *Cambridge Ancient History Vol XII: The Imperial Crisis and Recovery*. Cambridge: Cambridge University Press, pp. 297–351.

Milik, J. T. (1972), *Dédicaces Faites par des Dieux (Palmyre, Hatra, Tyr) et des Thiases Sémitiques à L'Époque Romaine: Recherches d'Épigraphie Proche-orientale*. Vol.1. Paris: P. Geuthner.

Millar, F. (1971), 'Paul of Samosata, Zenobia, and Aurelian: the Church, local culture and political allegiance in third-century Syria', *JRS*, 61, 1–17.

Millar, F. (1981), *The Roman Empire and its Neighbours*. 2nd edn. London: Duckworth.

Millar, F. (1993), *The Roman Near East 31 BC to AD 337*. Cambridge, MA: Harvard University Press.

Moliterno, P. (2001), 'Musiques pour Zénobie: Anfossi, Paisiello, Rossini', in J. Charles-Gaffiot, H. Lafange, J. -M. Hofman (eds.), *Moi, Zénobie, Reine de Palmyre 18 septembre –16 décembre 2001, Centre Culturel du Pantheon, Paris*. Milan: Skira Editore, pp. 153–6.

Nodelman, A. (1960), 'A preliminary history of Characene', *Berytus*, 13, 83–121.

Oppenheimer, A. (1983), *Babylonia Judaica in the Talmudic Period*. Beihefte zum Tubinger Atlas des Vorderen Orients no. 47. Wiesbaden: Dr Ludwig Reichert Verlag.

Paschoud, F. (ed.) (1971), *Zosime, Histoire Nouvelle*. Vol 1. Paris: Les Belles Lettres.

Paschoud, F. (1996), *Histoire Auguste: vol. 5.1 Vies d'Aurélien et de Tacite*. Paris: Les Belles Lettres.

Peachin, M. (1990), *Roman Imperial Titulature and Chronology AD 235–284*. Amsterdam: Gieben.

Périn, P. and Feffer, L. -C. (1987), *Les Francs: tome 1: à la Conquête de la Gaule*. Paris: Armand Colin.

Pflaum, H. -G. (1952), 'La fortification de la ville d'Adraha d'Arabie après des inscriptions récemment découvertes', *Syria* 29, 307–30.

Potter, D. S. (1990), *Prophecy and History in the Crisis of the Roman Empire: A Historical Commentary on the Thirteenth Sybilline Oracle*. Oxford: Clarendon Press.

Potter, D. S. (1996), 'Palmyra and Rome: Odaenathus's titulature and the use of *imperium maius*', *ZPE*, 113, 271–85.

Potter, D. S. (2004), *The Roman Empire at Bay AD 180–395*. London: Routledge.

Pucci. G. (2001), '*Zénobie* de la page à l'écran', in J. Charles-Gaffiot, H. Lafange, J. -M. Hofman (eds.), *Moi, Zénobie, Reine de Palmyre 18 septembre –16 décembre 2001, Centre Culturel du Pantheon, Paris*. Milan: Skira Editore, pp. 171–4.

Raschke, M. (1978), 'New studies in Roman commerce with the East', *ANRW* II .9.2, 604–1378.

Rey-Coquais, J. -P. (1978), 'Syrie romaine de Pompée à Dioclétien', *JRS* 68, 44–73.

Roland-Michel, M. (2001), 'Giambattista Tieplo et le cycle de la Ca' Zenobio',
    in J. Charles-Gaffiot, H. Lafange, J. -M. Hofman (eds.), *Moi, Zénobie, Reine
    de Palmyre 18 septembre –16 décembre 2001, Centre Culturel du Pantheon,
    Paris*. Milan: Skira Editore, pp. 143–4.

Saffrey, H. -D. (2001), 'La Reine Zénobie et le philosophe Longin', in J. Charles-
    Gaffiot, H. Lafange, J. -M. Hofman (eds.), *Moi, Zénobie, Reine de Palmyre
    18 septembre –16 décembre 2001, Centre Culturel du Pantheon, Paris*. Milan:
    Skira Editore, pp. 61–2.

Sajous-d'Orion, M. (2001), 'Palmyre en scène: décors pour *Aureliano in
    Palmira* de Rossini', in J. Charles-Gaffiot, H. Lafange, J. -M. Hofman (eds.),
    *Moi, Zénobie, Reine de Palmyre 18 septembre –16 décembre 2001, Centre
    Culturel du Pantheon, Paris*. Milan: Skira Editore, pp. 157–62.

Sartre, M. (1991), *L'Orient Romain: Provinces et Sociétés Provinciales en
    Mediterranée Orientale d'Auguste aux Sévères (31 avant J. -C. – 235 après
    J. -C.)*. Paris: Seuil.

Sartre, M. (2005a), *The Middle East Under Rome*. Cambridge, MA: Belknap
    Press of Harvard University Press.

Sartre. M (2005b), 'The Arabs and the desert peoples', in A. K. Bowman, P. Garnsey
    and A. Cameron (eds.), *Cambridge Ancient History Vol. 12: The Crisis of Empire
    AD 193–337*. 2nd edn. Cambridge: Cambridge University Press, pp. 498–520.

Saunders, R. T. (1992), *A Biography of the Emperor Aurelian*. Dissertation of the
    University of Cincinnati, published Ann Arbor: University of Michigan Press.

Schlumberger, D. (1943), 'Les gentilices romains des Palmyreniens', *BÉO* 9
    (1942–3), 53–82.

Schlumberger, D. (1972), 'Vorod l'agronome', *Syria*, 49, 339–41.

Schwarz, J. (1960), 'L'Empire romain et le commerce oriental', *Annales* Jan–Feb
    1960, 18–44.

Schwarz, J. (1976), 'Palmyre et l'opposition à Rome en Egypte', in *Palmyre:
    Bilan et Perspectives: Colloque de Strasbourg 18–20 Octobre 1973*. Strasbourg:
    Association pour l'Étude de la Civilisation Romaine, 138–51.

Seller, A. (1696), *The Antiquities of Palmyra Containing the History of the City,
    and its Emperors, From its Foundation to the Present Time: With an Appendix
    of Critical Observations on the Names, Religion, and Government of the
    Country and a Commentary on the Inscriptions Lately Found There*. London:
    S. Smith and B. Walford.

Seyrig, H. (1932), 'L'incorporation de Palmyre à l'empire romain', *Syria*, 13, 266–77.

Seyrig, H. (1933), 'Texts relatifs à la garnison romaine de Palmyre', *Syria*, 14, 152–68.

Seyrig, H. (1936), 'Inscriptions relatives au commerce maritime de Palmyre', in *Melanges Franz Cumont*, vol.1. Brussels: Université Libre de Bruxelles, pp. 397–402.

Seyrig, H. (1941), 'Inscriptions grecques de l'agora de Palmyre', *Syria*, 22, 44–8.

Seyrig, H. (1963), 'Les fils du Roi Odeinat', *AAS* 13, 171–2.

Southern. P. (2001), *The Roman Empire from Severus to Constantine*. London: Routledge.

Southern, P. (2006), *The Roman Army: a social and institutional history*. Santa Barbara: ABC-Clio; reprinted Oxford: Oxford University Press 2007.

Speidel, M. P. (1977), 'The Roman army in Arabia', *ANRW* II.8, 687–730.

Speidel, M. P. (1984), 'Palmyrene irregulars at Koptos', *BASP* 21, 221–4.

Starcky, J. and Gawlikowski, M. (1985), *Palmyre*. Paris: Librairie d'Amérique et d'Orient.

Stein, A. (1923), 'Kallinikos von Petra', *Hermes* 58, 448–56.

Stoneman, R. (1992), *Palmyra and its Empire: Zenobia's Revolt Against Rome*. Ann Arbor: University of Michigan Press.

Strobel, K. (1993), *Das Imperium Romanum in 3. Jahrhundert: Modell eine Historische Krise?* Historia Einzelschriften 75. Stuttgart: Franz Steiner Verlag.

Swain, S. (1993), 'Greek into Palmyrene: Odaenathus as *corrector totius orientis?*' *ZPE*, 99, 157–64.

Tavernier, J. B. (1676), *Les Six Voyages de Monsieur J. B. Tavernier, Écuyer Baron d'Aubonne, en Turquie, en Perse, et aux Indes, Pendant l'Éspace de Quarante Ans et par Toutes les Routes que l'on Peut Tenir: Accompagnez d'Observations Particuliers Sur la Qualité, le Réligion, le Gouvernement, les Coutumes et le Commerce de Chaque Pais*. 2 vols. Paris.

Teixidor, J. (1977), *The Pagan God: popular religion in the Graeco-Roman Near East*. Princeton, NJ: Princeton University Press.

Teixidor, J. (1984), *Un Port Roman du Désert: Palmyre et Son Commerce d'Auguste à Caracalla. Semitica* vol. 34. Paris: Librairie d'Amérique et d'Orient.

Teixidor, J. (1989), 'Les derniers rois d'Edesse d'aprés deux nouveaux documents syriaques', *ZPE* 76, 219–22.

Teixidor, J. (2001), 'Aperçu sur l'economie', in J. Charles-Gaffiot, H. Lafange, J. -M. Hofman (eds.), *Moi, Zénobie, Reine de Palmyre 18 septembre –16 décembre 2001, Centre Culturel du Pantheon, Paris*. Milan: Skira Editore, pp. 97–8.

Van Berchem, D. (1952), *L'Armeé de Diocletién et la Réforme Constantinienne*. Paris: P. Geuthner.

Van Berchem, D. (1954), 'Recherches sur la chronologie des enceintes de Syrie et de Mésopotamie', *Syria*, 31, 254–70.

Watson, G. R. (1969), *The Roman Soldier*. London: Thames and Hudson.

Watson, A. (1999), *Aurelian and the Third Century*. London: Routledge.

Wernsdorf, F. E. (1742), 'De Septimia Zenobia Pamyrenorum Augusta'. Dissertation, University of Leipzig.

Will, E. (1957), 'Marchands et chefs de caravans à Palmyre', *Syria*, 34, 262–77.

Will, E. (1985), 'Pline l'Ancien et Palmyre: un problème d'histoire ou d'histoire littéraire?', *Syria*, 62, 263–9.

Will, E. (1992), *Les Palmyreniens: La Venise des Sables*. Paris: Armand Colin.

Wood, R. and Dawkins, J. (1753), *The Ruins of Palmyra, Otherwise Tedmor in the Desart*. London: Robert Wood (Reprinted 1971, Farnborough: Gregg International).

Wright, W. (1895), *An Account of Palmyra and Zenobia, With Travels and Adventures in Bashan and the Desert*. London: T. Nelson and Sons.

Yon, J. -B. (2002), *Les Notables de Palmyre*. Beirut: Institut Français d'Archéologie du Proche-Orient.

Young, G. K. (2001), *Rome's Eastern Trade: International Commerce and Imperial Policy, 31 BC–AD 305*. London: Routledge.

Index